POVERTY AND POLITICIZATION

Herbert Hirsch

Poverty and Politicization

*Political Socialization
in an American Sub-Culture*

Fp | *The Free Press* NEW YORK
Collier-Macmillan Limited LONDON

To my three favorite Appalachians : Alma, Candy, and Diana, who make it all worthwhile.

Acknowledgments

This study was completed while the author was part of a larger interdisciplinary study whose primary purpose was to evaluate the effect of the "war on poverty" in Knox County, Kentucky. The data upon which this study is based was collected under Contract #693 between the University of Kentucky Research Foundation and the Office of Economic Opportunity. The grant was administered by the University of Kentucky, Center for Developmental Change, which also provided office space and research assistantships for the author. Computer time was furnished by the University of Kentucky, Computing Center.

Specific individuals also made significant contributions to the "cause." I gratefully acknowledge the cooperation of the Superintendent of the Schools of Knox County, Kentucky, who gave us access to his students; of the Director of the Testing Program of the Knox County schools, who administered the questionnaires; and of Ottis Murphy, who served as field representative for the overall project and expedited the collection of the data. I also wish to thank Robert Chanteloup, graduate student in sociology, whose programming and statistical assistance was instrumental in getting the data processed, and Professor Lewis Donohew, School of Communications, University of Kentucky, whose comments and conversation helped me to clarify my ideas regarding the role of the media. Special thanks are due to Professor Al Lott, Department of Psychology, for his comments on the manuscript and for initiating me into the world of social learning theory; to Professor Dean Jaros, whose comments on the manuscript are largely responsible for whatever clarity of thought and expression it contains; and to Professor S. Sidney Ulmer, whose overall influence upon me has been profound.

The two final acknowledgments are most important. First, a note of thanks to my parents, without whose aid none of this would have been possible. Second, I am especially grateful to Alma, whose patience and understanding were only exceeded by the assistance she provided in typing the entire first draft of this document.

Finally, of course, I grudgingly acknowledge that any errors in the document are my own.

H. H.
Austin, Texas

Contents

ACKNOWLEDGMENTS   *vii*

LIST OF TABLES   *x*

1   *Political Socialization:*   *1*
   REVIEW OF THE LITERATURE AND CRITIQUE

2   *Toward a Theory of Political Socialization*   *20*

3   *Methodology and Technique*   *27*

4   *Interpersonal Agents of Political Socialization:*   *33*
   THE FAMILY

5   *Interpersonal Agents of Political Socialization:*   *71*
   PEERS AND PEER GROUPS

6   *Interpersonal Agents of Political Socialization:*   *93*
   THE SCHOOL

7   *Impersonal Agents of Political Socialization:*   *118*
   THE MASS MEDIA AS SYMBOLIC MODELS

8   *Conclusion*   *137*

APPENDIX A   *144*

APPENDIX B   *153*

BIBLIOGRAPHY   *180*

INDEX   *199*

List of Tables

4.1   Child's Ranking of Agents of Information Transmission on Four Levels of Government: Local   *35*

4.2   Child's Ranking of Agents of Information Transmission on Four Levels of Government: State   *35*

4.3   Child's Ranking of Agents of Information Transmission on Four Levels of Government: National   *35*

4.4   Child's Ranking of Agents of Information Transmission on Four Levels of Government: International   *36*

4.5   The Mother as an Agent of Information Transmission on the Four Levels of Government   *37*

4.6   The Father as an Agent of Information Transmission on the Four Levels of Government   *37*

4.7   Principal Axis Factor Analysis, Varimax Rotation: Agents of Information Transmission   *38*

4.8   Gamma Correlations Between Party Preference of Child and Party Preference of Parents   *40*

4.9a b   Comparison of Party Identification of Child and Parent: Appalachian Mother and Both Parents of National Sample   *41*

4.10a b   Comparison of Party Identification of Child and Parent: Appalachian Father and Both Parents of National Sample   *42*

4.11   Gamma Correlations Between Party of Father and Party of Child Controlling Rank of Father as Information Agent   *43*

4.12   Gamma Correlations Between Party of Mother and Party of Child Controlling Rank of Mother as Information Agent   *43*

4.13   Gamma Correlations Between Party of Parent and Party of Child By Level of Political Information   *44*

4.14   Children's Preferred Source of Voting Advice   *44*

4.15   Comparison of Appalachian and New Haven Samples : Parents as a Preferred Source of Voting Advice by School Years   *45*

4.16   Preferred Sources of Voting Advice By School Year   *46*

4.17   Relationship Between Discussion of Politics With Family and Rank of Parents as Information Agents   *47*

4.18   Relationship Between Family Members Holding Political Office and Rank of Parents as Information Agents   *47*

4.19   Gamma Correlations Between Party of Parents and Party of Child : By Frequency of Discussion of Politics With Family   *48*

4.20   Gamma Correlations Between Party of Parents and Party of Child : By Family Member Holding Political Office   *48*

4.21   Relationship Between Child's Preferred Source of Voting Advice and Discussion of Politics with Family   *49*

4.22   Relationship Between Family Member Holding Political Office and Preferred Source of Voting Advice   *49*

4.23   Relationship Between Parents' Ranking as Agents of Information Transmission and the Age of the Child   *51*

4.24   Gamma Correlations Between Party of Parents and Party of Child : By Age of Child   *51*

4.25   Relationship Between Sex of Child and Ranking of Parents as Agents of Information Transmission   *54*

4.26   Percent of Child's Agreement With Party Identification of Father : By Sex of Child   *55*

4.27   Percent of Child's Agreement with Party Identification of Mother : By Sex of Child   *55*

4.28   Relationship Between Sex of Child and Preferred Source of Voting Advice   *55*

4.29   Parent Chosen as Preferred Source of Voting Advice : By Sex and School Year   *56*

4.30   Gamma Correlations Between Father's Employment and Child's Ranking of the Parents as Information Agents   *58*

4.31   Gamma Correlations Between Party Identification of Parents and Child : By Employment Status of Father   *59*

4.32   Relationship Between Employment Status of Father and Child's Preference for Parents as Sources of Voting Advice   *59*

4.33   Gamma Correlations Between Parents' Education and the Child's Ranking of the Parents as Information Agents   *60*

4.34   Gamma Correlations Between Party Identification of Parent and Child : By Father's Education   *60*

4.35 Gamma Correlations Between Party Identification of Parent and Child: By Mother's Education *60*

4.36 Relationship Between Education of Father and Child's Preferred Source of Voting Advice *61*

4.37 Relationship Between Education of Mother and Child's Preferred Source of Voting Advice. *61*

4.38 Comparison of Child's Ranking of the Parents as Information Agents: By Absence or Presence of the Father *62–63*

4.39 Relationship Between Absence of the Father and Party Identification of Father and Child *64*

4.40 Percent of Child's Agreement with Party Identification of Father: By Father-Absence *64*

4.41 Percent of Child's Agreement with Party Identification of Mother: By Father-Absence *64*

4.42 Relationship Between Absence of the Father and Parents as a Preferred Source of Voting Advice *64*

5.1 Rank of Peers as Agents of Information Transmission on Four Levels of Government *72*

5.2 Relationship Between Age and Rank of Peers as Information Agents *73–74*

5.3 Gamma Correlations Between Rank of Peers and Parents as Information Agents: By Age of Child *74–75*

5.4 Relationship Between Political Party of Peers and Political Party of Respondent *75*

5.5 Relationship Between Party Identification of Peers and Party of Respondent: By Age of Respondent *76*

5.6 Comparison of Gamma Correlations Between Party of Respondent and Party of Peers and Party of Respondent and Party of Parents: By Age of Respondent *77*

5.7 Relationship Between Sex of Child and Rank of Peers as Information Agents: By Sex of Child *78*

5.8 Gamma Correlations Between Party Identification of Peers and Respondent: By Sex of Respondent *79*

5.9 Relationship Between Child's Perception of Peers' Orientation to Political Stimuli and Rank of Peers as Information Agents *79–80*

5.10 Gamma Correlations Between Party Identification of Respondent and Party of Peers: By Peers' Interest in Politics *81*

5.11 Relationship Between Preferred Source of Voting Advice and Peers' Interest in Politics *81*

5.12 Gamma Correlations Between Child's Relationship-With-Father Score and Ranking of Peers as Information Agents *82*

5.13　Gamma Correlations Between Party Identification of Peers and Party of Respondent by Respondent's Relationship-with-Father Score　*83*

5.14　Relationship Between Child's Preferred Source of Voting Advice and Relationship with Father　*84*

5.15　Relationship Between Absence of the Father and Rank of Peers as Information Agents　*85–86*

5.16　Gamma Correlations Between Ranking of Peers and Parents as Information Agents : By Father-Absence (F-A) or Father-Presence (F-P)　*86*

5.17　Relationship Between Father-Absence and Party Identification of Respondent and Peers　*87*

5.18　Percent of Respondent's Agreement with Party Identification of Peers By Father-Absence　*87*

5.19　Relationship Between Membership in Youth Organizations and Desire to Maintain Status Quo　*88*

5.20　Relationship Between Membership in Youth Organizations and Interest in Politics　*89*

5.21　Relationship Between Membership in Youth Organizations and Discussion of Politics　*89*

6.1　Child's Ranking of the School as an Agent of Information Transmission on Four Levels of Government　*94*

6.2　Relationship Between Age of Child and Rank of School as an Information Agent　*96–97*

6.3　Gamma Correlations Between Rank of School and Peers, and School and Parents as Information Agents : By Age of Child　*97–98*

6.4　Gamma Correlations Between Party Preference of Child and Rank of the School as an Information Agent　*99*

6.5　Comparison of Appalachia and New Haven Samples : Teacher as a Source of Voting Advice　*100*

6.6　Relationship Between Sex of Child and Rank of School as an Information Agent　*101*

6.7　Relationship Between Child's Perception of Teacher's Orientation to Political Stimuli and Rank of School as an Information Agent　*102*

6.8　Relationship Between Teacher's Orientation to Political Stimuli and Preferred Source of Voting Advice　*102*

6.9　Relationship Between Teacher's Discussion of Candidates and Rank of School as an Information Agent　*103*

6.10　Relationship Between Discussion of Candidates and Preferred Source of Voting Advice　*104*

6.11　Relationship Between Attendance in a Civics Course and Rank of School as an Information Agent　*105–106*

6.12　Relationship Between Attendance in a Civics Course and Attention Paid to News in the Media　*107*

6.13   Relationship Between Attendance in a Civics Course and Reading a Newspaper   *107*

6.14   Relationship Between Attendance in a Civics Course and Interest in Politics   *107*

6.15   Relationship Between Attendance in a Civics Course and Political Knowledge   *108*

6.16   Relationship Between Exposure to Patriotic Rituals and Political Chauvinism   *109–110*

6.17   Relationship Between Attendance in a Civics Course and Political Efficacy   *111*

6.18   Gamma Correlations Between Relationship-With-Father Score and Rank of School as Information Agent   *112*

6.19   Relationship Between Father-Absence and Rank of School as an Information Agent   *113*

6.20   Gamma Correlations Between Rankings of Peers, Parents, and School as Information Agents: By Father-Absence (F-A) or Father Presence (F-P)   *113*

7.1   Child's Ranking of the Media as Agents of Information Transmission on Four Levels of Government   *119*

7.2   Relationship Between Rank of Radio as an Information Agent and Age of Child   *121*

7.3   Relationship Between Rank of Television as an Information Agent and Age of Child   *121*

7.4   Relationship Between Rank of Newspaper as an Information Agent and Age of Child   *121*

7.5   Relationship Between the Sex of the Child and Rank of Radio as an Information Agent   *122*

7.6   Relationship Between Sex of Child and Rank of Television as an Information Agent   *123*

7.7   Relationship Between Sex of Child and Rank of Newspaper as an Information Agent   *123*

7.8   Gamma Correlations Between Rank of Media and Rank of Mother as Agents of Information Transmission on Local Level of Government: By Sex of Respondent   *124*

7.9   Relationship Between Sex of Respondent and Attention Paid to News in Media   *124*

7.10   Relationship Between Sex and Frequency of Reading a News Story on Front Page of Newspaper   *125*

7.11   Gamma Correlations Between Child's Relationship-With-Father Score and Ranking of the Media as Information Agents   *126*

7.12   Relationship Between Father-Absence (F-A) or Father-Presence (F-P) and Rank of Media as Information Agents   *127–128*

7.13   Relationship Between Rate of Exposure to Television and Rank of Television as an Information Agent   *130*

7.14 Relationship Between Rate of Exposure to Radio and Rank of Radio as an Information Agent *130*

7.15 Relationship Between Reading a Newspaper and Rank of Newspaper as an Information Agent *131*

7.16 Relationship Between Frequency of Reading a News Story and Rank of Newspaper as an Information Agent *131*

7.17 Relationship Between Content Exposed to on Television and Rank of Television as an Information Agent *132*

7.18 Relationship Between Content Exposed to on Radio and Rank of Radio as an Information Agent *132*

7.19 Relationship Between Section of Newspaper Usually Read and Rank of Newspaper as an Information Agent *132*

7.20 Relationship Between Rate fo Exposure to Media and Political Knowledge *133–134*

7.21 Relationship Between Content Exposed to in Media and Political Knowledge *134*

7.14 Relationship between Rate of Exposure to Radio and Rank of Radio as an Information Agent   130

7.15 Relationship between Reading a Newspaper and Rank of Newspaper as an Information Agent   131

7.16 Relationship Between ... to Reading a Newsstory and Rank of Newspaper as an Information Agent   131

7.17 Relationship Between Content Exposed to for Television and Rank of Television as an Information Agent   132

7.18 Relationship between Newspaper Content Exposed to for Radio and Rank of Radio as an Information Agent   132

9.18 Relationship Between Section of Newspaper Reading Time and Rank of Newspaper as an Information Agent   132

7.20 Relationship between Rate to Exposure to Media and Political Knowledge   133   133

7.21 Relationship Between Content Exposed to for Media and Political Knowledge   133

POVERTY AND POLITICIZATION

1
Political Socialization

REVIEW OF THE LITERATURE
AND CRITIQUE

In the last decade, interest in political socialization—the process by which the child learns about the political culture in which he lives—has increased dramatically. Indeed, it "has emerged [as] a new specialization" within political science.[1] However, the study of political socialization is at the same time venerable. It would be unwarranted to claim that "today's behavioral political scientists have discovered a new problem. It is more accurate to credit them with refocusing attention on a classic concern of politics."[2]

Philosophers have been interested in and have speculated about the training of citizens and the means used by elites to inculcate loyalty,[3] and elites have continuously employed various practices to this end. Only recently, however, has empirical research begun to transform early philosophical speculation and the assumptions of political practice into more concrete knowledge of the factors involved in political learning. In addition, there has been an occasional piece of relevant empirical investigation. Research on civic training was conducted in the 1930s,[4] and interesting, though not specifically political, child development studies appeared in the psychological literature.[5] However, it was only following the publication in 1959 of *Hyman's Political Socialization* that political scientists have

Notes to Chapter 1 will be found on pp. 13–19.

evidenced any great concern over or conducted appreciable research on political socialization.

Hence the field, though vigorous, is young and relatively undeveloped. Stock needs to be taken of recent efforts (since 1959), and in the light of these efforts, new explanatory tacks need to be developed and new research needs to be proposed.

According to Greenstein:

While there is no generally accepted approach to the study of political socialization, much of what is known and of what ought to be known can be summed up in the following paraphrase of Lasswell's formulations of the general process of communication: (a) who, (b) learns what, (c) from whom, (d) under what circumstances, (e) with what effects?[6]

The discussion to follow will be organized around this formulation.

"WHO LEARNS?"

According to Froman, the primary question in political socialization is not "who learns?" but "how do children learn politically relevant attitudes and behaviors?"[7]

Most studies have attempted to answer this question by concentrating for the most part on young children.[8] The rationale for researching this population is based on two propositions: first, that basic orientations toward politics are learned in early childhood and adolescence,[9] and second, that this early socialization has important consequences for adult political behavior.[10]

There is indeed evidence to substantiate the first proposition. According to Greenstein, age is one of the most important factors influencing the political socialization of the child.[11] Easton and Hess have in fact claimed that "the truly formative years of the maturing member of a political system would seem to be the years between the ages of three and thirteen."[12] Indeed, a prominent finding of many studies is that the young child acquires certain political orientations at an early age.[13]

For example, at a very young age the child has an awareness of the President. The child's image of the President is positive and highly idealized, but suffers diminution as the child gets older.[14] Other findings related to age are: (1) that by the time the child is in the fourth grade, six out of ten "were able to state whether their party preference was Republican or Democratic . . . "[15]; (2) a cynical attitude toward politics increases as age increases[16]; and (3) as the child gets older he is less likely to state that he would ask his parents for voting advice.[17] It is evident, therefore, that at an early age the child has become aware of, and loyal to, political figures, has begun to express support for the system, has acquired a preference for a political party and holds certain political attitudes. These factors appear early in the life cycle, but are subject to change as the child matures.

Thus, indeed children learn, but there is differential learning influenced by certain characteristics of the child, the investigation of which gives a more detailed answer to the question of "who?" The two primary characteristics are sex and social class.[18]

Regarding sex, findings are similar to, but not as conclusive as, those concerning the political behavior of adults—that is, boys know more about politics than girls[19]; boys are more interested in and active in politics than girls; and boys are more likely to read about politics in the newspaper.[20] Gender does not have any relationship to the child's future expectation of whether or not he will vote when he is twenty-one.[21]

In regard to class, one finds that, in general, children of the upper socioeconomic strata are more likely to express an interest in politics and to be more active politically than children of lower status.[22] The relationship between socioeconomic status and political socialization, however, is not always clear. For example, Greenstein found that there is no difference between the classes in ability to identify political figures, and that children in both status groups indicate that they prefer one political party over another.[23] According to Greenstein, these differences in political socialization, which are related to sex and social class factors, "have already begun to be established by nine years of age. . . . "[24] Hence it appears that many frequently observed differences in adult political attitudes by sex and social class have their precursors in youth.

The young child, consequently, does indeed acquire certain political orientations at an early age. However, the question of the extent to which these early years are the "truly formative years" in the development of political attitudes has not been, and cannot be, answered from the data gathered by any of the studies thus far concluded. Only a design incorporating a sample composed of a wide dispersion of ages, either a cross-sectional or a longitudinal study, could adequately answer this question.[25]

Indeed, there is evidence that counsels caution in accepting the more extravagant claims about the efficacy of childhood political learning. In a review of the psychological and sociological literature on socialization, William Sewell demonstrates that, while early learning is important, social-role learning persists throughout a person's life cycle.[26] Clearly, at least some kinds of political socialization occur after childhood. For example, studies of the socialization of American state legislators point out the fact that, while a large percentage of them remembers being socialized in childhood, a considerable percentage was socialized later in life.[27]

Thus, while early socialization experiences may be important, concentration of attention on children of a particular age group, as has characterized political science research, threatens to trap the investigator in a static conception of socialization.[28] By so restricting their attention, scholars have been unable to deal directly with a basic assumption upon which research into childhood socialization is based. They have been unable to answer what is perhaps the key theoretical question: "How does early socialization relate to later political behavior?"[29]

In seeking to answer this question, it behooves the student of children's political orientations to consider that the relationship is neither direct nor complete, that events subsequent to childhood may importantly condition the impact of acquisitions during the early years.

"WHAT IS LEARNED?"

By far the greatest concern of scholars of political socialization has been with the content of early political learning. Greenstein makes a distinction between "politically relevant aspects of personality development" and "specifically political learning."[30] The former has been virtually ignored by political scientists, who have preferred to devote most attention to the substantive questions of the latter.[31] Greenstein divides "specifically political learning" into three sections:

1. Learning connected with the citizen role (partisan attachment, ideology, motivation to participate).
2. Learning connected with subject role (national loyalty, orientations toward authority, conception of the legitimacy of institutions).
3. Learning connected with recruitment to and performance of specialized roles, such as bureaucrat, party functionary, and legislator.[32]

In regard to citizen-role learning, studies have shown that most children express a preference for one political party over another, that most agree with their parents' party preference, and that this identification is not based on in-depth knowledge of politics.[33] Party loyalty, however, is not the whole of politics. Also important in forming the citizen's role are motivation to participate and ideology. Unfortunately, neither of these has received much research attention. Most of the children interviewed state that they will vote when they are old enough.[34] This does not fully tap the question of motivation. Intention to vote is apparently associated with feelings of duty. Though interesting, this begs the question of why children think it is their duty to vote.

In regard to what Greenstein labels "ideology," one finds that children "were not sufficiently well informed to understand the sorts of statements which make up liberalism–conservatism scales,"[35] and that most of them could not distinguish between the two major political parties.[36] Greenstein suggests that this is due to the fact that the young child has not yet reached the "stage of ideolgy–readiness" that is necessary "before he can become, in the generic sense of the terms, either a little liberal or else a little conservative."[37]

Due, however, to the lack of theoretical frameworks, these findings seem to be merely isolated bits of knowledge floating in a sea of relative ignorance. The student of political socialization has probably only scratched the surface of the relevant citizen's orientations of children. Neither participation as such nor the direction of participation has been thoroughly researched.

Considerable attention has been devoted to childhood learning of the subject role.[38] Children generally have a greater awareness and knowledge about the national government than of the state.[39] This awareness usually carries with it a benevolent and favorable view of the government. As Easton and Dennis report, children at all grade levels of their sample (2–8) "roundly approve of government."[40] One group of studies point out that children trust the government and do not display as cynical an attitude toward politics and politicians as do their parents.[41] However, the content of this critical area of political affect, though generally favorable, appears to vary with many factors. Ziblatt notes that students who participate in extracurricular activities are more likely to trust the government than those who do not participate.[42] Though suggestive of an interesting kind of transfer, this relationship may be a function of the correlation of such participation to high socioeconomic status.[43] There are, moreover, cultural factors to be considered. Students from Appalachia are more cynical than their counterparts elsewhere.[44] Pinner has demonstrated that Belgian and French students "exhibit more political distrust than do the Dutch high school and university students."[45] Clearly, more research on the child's attitude toward political authority is called for.

While the relationships are complicated, it has been fairly well established, as noted above, that the child has a positive image of executive figures (the President in the U.S. is the first political figure about which the child has information).[46] Various explanations have been posited to account for this relationship. Most interesting for the present paper is the fact that no data have been gathered which empirically test a learning theory formulation of the acquiring of attitudes toward politial authority.

Finally, "learning connected with recruitment to performance of specialized roles, such as bureaucrat, party functionary, and legislator,"[47] is also very much under-investigated.[48] Though more attention is desirable, the primary focus of the present work will include only the first two content areas.

"FROM WHOM?" THE AGENTS OF POLITICAL SOCIALIZATION

The question of "From Whom?" the child learns about politics reminds one of Mark Twain's oft-quoted statement about the weather. To paraphrase, one could say that everyone talks about the agents of socialization but no one does anything about them. Most scholars agree, with little or no data to back them up, that all of the following act as agents of political socialization: family, school, church, peer groups and youth organizations, social class, ethnic origin, geographic region, and mass media.[49] All of these formulations are hypothetical. By far the most comprehensive inquiry into the agents of political socialization is that of Hess and Torney. They divide "socializing contexts" into three general types.

The first type includes institutions of well-defined structure and organization: the family, school and church.

The second type of socializing influence occurs in larger social settings. The most important of these social contexts are: social class, ethnic origin, and geographical region.

A third type of influence in the socializing process derives from the child's personal characteristics.[50]

According to these writers, the first type influences the child by "direct teaching of political attitudes and values and by inducting him into the behavior and roles appropriate to family, school, or church membership. These values are then generalized to attitudes toward political life of the community and nation."[51]

Most scholars agree that the family is one of the most potent sources of political socialization. According to Hess and Torney, the family acts as an agent in three ways. First, it transmits attitudes to the child; second, the parent serves as a model to the child; third, role definitions and expectations within the family structure are generalized to political objects.[52]

Probably the strongest finding to date, involving the family as an agent, is the child's tendency to assimilate the party preference of his parents.[53] The parent also is the most preferred source of voting advice for the child.[54] But, again, there appear to be important conditioning factors. Hess and Torney demonstrate that age acts as an important variable. As the child grows older, he looks less to the parent for political information.[55] Hence, the parent is more salient as an agent to the youngest child.

Hess and Torney find that other factors had little influence on the parent as an agent. The two factors they investigated were the absence or presence of the father in the home and the status of inter-familial relationships.[56] They find that father-absence makes no difference in attitudes toward authority[57] and that "children who see their fathers as being powerful tend to be more informed and interested in political matters."[58]

The second well-defined structure that acts as an agent of political socialization is the school. Hess and Torney disagree with Greenstein. While the latter regards the family as the primary agent, the former feel that "the public school is the most important and effective instrument of political socialization in the United States."[59] The school operates as both a manifest and a latent form of transmission.[60] It is manifest when it socializes directly through classroom instruction, class rituals and ceremonies, such as pledging allegiance to the flag, singing patriotic songs, and celebrating patriotic holidays.[61] It is latent when it socializes role behavior within the school structure which may be transferred to other behavior outside the school. Contextually, the school socializes respect and awe for the government and stresses "the structure rather than the dynamics of government."[62] It tells the child little concerning the role of political parties and tends to "stress certain consensus values, such as the importance of voting and the criteria one should use to determine his voting choice."[63] Even in the area of political orientations, "There is a lack of evidence that the civics curriculum has a significant effect on the political orientations of the great majority of American high school students."[64]

Though they present an impressive array, many of the statements above are not based on empirical data. They could more realistically be labeled hypotheses. The role of the school as an agent of political socialization requires a great deal more investigation.

Two final well-defined structures that act as agents are the church and peer group. There is practically no data at all on the church as an agent of political socialization. The only finding is from Hess and Torney, who report that religious affiliation affects party preference.[65] Needless to say, more work is needed here.

Regarding the peer group, there are some preliminary findings. For example, peer group activities in which the child may participate are of three basic types:

Children's service organizations (YMCA, Scouts, etc.); school sponsored clubs (band, sports, etc.); and positions of leadership (holding office, etc.) in these groups.[66]

It has been found that "students who join groups express more interest in political affairs, are more actively involved in conversations about politics and current events, and defend their opinions on those issues."[67]

The second type of socializing influence is that which occurs in the larger social setting. Three types have been identified: social class, ethnic origin, geographic region. There is little research on children regarding these factors.[68] There is, however, one other agent that operates in the larger social setting. In regard to the mass media as an agent of socialization, one is able to find little data other than those dealing with how much television the child watches.[69] Important work on media effects has been done by scholars in disciplines other than political science, but discussion of these studies is deferred until the substantive section dealing with this topic.

The third type of socializing influence is the personal characteristics of the child. According to Hess and Torney, "these *individual characteristics* influence socializing efforts of the family, school and other agents, and limit the extent of learning."[70] These authors state that the main factor that limits the child's ability to assimilate what is taught is intelligence.[71] But overall personal characteristics have received even less attention as childhood socialization agents than the media. Rosenberg demonstrates that self-esteem is related to interest in, and discussion of, public affairs[72]; and Jaros has shown that the anxiety displayed by the child is related to authoritarianism, which in turn is related to attributed presidential strength and power.[73]

In summary, one must conclude that, other than from the family, we have no hard data concerning the relative influence of the different agents. The question of "From Whom?" has not been adequately researched.

"UNDER WHAT CIRCUMSTANCES?"

Inquiring about the circumstances under which socialization occurs is very similar to asking who learns. By "circumstances" Greenstein refers to culture. There has been an ever-increasing number of studies that investigate socialization in different cultures. Most of them naturally reflect the main thrust of political socialization research in the United States—that is, they focus primarily on the content of what is socialized and virtually exclude any discussion of the agents involved.[74] There are some exceptions.

Converse and Depeux, in a comparative study of France and the United States, found that in France there is less political communication between parent and child. While 80% of American adults are able to remember what their parents' party preferences were, for French adults the figure is only 30%.[75]

Hess compared attitudes toward the main political authority figure in five different countries: United States, Chile, Puerto Rico, Japan, and Australia.[76] He found similarities and differences. All displayed (a) "less idealization of prominent authority figures and (b) increased awareness of role and competence qualities" as the child grew older.[77] Differences suggested "(a) differential effects of social class upon political socialization in different countries and (b) different levels of influence of home and school as socializing agents."[78]

Both Hess and Converse and Depeux found differences in the family as an agent in different cultures. A study of an American sub-culture by Jaros, Hirsch, and Fleron also indicated that the agents may act differently in different cultural contexts,[79] and pointed out that culture seems to influence the political attitudes of youth.[80]

In general, these studies lend support to the warning that the major findings of political socialization research are "culture bound" and that (as has been suggested) the laws of socialization are non-universal.[81] More sub- and cross-cultural data are clearly called for.

"WITH WHAT EFFECTS?"

As stated earlier, there is really no way, using the data gathered up to this point, to test the effects of socialization. Greenstein speculates that early learning is important because it "takes place during a formative period and (because) early learning affects later learning."[82] In regard to the effects of socialization on the political system, there are no data to speak of. Greenstein as well as Easton and Dennis give us the near-truism that socialization may be either a stabilizing influence or a "potential source of change."[83]

Easton and Dennis claim that their research "concentrates on the stress that may arise from the inability of a system to keep the input of support at some minimal level."[84] In their own words, however, they tell us what they have actually done: "Once we establish the objects toward which members of a system are capable of reacting, we need to inquire into how they feel about what they see."[85] Despite the importance of their book, this is all they have done. Indeed, it takes an inferential leap of grand magnitude to proceed from this description to statements regarding the persistence of political systems. It is, moreover, possible that what Easton and Dennis have examined is merely another inquiry into the authoritarian syndrome. That is, by asking children how they feel about authority one may be tapping the dimension of authoritarianism rather than that of support for the political system. This is indeed important and undoubtedly has implications for the system, but caution should be exercised in making the leap.

This literature does, however, raise some interesting points about the possible precursors of revolutionary and iconoclastic political behavior. These, as well as conventional behavior, must somehow be learned. But in all honesty political scientists have not gotten beyond the realm of speculation in answering this important question. To reiterate, it is in this area that the need for longitudinal studies is most apparent.

CRITIQUE

Many shortcomings of extant research are outlined in the preceding pages. Such considerations as the need for longitudinal data,[86] the lack of studies dealing with the socialization of adults, and the lack of data on the effect of early socialization on later behavior, occupied our attention.[87] In addition one might cite the need to supplement questionnaires by personal interviews and both of these techniques by methods such as observation, projective techniques, and laboratory experiments.[88]

According to Sigel, "socialization is a misnomer for what we study because we study *what* children have learned (the output) not *how* they learned it."[89] We have in other words *not* been looking at the *process* of political socialization, we *have* been looking at the *content*. The preceding review of the literature has demonstrated this imbalance. The large amount of work examining "what is learned" as compared to the dearth of studies dealing with the question of "from whom?" is evident. As Sigel further states, once we have enumerated the content, we then compare the answers "by age, and if we find systematic differences over age, we assume they are due to development" of the child.[90]

This procedure is highly inferential. The differences observed could just as easily be the result of other factors, such as exposure to media. With conspicuous exceptions, political scientists have not been too imaginative in their quest for variables. They have used factors such as age and social class as direct agents of socialization, when in fact they probably mediate between the agents and the content.

More about this later. For now, one may say that the political scientist has primarily concerned himself with "describing the content of children's political evaluations."[91] This "static and homogeneous" conception of political socialization is partially the result of the main theoretical frameworks that have been used to analyze political socialization. While Sigel is correct in stating that a theory of political socialization does not exist,[92] one is able to identify a theoretical strand running through most of the research. It is primarily Freudian or psychoanalytic.[93] In their analysis of the role of the parent as an agent of socialization and the generalization of attitudes from parental authority figures to political authority figures, Greenstein and Easton and his colleagues demonstrate heavy reliance on this approach.[94]

As demonstrated by the above discussion, this theory is not adequate. Froman presents a detailed analysis of the limitations involved in the use of psychoanalytic thinking. According to him:

(1) it draws attention away from possible agents of learning other than parents, such as peer groups, mass media, and school sources. . . .
(2) it has not been adequately tested.
(3) more importantly, it tends to blend together the component parts of what have been referred to as "images" at the cost of theorizing about the learning process.[95]

In other words, the psychoanalytic framework has restricted the investigation of the agents of socialization largely to the family. Sigel argues that this has led to a "simplistic and static" model of political socialization, and that the political scientist must ground his study of socialization on more appropriate "theoretical underpinnings."[96] She recommends learning theory[97] because it raises additional questions to which little attention has been given.

A learning-theory framework, according to Sigel, would cause the political scientists to ask questions other than "what does the child know about the President, about justice, etc. ?"[98] It would focus attention on "the same agents or forces that influence all social behavior: first and foremost, the family, the socially relevant groups or institutions, such as school, church and social class; and—last but not least—society at large and the political culture it fosters."[99]

Up to now, the student of political socialization has not based his inquiry upon a theoretical framework that could operate to bring some order to his data. Additional approaches are necessary and the present work will attempt to formulate a theoretical framework that should provide some insight into the process of political socialization.

Notes

Chapter 1

[1] Jack Dennis, *Recent Research on Political Socialization: A Bibliography of Published, Forthcoming, and Unpublished Works, Thesis, and Dissertations, and a Survey of Projects in Progress* (Medford, Mass.: Lincoln Filene Center for Citizenship and Public Affairs, 1967), p. 1. Surveys of the field have begun to appear. See: Richard Dawson, "Political Socialization," in James H. Robinson (ed.), *Political Science Annual: An International Review*, Vol. 1 (Indianapolis: Bobbs-Merrill, 1966), pp. 1–94: Jack Dennis, "Major Problems of Political Socialization Research," *Midwest Journal of Political Science*, XII (February, 1968), pp. 85–114; and Richard E. Dawson and Kenneth Prewitt, *Political Socialization* (Boston: Little, Brown and Company 1969).

[2] Dean Jaros, *Children's Orientations Toward Political Authority: A Detroit Study*. Unpublished Ph.D. dissertation submitted to the Department of Political Science, Vanderbilt University, June, 1966, p. 4.

[3] There are several reviews of this literature: *Ibid.,* pp. 4–9; and Fred I. Greenstein, *Children and Politics* (New Haven: Yale University Press, 1965), pp. 1–5.

[4] The volumes in this series are: Bessie Louise Pierce, *Citizen's Organizations and the Civic Training of Youth* (New York: Scribners, 1944); Charles E. Merriam, *The Making of Citizens: A Comparative Study of Civic Training* (University of Chicago Press, 1931); and Charles E. Merriam, *Civic Education in the United States* (New York: Scribners, 1934). This literature is reviewed in Greenstein, *op. cit.,* pp. 5–7; and Jaros, *op. cit.,* p. 17.

[5] This literature is given a comprehensive review by: Herbert Hyman, *Political Socialization: Study in the Psychology of Political Behavior* (New York: The Free Press, 1959); and Greenstein, *op. cit.,* pp. 7–9.

[6] Fred I. Greenstein, "Political Socialization," Mimeo prepared for the *International Encyclopedia of the Social Sciences* (New York: Crowell-Collier, 1968), p. 3; a similar formulation has been proposed by William C. Mitchell, *The American Polity* (New York: The Free Press, 1962), p. 146.

⁷ Lewis A. Froman, Jr., "Learning Political Attitudes," *Western Political Quarterly,* 15 (June, 1962), p. 305. There is, however, even substantial disagreement on this basic point. For Easton and Dennis the primary question is not related to the process by which the child learns political attitudes and behaviors, but ". . . to determine the relevance of socialization for the operation of a political system as a whole." David Easton and Jack Dennis, *Children in the Political System: Origins of Political Legitimacy* (New York: McGraw-Hill, 1969). p. 42. We have, indeed, even been warned that "Political scholars should guard against letting their intellectual energies and research resources be drained into social-psychological queries, however important the latter may be." Richard E. Dawson and Kenneth Prewitt, *Political Socialization* (Boston: Little, Brown and Company, 1969), p. 14. As will become evident, my sympathies are not in accord with these views.

⁸ The only study using older subjects is: M. Kent Jennings and Richard G. Niemi, "The Transmission of Political Values from Parent to Child," *The American Political Science Review,* LXII (March, 1968), pp. 169–184.

⁹ Robert D. Hess and Judith V. Torney, *The Development of Basic Attitudes and Values Toward Government and Citizenship During the Elementary School Years,* Part I (Chicago: The University of Chicago, 1965), p. 4. This report is very much like the later book which grew out of it. See: Robert D. Hess and Judith V. Torney, *The Development of Political Attitudes in Children* (Chicago: Aldine Publishing Company, 1967), esp. Chaps. 1 and 2. Since they are so much alike, page numbers referred to throughout this study, unless otherwise noted, will refer to the earlier report. Also see: Greenstein, *International Encyclopedia,* p. 7; and David Easton and Robert D. Hess, "The Child's Political World," *Midwest Journal of Political Science,* VI, 3 (August, 1962), p. 236.

¹⁰ Robert D. Hess, "The Socialization of Attitudes Toward Political Authority: Some Cross National Comparisons." *International Social Science Journal,* XV (1963), p. 544; Roberta S. Sigel, "An Exploration Into Some Aspects of Political Socialization: School Children's Reactions to the Death of a President," in Martha Wolfenstein and Gilbert Kliman (eds.), *Children and the Death of a President: Multi-Disciplinary Studies* (New York: Doubleday, 1965), p. 31. Easton and Dennis, *Children in the Political System, passim.*

¹¹ Greenstein, *International Encyclopedia,* p. 6.

¹² Easton and Hess, *Midwest Journal,* p. 236; also Hess, *International Social Science Journal,* p. 544.

¹³ Dawson and Prewitt, *op. cit.,* Chap. IV, pp. 41–62.

¹⁴ Fred I. Greenstein, "The Benevolent Leader: Children's Images of Political Authority," the *American Political Science Review,* LIV (December, 1960); Greenstein, Children and Politics: Robert D. Hess and David Easton, "The Child's Changing Image of the President," *Public Opinion Quarterly,* Vol. 24 (1960), pp. 632–644; Hess, *International Social Science Journal;* Hess and Torney, p. 97; Roberta Sigel, "An Exploration into Some Aspects of Political Socialization," p. 33; and Dean Jaros, "Children's Orientations Toward the President: Some Additional Theoretical Considerations and Data," *The Journal of Politics,* 29, 2 (May, 1967), pp. 368–387.

¹⁵ Greenstein, *Children and Politics,* p. 71.

¹⁶ *Ibid.,* p. 57.

¹⁷ *Ibid.,* p. 104.

¹⁸ Greenstein, *International Encyclopedia,* p. 3; Dawson and Prewitt, *op. cit.,* pp. 181–194. Also see: Hess and Torney, *The Development of Political Attitudes in Children,* Chaps. 7 and 8, pp. 126–194.

[19] Fred I. Greenstein, "Sex-Related Political Differences in Childhood," *Journal of Politics,* 23, 2 (May, 1961), p. 358.

[20] Greenstein, *Children and Politics,* pp. 115, 117.

[21] *Ibid.*

[22] Greenstein, *International Encyclopedia,* p. 3; and *Children and Politics,* pp. 58–59.

[23] Greenstein, *Children and Politics,* p. 73.

[24] Greenstein, *International Encyclopedia,* p. 3.

[25] The only study, of which the author has knowledge, which uses a sample of children in grades 5 through 12 is: Dean Jaros, Herbert Hirsch, and Frederic Fleron, "The Malevolent Leader: Political Socialization in an American Sub-Culture," *The American Political Science Review,* LXII, 2 (June, 1968), pp. 564–575.

[26] William H. Sewell, "Some Recent Developments in Socialization Theory and Research," *The Annals of the American Academy of Political and Social Science* (September, 1963), pp. 163–181. Sewell cites a study which demonstrates that in later life a role reversal occurs and adult children become agents of socialization for their aged parents. See Raymond Payne, "Some Theoretical Approaches to the Sociology of Ageing," *Social Forces* (May, 1960). Also see: Orville G. Brim and Stanton Wheeler, *Socialization After Childhood* (New York: John Wiley, 1966), and Orville G. Brim, Jr., "Adult Socialization," in John A. Clausen (ed.), *Socialization and Society* (Boston: Little, Brown and Company, 1968), pp. 182–226.

[27] Heinz Eulau, *et al.,* "The Political Socialization of American State Legislators," *Midwest Journal of Political Science,* Vol. 3 (1959), pp. 188–206; and Herbert Hirsch, "The Political Socialization of State Legislators: A Re-Examination," in Herbert Hirsch and M. Donald Hancock, (eds.), *Comparative Legislative Systems: A Reader in Theory and Research* (New York: The Free Press, forthcoming).

[28] A similar comment concerning the static nature of the political scientist's model of socialization has been made by Roberta S. Sigel, *Political Socialization: Some Reactions on Current Approaches and Conceptualizations.* Paper delivered at the 1966 Annual Meeting of the American Political Science Association, Statler-Hilton Hotel, New York City, September 6–10, p. 14.

[29] For a similar statement see: Kenneth Prewitt, "Political Socialization and Leadership Selection," *The Annals of the American Academy of Political and Social Science,* Vol. 361 (1965), p. 97.

[30] Greenstein, *International Encyclopedia,* p. 4, Easton and Hess also propose a classification of the content of political learning. David Easton and Robert D. Hess, "Youth and the Political System," in Seymour Martin Lipset and Leo Lowenthal (eds.), *Culture and Social Character* (New York: The Free Press, 1961), pp. 226–251; and by the same authors, *Midwest Journal.*

[31] For a review of some early studies see: Hyman, *op. cit.,* pp. 206–223. The author is aware of only two articles on political socialization which make use of personality variables. The first is mainly a theoretical discussion with no data, the second is more empirical and has data on authoritarianism and anxiety. See: Fred I. Greenstein, "Personality and Political Socialization: The Theories of Authoritarian and Democratic Character," *The Annals,* Vol. 361 (1965), pp. 81–95; and Dean Jaros, *Children's Orientations Toward Political Authority: A Detroit Study.* Ph.D. dissertation, June, 1966; and by the same author, "Children's Orientations Toward the President: Some Additional Theoretical Considerations and Data," *The Journal of Politics,* 29, 2 (May, 1967), pp. 368–387.

[32] Greenstein, *International Encyclopedia,* p. 4.

[33] Greenstein, *Children and Politics,* pp. 55–83; and Hess and Torney, pp. 44–45,

147–167; and James C. Davies, "The Family's Role in Political Socialization," *The Annals,* Vol. 361 (1965), pp. 10–19. On the inheritance of party identification see: Paul Lazarsfeld, *et al., The People's Choice* (2nd ed., New York: Columbia University Press, 1948), p. 142; Bernard Berelson, *et al., Voting* (Chicago: University of Chicago Press, 1954), p. 89; Angus Campbell, *et al., The Voter Decides* (Evanston, Ill.: Row Peterson, 1954), pp. 97–107; Angus Campbell, *et al., The American Voter,* Chaps. 6 and 7; and Hyman, *Political Socialization,* Chap. 5.

[34] Hess and Torney, pp. 147–167; Greenstein, *American Political Science Review,* p. 938.

[35] Greenstein, *Children and Politics,* p. 67.

[36] *Ibid.,* pp. 67–71.

[37] *Ibid.,* p. 71.

[38] Greenstein, *International Encyclopedia,* p. 4.

[39] Greenstein, *Children and Politics,* p. 61; David Easton and Jack Dennis, "The Child's Image of Government," *The Annals,* Vol. 361 (1965), pp. 40–57; and M. Kent Jennings, "Pre-Adult Orientations to Multiple Systems of Government," *Midwest Journal of Political Science* (August, 1967), p. 96.

[40] Easton and Dennis, *Annals,* p. 52, and more recently, *Children in the Political System, passim.*

[41] Greenstein, *The American Political Science Review,* 1960, p. 935; and Jennings and Niemi, *op. cit.*

[42] David Ziblatt, "High School Extracurricular Activities and Political Socialization," *The Annals,* Vol. 361 (1965), pp. 20–31.

[43] *Ibid.*

[44] Jaros, Hirsch, and Fleron, *op. cit.*

[45] Frank A. Pinner, "Parental Overprotection and Political Distrust," *The Annals,* Vol. 361 (1965), pp. 58–70.

[46] Hess and Easton, *Public Opinion Quarterly,* p. 636; Robert Hess and David Easton, "The Role of the Elementary School in Political Socialization," *The School Review,* LXX, 3 (Autumn, 1962), pp. 260–261; Hess, *International Social Science Journal,* pp. 12–13; Greenstein, *Children and Politics,* pp. 27–54; Fred I. Greenstein, "Popular Images of the President," *The American Journal of Psychiatry,* CXXII, 5, and for the most comprehensive inquiry into childhood orientations toward political authority see: Easton and Dennis, *Children in the Political System* (November, 1965), p. 524; Hess and Torney, pp. 102–105; and Jaros, *Journal of Politics.* There is, to date, only one study reporting deviant findings. It demonstrates that children in the Appalachian sub-culture are not as favorably disposed to the President as their contemporaries. See: Jaros, Hirsch, and Fleron, *op. cit.*

[47] Greenstein, *International Encyclopedia,* p. 4.

[48] For a series of studies see: Eulau, *et al., Midwest Journal*; Allan Kornberg and Norman Thomas, "The Political Socialization of National Legislative Elites in the United States and Canada," *Journal of Politics,* 27 (November, 1965), pp. 761–775; Heinz Eulau and John D. Sprague, *Lawyers in Politics* (Indianapolis, Indiana: Bobbs-Merrill, 1964), esp. Chap. 3, "The Political Socialization of Lawyers," pp. 56–64; and James David Barber, *The Lawmakers: Recruitment and Adaptation to Legislative Life* (New, Haven: Yale University Press, 1965), esp. Chap. 6, "The Development of Political Personalities," pp. 212–258; Hirsch, *op. cit.*; Kenneth Prewitt, *et al.,* "Political Socialization and Political Roles," *Public Opinion Quarterly,* 30 (1966–67), pp. 569–582.

[49] On the agents of socialization see: Easton and Hess, "Youth and the Political System," p. 251; Greenstein, *Children and Politics,* pp. 9–15; and by the same author, *International Encyclopedia,* p. 6; Lewis A. Froman, Jr., "Personality and Political Socializa-

tion," *Journal of Politics*, 23, 2 (May, 1961), pp. 341–352; William C. Mitchell, *The American Polity* (New York: The Free Press, 1962), esp. Chap. 7, "The Socialization of Citizens," pp. 145–178; Hess and Torney, *op. cit.*, pp. 182–228; and Dawson and Prewitt, *op. cit.*, pp. 105–200.

[50] Hess and Torney, *op. cit.*, pp. 182–184; in the book, pp. 93–94.

[51] *Ibid.*, p. 182.

[52] *Ibid.*, p. 184. For Greenstein the family is the primary agent of socialization. See: *Children and Politics,* p. 44.

[53] Hess and Torney, p. 195. For other studies dealing with the inheritance of party identification see footnote 33.

[54] *Ibid.*, p. 165; and Greenstein, *Children and Politics,* p. 103, and p. 119.

[55] Hess and Torney, p. 165.

[56] *Ibid.*, pp. 187–200.

[57] *Ibid.*, pp. 193–195.

[58] *Ibid.*, p. 200.

[59] *Ibid.*

[60] Gabriel A. Almond and G. Bingham Powell, Jr., *Comparative Politics: A Developmental Approach* (Boston: Little, Brown and Company, 1966), pp. 65–66.

[61] Hess and Torney, p. 200; Greenstein, *International Encyclopedia,* p. 6; and Mitchell, *op. cit.*, p. 161.

[62] Greenstein, *International Encyclopedia*, p. 6; and Hess and Torney, p. 202.

[63] Hess and Torney, pp. 154 and p. 210.

[64] Kenneth Langton and M. Kent Jennings, "Political Socialization and the High School Civics Curriculum," *The American Political Science Review,* LXII (September, 1968), p. 866. Also see: Dean Jaros, "The Teacher and Political Socialization: Transmitting the Civic Culture," *Social Science Quarterly* (September, 1968), pp. 284–295.

[65] Hess and Torney, pp. 216–217.

[66] *Ibid.*, p. 222.

[67] *Ibid.*

[68] *Ibid.*, p. 183.

[69] Greenstein, *International Encyclopedia*, p. 6. Two suggestive studies are: Roberta Sigel, "Television and the Reactions of School Children to the Assassination," in Bradley S. Greenberg and Edwin B. Parker (eds.), *The Kennedy Assassination and the American Public* (Stanford University Press, 1965), pp. 199–219; and Herbert Hyman, "Mass Media and Political Socialization: The Role of Patterns of Communication," in Lucian Pye (ed.), *Communication and Political Development* (Princeton University Press, 1963), pp. 128–148.

[70] Hess and Torney, pp. 183–184.

[71] *Ibid.*, p. 184. For the latest, and not too fruitful, attempt to relate intelligence to the development of a "regime norm" see: Elliott S. White, "Intelligence and Sense of Political Efficacy in Children," *Journal of Politics,* 30 (August, 1968), pp. 710–731.

[72] Morris Rosenberg, *Society and the Adolescent Self-Image* (Princeton: Princeton University Press, 1965), pp. 206–223.

[73] Jaros, *Journal of Politics*, p. 385.

[74] These studies are important, for they do indeed add an important dimension to our understanding of the incipient citizen. See: Reid Reading, "Political Socialization in Columbia and the United States: An Exploratory Study," *Midwest Journal of Political Science*, pp. 352–381; Kenneth N. Walker, "Political Socialization in Universities," in Seymour Martin Lipset and Aldo Solari (eds.), *Elites in Latin America* (New York: Oxford University Press, 1967), pp. 408–430; Jack Dennis, *et al.*, "Political Socialization

to Democratic Orientations in Four Western Systems," *Comparative Political Studies,* 1 (1968), pp. 71–101; Timothy M. Hennessey, "Democratic Attitudinal Configurations Among Italian Youth," *Midwest Journal of Political Science,* XIII (May, 1969), pp. 167–193. For a study using adults as subjects, see: Frederick W. Frey, "Socialization to National Identification Among Turkish Peasants," *Journal of Politics,* 4 (November, 1968), pp. 934–965.

[75] Philip E. Converse and George Depeux, "Politicization of the Electorate in France and the United States," *Public Opinion Quarterly,* XXVI, 1 (Sping, 1962), pp. 1–23.

[76] Hess, *International Social Science Journal,* pp. 542–559.

[77] *Ibid.,* p. 557.

[78] *Ibid.*

[79] Jaros, Hirsch, and Fleron, *op. cit.*

[80] *Ibid.*

[81] Michael Argyle and Peter Delin, "Non-Universal Laws of Socialization," *Human Relations,* 18, 1 (February, 1965), pp. 77–86; also Sigel, *Political Socialization: Some Reactions on Current Approaches and Conceptualizations,* p. 14; where she states that one ". . . cannot talk about socialization in a universalistic sense: one is socialized to a specific system."

[82] Greenstein, *Children and Politics,* p. 79.

[83] Greenstein, *International Encyclopedia,* pp. 7–8; Easton and Dennis, *Children in the Political System, passim.*

[84] Easton and Dennis, *Children in the Political System,* p. 57.

[85] *Ibid.,* p. 105.

[86] Sigel, *A.P.S.A.,* p. 3; and Lewis A. Froman, Jr., "Learning Political Attitudes," *Western Political Quarterly,* 15 (June, 1962), pp. 305–306 also note the need for longitudinal studies.

[87] Sewell, *The Annals,* pp. 173–179, gives a detailed account of the lack of and need for studies of the socialization of adults.

[88] Sigel, *A.P.S.A.,* pp. 10–11. For an interesting account of the weaknesses of depending solely on interview data see: Robert Rosenthal, *Experimenter Effects in Behavior Research* (New York: Appleton-Century-Crofts, 1966), and for a delightful account of alternatives and supplements to interviews and questionnaires see: Eugene J. Webb, *et al., Unobtrusive Measures: Nonreactive Research in the Social Sciences* (Chicago: Rand McNally and Company, 1966).

[89] Sigel, *A.P.S.A.,* p. 3.

[90] *Ibid.,* p. 2.

[91] Froman, *Western Political Quarterly,* p. 312.

[92] Sigel, *A.P.S.A.,* p. 11.

[93] Froman, *Western Political Quarterly,* pp. 304–305; Hess, *International Social Science Journal,* p. 542.

[94] A number of studies rely upon a combination of systems theory and psychoanalytic theory. These scholars rely heavily upon De Grazia's Freudian account of the role played by the family in forming attitudes toward political authority figures (Sebastian De Grazia, *The Political Community: A Study of Anomie* (Chicago: University of Chicago Press, 1948), p. 11). They add a systems framework under the influence of their major hypothesis, i.e.

"that if a political system is to persist, one of its major tasks is to provide for the input of at least a minimal level of support for a regime of some kind." (David Easton and Jack Dennis, "The Child's Acquisition of Regime Norms: Political Efficacy," *The American Political Science Review,* LXI (March, 1967), p. 25.

Systems theory is offered as a means of incorporating the study of political socialization onto the macro-level of analysis. It is supposed to demonstrate how political socialization affects the operation of the political system. Thus far, I think, it has not been successful. As noted previously, to go from a description of the content of what the child learns about politics to statements about system implications requires an inferential leap of great magnitude. The concept of socialization seems to me to be singularly oriented toward the individual. We are interested in what society, i.e. system, does to the individual. This is not to say that the converse of this is not equally, if not more, important. It is much more difficult to get at empirically. For Easton and Dennis, however, the state is the end, i.e. how does socialization affect the system? If systems are aggregates of individuals, and they may not in fact be such, then examining the *process* and *content* of the political socialization of the individual inevitably leads to certain implications for the system. Empirical verification of the systemic consequences of individual political socialization still await discovery. The main studies are: Easton and Dennis, *American Political Science Review*; Hess and Easton, *The School Review*; Easton and Hess, "Youth and the Political System;" and Easton and Hess, *Midwest Journal of Political Science*; Easton and Dennis, *Children in the Political System*.

[95] Froman, *Western Political Quarterly*, p. 305.

[96] Sigel, *A.P.S.A.*, p. 2.

[97] There are three works that attempt to use a learning theory framework. Hess and Torney, p. 3, state that their report "analyzes political involvement from the viewpoint of learning processes regarding political behavior as acquired response patterns rather than as expressions of deep psychic needs." This is only partially true. They do not deduce their hypotheses from a learning theory, rather they have taken them from prior political socialization literature. One is really not able to see how this data relates to learning theory. The other two works are basically theoretical discussions which translate certain political science concepts into a learning theory framework. See: Henry Teune, "The Learning of Integrative Habits," in Philip E. Jacob and James V. Toscano (eds)., *The Integration of Political Communities* (Philadelphia: J. B. Lippincott Co., 1964), pp. 247–282; and Richard M. Merelman, "Learning and Legitimacy," *The American Political Science Review*, LX, 3 (September, 1966), pp. 548–561.

[98] Sigel, *A.P.S.A.*, p. 4.

[99] Roberta S. Sigel, "Assumptions About the Learning of Political Values," *The Annals*, Vol. 361 (1965), p. 4.

2
Toward a Theory
of Political Socialization

Having reviewed the political socialization literature we shall now attempt to formulate a more adequate theory of political socialization. This theoretical formulation will be composed of an eclectic mixture of (1) prior studies of political socialization, (2) social learning theory, and (3) some propositions derived from culture theory and personality theory.[1]

Most studies of political socialization display an implicit or explicit conceptualization of political socialization as a learning process. Unfortunately, however, Hyman's remark of almost ten years ago, though concurred in by most recent observers, goes yet unheeded: "One seeks far and wide for any extended treatment of political behavior as learned behavior, despite the fact that this is patently the case."[2] It is a fairly well established axiom that socialization processes operate " . . . mainly through the mechanisms of learning. . . ."[3] In other words, if political socialization operates in the same manner as the process of socialization in general, then it too must be a learning process. Therefore, a learning theory that takes account of social variables, i.e., a social learning theory, should provide the political scientist with additional insights into the workings of the process.

Indeed, scholars see the broad applicability of the canons of learning

Notes to Chapter 2 will be found on pp. 25–26.

theory. According to Mowrer, however, on the basis of learning theory alone:

One cannot at all accurately foretell what an organism will or will not do. One must also know what both his internal environment (tissue needs) and his external environment (physical and social) are going to be. A psychology of the total person must, therefore, be anchored no less in sociology, history, culture theory, and even geography than it is in biology.[4]

It is the object of this work to add political science to Mowrer's list, for it is political stimuli in which we are interested. Not only may this offer new approaches to traditional political concerns, but it may have implications for broader social theory as well.

SOCIAL LEARNING THEORY: A BRIEF DEVELOPMENTAL ACCOUNT

Historically, the emergence of social learning theory dates from 1941 when Miller and Dollard's classic study, *Social Learning and Imitation*, was published.

Miller and Dollard took learning theory out of the laboratory and extrapolated its propositions to social behavior. According to their basic formulation, the "first factor involved in learning is drive. . . . Drive impels the subject to act or respond. Response is the second factor involved in learning. . . . Responses are elicited by cues. . . . Finally, comes the reward."[5] The main type of response behavior is "imitation," which consists of three sub-types: "same behavior, matched–dependent behavior, and copying,"[6] The latter two receive the greatest amount of discussion in regard to the socialization of children.[7]

In "matched–dependent" behavior,

the leader is able to read the relevant environmental cues, but the follower is not; the latter must depend upon the leader for the signal as to what act is performed and where and when.[8]

In "copying,"

the copier must slowly bring his response to approximate that of a model and must know, when he has done so, that his act is an acceptable reproduction of the model act.[9]

Therefore,

the essential difference between the two processes is that in matched–dependent behavior the imitator responds only to the cue from the leader, while in copying he responds to the cues of sameness and difference from his own and his model's response.[10]

Bandura and Walters[11] have expanded on Miller and Dollard's basic formulations. "Their studies have been conducted in natural field settings, in the laboratory, and in the clinic with children and adolescents. As a consequence, among the learning theorists, their work shows most clearly the relevance of this approach to the understanding of human social behavior."[12]

Miller and Dollard

posit that initially the imitative act occurs by chance and the act can only be reinforced if some drive is reduced following the execution of the response. According to this view only direct reward from the social environment, like praise or affection, can strengthen the person's tendency to imitate a model.[13]

But Bandura indicates that this conceptualization presents two important theoretical problems:

First, it requires the subject to perform some approximation of the response before he can learn it. . . . Second, traditional behavior theories assume that the subject somehow suspends learning until the occurrence of reinforcing consequences following the termination of the response. Thus, if an experimenter were to inform a child that Columbus discovered America in 1492, the acquisition of this knowledge is presumably delayed and made contingent on the occurrence of a rewarding payoff.[14]

Along with the traditional learning paradigm, Bandura feels that "no trial" or "observational" learning is "highly prevalent among homo sapiens, exceedingly efficient and, in cases where errors are dangerous or costly, becomes an indispensable means of transmitting and modifying behavioral repertories."[15] It is not likely, Bandura points out, that one would teach a child to swim, or a woman to drive a car, by relying on trial and error. Observational learning depends upon the learner's being exposed to "real-life models who perform, intentionally or unwittingly, patterns of behavior that may be imitated by others."[16] In observational learning the subject neither makes a response nor gets a reward—he does not have to manifest any overt behavior. Imitation, for Bandura, does not mean behavior matching. The modeling process, or the process of observational learning, starts behavior, but matching does not have to be overt. It simply means that a person will have a tendency to "reproduce the actions, attitudes, or emotional responses exhibited by real-life or symbolized models."[17]

Defining socialization as the process by which the person learns the political attitudes and behaviors of his culture emphasizes its congruence with this modeling process. Indeed, Bandura notes that observational learning is "utilized in all cultures to promote the acquisition of socially sanctioned behavior patterns."[18] We merely add that the behavior patterns in which we are interested are political. Hess and Torney have in fact noted that one of the ways in which the family can act as an agent of political socialization is by serving as a model for the child.[19]

SOCIAL LEARNING THEORY AND THE AGENTS OF POLITICAL SOCIALIZATION

The modeling scheme focuses our attention on cue stimuli and their generators—the agents of political socialization.

An implicit assumption involved in viewing political socialization as a process of learning is that the customary mode of political behavior within a culture is continuously passed from adults to children. In accepting this we focus on learning that occurs during childhood not because we discount the fact that socialization is a continuous process, but because, as Brim notes ". . . early learning interferes with and limits later learning,"[20] and because behavior learned in childhood is particularly hard to extinguish since it is "learned under conditions of partial reinforcement."[21] Political orientations are to be viewed in the same manner as they are viewed by Hess and Torney—as acquired response patterns.[22] A particularly acquisitive period in life is childhood.

The agents from whom the child acquires his response patterns are, therefore, keys to understanding the process of political socialization. Socializing agents can be defined as "resource mediators or resource administrators."[23] In this case, political information and attitudes are the resources, and it is our aim to find out who administers and mediates them for the child. Who, in fact, are the agents of political socialization?

THE AGENTS: A THEORETICAL FORMULATION

Students of political socialization have claimed that all of the following act as agents of political socialization: family, school, church, peer groups and youth organizations, social class, ethnic origin, geographic region, and mass media.[24]

The agents that have been posited as influential by political scientists are the same as those that learning theorists have identified as models in the learning process. Accordingly, it requires no great extension to use the relatively coherent principles of learning theory to interpret more fully generalizations about political socialization. More importantly, the theory also leads to additional hypotheses concerning the activities of the jointly acknowledged agents. Finally, by so emphasizing a *process* of socialization, learning theory illuminates the possibility of functional equivalence among several teachers or agents. Under certain circumstances, altogether unsuspected variables may be operative. Learning theory may lead us to them.

This work is concerned with one of these circumstances. The investigation of the role of political socialization agents in the sub-cultural setting of Appalachia has been stimulated by these theoretical considerations.[25] Appalachia may be classified as a sub-culture for at least two reasons. First, "many cultural norms of Appalachia differ radically from those considered to be standard middle-class imperatives. Second, the abject poverty of the region imposes characteristics that differentiate it from most other areas in the country."[26]

While learning theory is consistent with many of the findings of previous socialization studies, it suggests that altogether different agents are operative in the specific milieu under investigation here. Should these hypotheses prove to be true empirically, not only will learning theory have served as an impetus to new investigation, but it will also have been shown to be of sufficient generality to explain the most diverse findings.

In social learning theory terms, the family is an early and pervasive model. This research not only seeks to explain the operation of this model, but also to investigate its possible replacement by other, more salient models as the child matures. Conducting the study in the Appalachian setting allows us to determine what happens when family models are impaired by the environmental factors found in a poverty sub-culture.

It is to the design and execution of the Appalachian study that we now turn.

Notes

Chapter 2

[1] When one attempts to formulate a relatively new theoretical approach to an established area of study he is open to the criticism that he could have utilized a theoretical framework proposed by earlier scholars. This notion is partially rejected here because concentration on one man's theory would be stultifying. Our purpose is to uncover new knowledge, and, therefore, a cross-cultural comparison using prior political socialization work as the theoretical basis, while useful, would not lead one to examine new variables and the effect or non-effect they might have upon the process of political socialization. The criticism is not completely rejected for we do incorporate prior political socialization findings into the theory.

[2] Hyman, *Political Socialization*, p. 17.

[3] Talcott Parsons and Edward A. Shils, *Towards a General Theory of Action* (New York: Harper & Row, 1962: paperback edition), p. 227; and Neal E. Miller and John Dollard, *Social Learning and Imitation* (New Haven: Yale University Press, 1941), p. 4.

[4] O. Hobart Mowrer, *Learning Theory and Behavior* (New York: John Wiley, 1960), p. 10.

[5] Miller and Dollard, *op. cit.,* pp. 16–17.

[6] *Ibid.,* p. 91.

[7] *Ibid.,* pp. 92, 93 and 162.

[8] *Ibid.,* p. 11.

[9] *Ibid.*

[10] *Ibid.,* p. 154.

[11] Albert Bandura and Richard H. Walters, *Social Learning and Personality Development* (New York: Holt, Rinehart and Winston, 1963).

[12] Morton Deutsch and Robert M. Krauss, *Theories in Social Psychology* (New York: Basic Books, Inc., 1965), p. 94.

[13] Jerome Kagan, "The Concept of Identification," *Psychological Review*, 65, 5 (1958), p. 296.

[14] Albert Bandura, "Behavior Modifications Through Modeling Procedures," in L. Krasner and L. Ullman (eds.), *Research in Behavior Modification* (New York: Holt, Rinehart and Winston, 1965), p. 312.

[15] *Ibid.*

[16] *Ibid.,* p. 314.

[17] Bandura and Walters, *op. cit.,* p. 89.

[18] Albert Bandura, "Vicarious Processes: A Case of No-Trial Learning," in Leonard Berkowitz (ed.), *Advances in Experimental Social Psychology*, Vol. 2 (New York: Academic Press, 1965), p. 29.

[19] Hess and Torney, p. 184.

[20] Brim and Wheeler, p. 22.

[21] Brim, "Personality Development as Role-Learning," p. 129; and Brim and Wheeler, p. 21. Also see: Irwin L. Child, "Socialization," in Gardner Lindzey (ed.), *Handbook of Social Psychology*, Vol. II (Cambridge, Mass.: Addison-Wesley Publishing Company, Inc., 1954), p. 678.

[22] Hess and Torney, p. 3.

[23] John W. M. Whiting, "Resource Mediation and Learning by Identification," in Ira Iscoe and Harold W. Stevenson (eds.), *Personality Development in Children* (Austin, Texas: University of Texas Press, 1960), p. 115.

[24] See: Easton and Hess, "Youth and the Political System," p. 251; Greenstein, *Children and Politics*, pp. 9–15; and by the same author, *International Encyclopedia*, p. 6; Froman, *Journal of Politics*, pp. 341–352; Mitchell, *op. cit.,* chap. 7, pp. 145–178; and Hess and Torney, 182–228.

[25] Brim has noted that: "In different cultures, the conception of the desirable adult may differ and different ends may be sought in socialization." Brim, "Personality Development as Role-Learning," p. 152. Also see: Brim and Wheeler, *Socialization After Childhood*, p. 19; Easton and Hess, "Youth and the Political System," p. 242; Sewell, *op. cit.,* p. 167; Sigel, *Political Socialization: Some Reactions on Current Approaches and Conceptualizations*, p. 14; and Almond and Powell, *op. cit.,* p. 23.

[26] Jaros, Hirsch, and Fleron, *op. cit.,* p. 565. Also see: Jack E. Weller, *op. cit.*; Harry M. Caudill, *Night Comes to the Cumberlands* (Boston: Little, Brown and Co., 1963); and Thomas R. Ford (ed.), *The Southern Appalachian Region: A Survey* (Lexington: University of Kentucky Press, 1960).

3
Methodology and Technique

SELECTION OF THE SAMPLE

The sample upon which this study is based includes the entire population of fifth through twelfth-grade school children in rural Knox County, Kentucky. Excluded from the sample are those areas of Knox County that have been defined as "non-rural." The population is designed to represent a "model" rural Appalachian poverty area. Knox County is neither the poorest nor the richest county in Appalachia; it contains elements of extreme poverty as well as some "better-off." Criteria of selection included distributions of sex, age, birth rate, out-migration, education, income, employment and industry.[1] The identification of the population within Knox County was accomplished through (1) conferences with local officials and (2) from a complete household census and detailed mapping of the area. Consequently, data have been gathered from a carefully selected population designed to represent a "typical" Appalachian poverty area.

For statistical purposes this population will be construed as a sample of the rural Appalachian poverty culture. This conceptualization enables one to utilize tests of significance.[2]

Notes to Chapter 3 will be found on pp. 31–32.

DEVELOPMENT OF THE QUESTIONNAIRE

A preliminary written questionnaire was designed in the summer of 1966. During the months of July and August, 1966, a pre-test of this schedule was administered to a group of 60 children, grades seven through nine, who were attending a summer camp program (Camp UNICO) in Barbourville, Kentucky. These children came to the camp from all portions of Kentucky's Appalachian counties, with one or two from Tennessee. Particularly disadvantaged, many of them verged on functional illiteracy.

It was particularly appropriate to conduct the pre-test on this group. Not only did it embody the region-specific characteristics of the Knox County youth to be studied, but it also provided a margin for error in designing a comprehensible instrument for use in Appalachia. Children in the area are badly under-educated and under-developed intellectually. There was, therefore, some danger that instruments reflecting experience with other American children would be pitched "over the heads" of these mountain youngsters. By pre-testing on an especially backward group and observing that even these children could understand the requirements of various item responses, assurance was gained that more able but still sub-standard Appalachian youth would have no difficulties in comprehending the items.

The pre-test questionnaire contained an extremely large number of items, derived from appropriate literature using the following criteria: (1) relationships of the item to learning and socialization theory; (2) ability to permit comparisons with existing bodies of data. This omnibus instrument took two hours to administer, and was given in two separate sittings.

Pre-test results required the elimination of about 150 items. Criteria for rejection included: (1) properties of the responses such as the shape of the distribution and frequency of "don't know" responses; (2) indications of sensitivity (presumably due to peculiar local values) to item content. Questions about the work habits of parents, for example, were not retained. The latter criterion also served as a basis for modification of certain items. For example, on this basis the word "damn" contained in one question was changed to "hang". In other words, the wording of questions was changed to fit the cultural context. Finally, an item analysis of all scales was run. As a result it was possible to eliminate a number of scale items as "non-discriminating" in the cultural context of Appalachia.[3]

The revised questionnaire was administered during the months of January through March, 1967, by the supervisor of Knox County Public Schools, who is responsible for conducting the county testing program and who holds a Master's degree in guidance and a certificate from the Educational Testing Service. This gentleman is a native of Knox County and was extremely helpful in securing access to the schools.

A single form of the questionnaire was used for all grades. All fifth through twelfth-grade school children in the selected population in attendance on the days of administration ($N = 2,544$) were questioned. The rate of absence was between 15 and 20%. There is no reason to believe that absences were not randomly distributed throughout the population.[4]

SCALES AND SCORES

Many of the variables in this study are measured by responses to single items; the reliance here is on face validity. This is as it must be, for the task of variable identification, to say nothing of instrumentation, has hardly begun for childhood political socialization.

However, for several key variables there are scalar devices.

. . . Cynicism is a basic orientation toward political actors and activity. Found empirically to be related to political participation, the presence of distrust and skepticism presumably pervades all encounters with political objects. . . . Political cynicism appears to be a manifestation of a deep-seated suspicion of other's motives and actions.[5]

Jennings and Niemi report five items forming a Guttman scale when administered to both parents and children of a national random sample (coefficient's of reproducibility, .93 and .92 respectively).[6]

Similarly important to democratic citizenship is the feeling of political efficacy. There are:

a number of elements which might serve as part of the meaning of political efficacy: a sense of the direct political potency of the individual; a belief in the responsiveness of the government to the desires of individuals; the idea of comprehensibility of government; the availability of adequate means of influence; and a general resistance to fatalism about the tractability of government to anyone, ruler or ruled.[7]

To tap these sub-dimensions of efficacy, Easton and Dennis developed an eight-item scale. Analysis of their data yielded the surprising finding that by "grade 3 children have already begun to form an attitude . . . which we could call a sense of political efficacy."[8]

Attitude toward civil rights is measured by the five-item "civil rights score."[9] The civil rights items deal with racial attitudes. Hyman *et al.* give no data on the scale's unidimensionality. We have found through item analysis that all items discriminate and that for all intents and purposes they form a unidimensional Guttman scale (CR = .88; MMr = .37).

The political chauvinism score, adopted from Litt, measures

references to the unique and nationalistic character of "democracy" or "good government" as an American monopoly, and glorified treatment of American political institutions, procedures and public figures.[10]

The coefficient of reliability as reported by Litt equals .932.[11]

These procedures permit the collection of data bearing on many hypotheses about socialization in a sub-culture. In short, they allow a test of observational learning theory to act as a stimulus to the discovery of knowledge concerning the agents of socialization.

Notes
Chapter 3

[1] On the research population see: Paul Street, *et al., The Knox County Community Action Program of the Office of Economic Opportunity.* Preliminary report to the Office of Economic Opportunity, May, 1967, pp. 1–25. The study is part of a larger study financed under contract #693 between the University of Kentucky Research Foundation and the Office of Economic Opportunity.

[2] A debate concerning the appropriateness of significance tests in survey research has been carried on in the sociology literature for many years. See, for example: Hanan C. Selvin, "A Critique of Tests of Significance in Survey Research," *American Sociological Review,* 22 (October, 1957), pp. 519–527; Robert McGinnis, "Randomization and Inference in Sociological Research," *American Sociological Review,* 23 (August, 1958), pp. 408–414; Leslie Kish, "Some Statistical Problems in Research Design," *American Sociological Review,* 24 (1959), pp. 328–338; and Leslie Kish, *Survey Sampling* (New York: John Wiley and Sons, Inc., 1965), especially Chap. 14, "Some Issues of Inference from Survey Data," pp. 574–597. Due to the prohibitive costs involved a true all Appalachian sample could not be obtained.

[3] On the use of item analysis for attitude scales see: Allen L. Edwards, *Techniques of Attitude Scale Construction* (New York: Appleton-Century-Crofts, Inc., 1957).

[4] Even the most remote schools were covered. This was done so that the isolated children were included.

[5] The scale of political cynicism is taken from: Jennings and Niemi, *op. cit.,* p. 13

[6] *Ibid.,* p. 14.

[7] Easton and Dennis, *American Political Science Review,* p. 29. A comprehensive discussion of the concept "efficacy" may be found there.

[8] *Ibid.,* p. 31.

[9] The "Civil Rights Score" is adopted from: Herbert H. Hyman, Charles R. Wright and Terrence K. Hopkins, *Applications of Methods of Evaluation: Four Studies of the*

Encampment for Citizenship (Berkeley and Los Angeles: University of California Press, 1963), p. 308.

[10] Edgar Litt, "Civic Education, Community Norms, and Political Indoctrination," *American Sociological Review*, XXVIII, I (February, 1963), pp. 69–75.

[11] *Ibid.*, p. 70.

4

Interpersonal Agents of Political Socialization:

THE FAMILY

Most scholars of political socialization agree that the family is one of the most pervasive agents of political socialization. This is to be expected, for the child is usually exposed to familial influence for a long period of time. Studies have demonstrated, for example, that the child tends to assimilate the party preference of the parent and to look to the parent as a source of political advice.[1] However, as the child grows older and as contact with other agents increases, the parents' influence appears to decline.[2]

Social learning theorists cite similar findings, but have more data upon which to base their contention that the family is of primary importance as an agent of socialization. According to Bandura and Walters, behavior learned from parents is pervasive. In fact, "behavior and values transmitted from the home may govern the selection and rejection of extra familial models, thus reducing the possibility of marked changes in behavior patterns that are established during earlier stages of development."[3] The parent acts as an influential model that orients a person to stimuli, then the response to these stimuli may become that person's own.[4]

Several classes of behavior may be acquired through the observation of parental models. Experimental evidence tends to focus on aggression.

Notes to Chapter 4 will be found on pp 67–70.

Aggressive parents have been found to have aggressive children, and differences between aggressive and inhibited children are "due at least in part to imitative learning."[5] Similarly, "parents who are highly anxious about sexual matters tend to have children who also display high sex anxiety."[6]

Parental models may also transmit deviant behavior. Bandura cites a study by Fleck which "describes a young schizophrenic whose bizarre hospital behavior evidently paralleled, often in detail, the deviant pattern of home life displayed by his father."[7] Other data demonstrate that such behavior as incestuousness, homosexuality and autism may be transmitted from parental models to offspring.[8] Less spectacular forms of children's responses have also been linked to parental modeling. Dependency behavior and achievement motivation may be added to the empirically established list.[9] Finally, and most generally, Harris, Gough and Martin demonstrated that there was a "positive and appreciable correlation between attitudes of children and of their parents in various attitude areas."[10] Taken together, this is an impressive array of evidence. Fully consistent with the above noted observations about youthful party identification and political advice seeking, it suggests that parents are indeed an extremely important model. If this dynamic extends to many political objects, several childhood phenomena should be observed.

Hypothesis 4.1: The child will rank the parents significantly higher than any other agent of transmission of political information.

In examining the relationships one must take account of additional variables. While learning theory alone does not give one any reason to expect the child to perceive the parent as being a more salient agent on any one particular dimension of political stimuli, it may be well to control for differential cognitions on various dimensions. Jennings found that high school students have different levels of information about, and different perceptions of, four levels of government—local, state, national, and international.[11] We shall want to know, therefore, how the parents are ranked as agents of information transmission on all the levels. The data are presented in Tables 4.1 through 4.4.

The data demonstrate some rather remarkable patterns. Overall, it is evident that the Appalachian parent does not rank significantly higher than the other proposed agents.

The chief agent of information transmission concerning the local level of government is the radio. Friends rank second, TV third, mothers

Table 4.1
Child's Ranking of Agents of Information Transmission on Four Levels of Government: Local

AGENT				RANK						
	1	2	3	4	5	6	7	8	Total %	N
Radio	39	18	12	10	9	6	4	2	100	1805
TV	17	16	9	7	8	13	26	10	100	1623
Newspaper	10	19	20	10	15	12	10	4	100	1667
School	10	11	17	26	9	13	10	4	100	1674
Mother	12	16	15	18	20	11	6	1	99*	1682
Father	11	14	13	15	19	16	8	4	100	1601
Friends	18	9	14	11	14	16	15	3	100	1725

G = .13   P = .001

* Percent does not equal 100 due to rounding.

Table 4.2
Child's Ranking of Agents of Information Transmission on Four Levels of Government: State

AGENT				RANK						
	1	2	3	4	5	6	7	8	Total %	N
Radio	47	24	12	6	5	3	2	2	101*	1817
TV	31	23	15	8	6	6	7	4	100	1755
Newspaper	15	26	31	7	7	5	6	3	100	1703
School	4	5	14	29	11	18	14	5	100	1615
Mother	7	10	10	20	27	16	8	2	100	1619
Father	8	10	10	17	24	20	8	4	101*	1555
Friends	3	4	9	10	15	22	32	5	100	1595

G = .46   P = .001

* Percent does not equal 100 due to rounding.

Table 4.3
Child's Ranking of Agents of Information Transmission on Four Levels of Government: National

AGENT				RANK						
	1	2	3	4	5	6	7	8	Total %	N
Radio	25	39	23	4	4	2	2	1	100	1772
TV	63	20	6	3	2	2	1	3	100	1874
Newspaper	9	25	45	7	4	3	4	2	99*	1694
School	2	5	9	38	9	16	15	7	100	1595
Mother	4	5	6	20	34	18	9	3	99*	1570
Father	4	5	6	20	29	24	9	4	101*	1511
Friends	2	2	5	8	14	25	39	6	101*	1554

G = .61   P = .001

* Percent does not equal 100 due to rounding.

Table 4.4
Child's Ranking of Agents of Information Transmission on Four Levels of Government: International

AGENT				RANK						
	1	2	3	4	5	6	7	8	Total %	N
Radio	23	41	23	5	3	2	2	1	100	1733
TV	66	18	5	2	2	2	2	3	100	1850
Newspaper	8	25	47	6	5	3	4	2	100	1660
School	3	3	8	41	10	16	13	6	100	1545
Mother	4	5	6	18	33	20	9	5	100	1522
Father	3	6	6	17	27	26	10	4	99 *	1469
Friends	2	3	5	9	13	21	42	6	101 *	1511

$G = .76$ $P = .001$

* Percent does not equal 100 due to rounding.

fourth, with the father a poor fifth, not too far above newspapers and the school. Moving on to the child's ranking of information agents on the state level one finds a similar pattern, i.e., radio ranks first, TV second, this time newspapers rather than friends are third, and again mother and father are ranked fourth and fifth respectively.

An examination of Tables 4.3 and 4.4 shows a rather striking difference in the child's perception of agents of information transmission, though parents' positions are hardly improved. Regarding information about the federal level of government, one finds that television is ranked far above any of the other agents. In Table 4.3 one notices that gamma has increased to .61, indicating that there is 61% agreement on the child's ranking of information agents. One may say, therefore, that television is ranked significantly higher than the other agents. Television seems to be the main agent of transmission regarding information concerning the federal level of government.

Turning our attention to the agents of information about the international or "world" level, we find exactly the same results as on the federal level, except that gamma is even larger, indicating even greater agreement. Mother and father are ranked at the same low level.

At this point, then, one is forced to conclude that there is no evidence to substantiate Hypothesis 1, and it must be rejected. Parents are not ranked as the most salient agents of information transmission. The media predominate.

Turning our attention to the question of whether the parent ranks the same as an agent of transmission concerning all four levels of government, Tables 4.5 and 4.6 demonstrate that they do not. While it is a fact

Table 4.5
The Mother as an Agent of Information Transmission on the Four Levels of Government

LEVEL OF GOVERNMENT	RANK OF MOTHER									
	1	2	3	4	5	6	7	8	Total %	N
Local	12	16	15	18	20	11	6	1	99*	1682
State	7	10	10	20	27	16	8	2	100	1619
National	4	5	6	20	34	18	9	3	99*	1570
International	4	5	6	17	34	20	9	5	100	1522

$G = .25$ $P = .001$

* Percent does not equal 100 due to rounding.

Table 4.6
The Father as an Agent of Information Transmission on the Four Levels of Government

LEVEL OF GOVERNMENT	RANK OF FATHER									
	1	2	3	4	5	6	7	8	Total %	N
Local	11	14	13	15	19	16	8	4	100	1601
State	8	10	10	17	24	20	8	4	101*	1555
National	4	5	6	20	29	24	9	4	101*	1511
International	3	6	6	17	27	26	10	4	99*	1469

$G = .28$ $P = .001$

* Percent does not equal 100 due to rounding.

that the parents' ranking on all levels is extremely low, one finds that there is a significant difference among the rankings. Both parents rank higher as agents concerning local and state affairs and lower as agents of information about national and international affairs. That these responses in fact reflect information absorption from the media is suggested by the radio-TV differential with respect to various levels of government. Radio probably does transmit more local and state information, while TV undoubtedly has a wider coverage. Response patterns are congruent with this.

Again, these findings are somewhat surprising in a parochial sub-culture. Appalachian parents are probably more locally oriented. To the extent that this is true, there is some slight support for Hypothesis 1.

The findings also suggest that the different governmental levels are dimensions that must be considered in specifying the content of what the child learns and from where he learns it. Even from this initial analysis, it is becoming clear that the answers to the questions, "what is learned?" and

*Interpersonal Agents of Political Socialization:
The Family*

"from whom?" are (1) not obvious, and (2) involve variable interaction of a highly complex nature.

Moreover, there is evidence to indicate that the agents that communicate political information to the child are of two quite distinct types. Table 4.7, a "principal (sic) axes" factor analysis, varimax rotation, performed on the measures of agent performance, demonstrates the presence of two principal factors that account for 64.4% of the variance.

Table 4.7
Principal Axis Factor Analysis, Varimax Rotation: Agents of Information Transmission

AGENTS AND GOVERNMENTAL LEVEL	FACTOR LOADINGS	
	Factor 1	Factor 2
Radio-Local	.36	.53
TV-Local	.57	.38
Newspaper-Local	.45	.57
School-Local	.57	.44
Mother-Local	.71	.26
Father-Local	.72	.25
Friends-Local	.60	.33
Radio-State	.21	.72
TV-State	.34	.58
Newspaper-State	.31	.72
School-State	.67	.44
Mother-State	.84	.23
Father-State	.84	.20
Friends-State	.82	.29
Radio-National	.33	.72
TV-National	.05	.78
Newspaper-National	.39	.71
School-National	.71	.42
Mother-National	.86	.24
Father-National	.85	.24
Friends-National	.85	.30
Radio-International	.33	.72
TV-International	.05	.78
Newspaper-International	.39	.72
School-International	.72	.43
Mother-International	.86	.22
Father-International	.85	.22
Friends-International	.84	.29
Variance accounted for	54.81%	9.66%

On the one hand, there are the agents that operate through inter-personal interaction, i.e. family, friends and school. We shall call these the "personal" agents of information transmission. On the other hand, there are the agents that operate more impersonally, i.e., radio, TV and news-papers.[12]

The above evidence indicates that there is empirical justification for altering the conceptualization of the agents that has been proposed by Hess and Torney.[13] Instead of dividing the agents into "institutions of well-defined structure and organization" and "influence that occurs in the larger social setting,"[14] a division into "personal" and "non-personal" agents of information transmission appears to have more empirical meaning.

Given the findings reported in the review of the literature that demon-strate that the parents or the school are the most influential agents of political socialization,[15] why are they ranked so low as agents of information transmission? (The question of the school will be investigated in the next chapter.) Two possible explanations are available. The first may lie in the fact that the relationships discovered are sub-cultural phenomena. The second (and more plausible) is that the studies heretofore discussed did not tap the dimension of information transmission, but concentrated instead on variables such as the inheritance of party identification. It is possible, therefore, that the parent could in fact be the chief agent passing on his or her party identification to the child while at the same time ranking extremely low as an agent of information transmission. We shall examine this notion first by investigating the dimension of party identification and the rankings of the parents as transmitters of this variable. A more detailed discussion of the rankings of the other agents is deferred until the appro-priate chapter. Most studies agree that the family's greatest impact on the socialization of the child is in the area of political party preference.[16] Modeling this dimension appears extensive.

Hypothesis 4.2: There will be a significant relationship between the party preference of the parent and the political party preference of the child.

Table 4.8 indicates that there is indeed a strong association between the party preferred by the parent and that preferred by the child. It is ob-vious, however, that the child is more likely to look to the mother than to the father. The Appalachian child expresses 87% agreement with the party of his mother, but only 30% agreement of that with his father. This finding is in contradiction to the theoretical literature, which notes that

Table 4.8
Gamma Correlations Between
Party Preference of Child and
Party Preference of Parents

Parent	Gamma	Significance Level
Mother	.87	.0000
Father	.30	.0001

the father is the main source of political party preference. It also differs from the finding of Jennings and Niemi that "59 percent of the students fall into the same broad category as their parents. . . ."[17] The data presented above demonstrate that there is a great difference between the two parents. Far fewer than 59% agree with the father, while many more than 59% agree with the mother. While Jennings and Niemi do not differentiate between parents, the large differences between father and mother leads one to speculate that the Appalachian culture—in this case a distinct poverty culture—has led to a situation in which matriarchal influence is greater than patriarchal influence. We are probably in the presence of a matriarchal culture in which the child looks to the mother for political cues.

In order to examine the cultural variable, the Appalachian data will be compared with the national sample of high school seniors reported on by Jennings and Niemi. In the process, two points must be kept in mind. First, that the national sample identified the parents' party preference by directly interviewing the parent, while in the Appalachian sample the parent's party is identified by the child's perception of the parent's party. The second point is that the Appalachian questionnaire included a "don't know" category which yielded a relatively large number of responses. Consequently, while the data are not directly comparable, they may still yield valuable insights regarding the salience of the cultural factor.

Tables 4.9a and b and 4.10a and b demonstrate that there is indeed a significant difference between the two samples. Not only is the matriarchal tendency made more evident, but parental influence—maternal or paternal —is more efficacious in Appalachia than the nation as a whole. A direct comparison of seniors underlies this fact, though Democratic fathers are not significantly more successful than their national-sample counterparts. In order to explore these findings fully one would have to have a national sample with a wide dispersion of ages. One hopes that such data will be forthcoming.

One must conclude that the Appalachian child is more, rather than less, likely to agree with the party identification of his parents. Due to the

Table 4.9a
Comparison of Party Identification of Child and Parent: Appalachian Mother and Both Parents of National Sample

PARTY IDENTIFICATION		ENTIRE APPALACHIAN SAMPLE	NATIONAL SAMPLE†	SMIRNOV TWO-SAMPLE TEST
Parent	Child			
Democrat	Democrat	80.2	65.9	D = .14
Democrat	Independent	1.2	26.8	P = .001
Democrat	Republican	18.0	7.3	
Total %		99.4*	100.0	
		N = 440	N = 914	
Republican	Democrat	8.8	12.7	D = .39
Republican	Independent	1.1	36.5	P = .001
Republican	Republican	90.0	50.8	
Total %		99.9*	100.0	
		N = 613	N = 495	

Table 4.9b
Comparison of Party Identification of Child and Parent: Appalachian Mother and Both Parents of National Sample

PARTY IDENTIFICATION		APPALACHIAN SENIORS	NATIONAL SAMPLE	SMIRNOV TEST
Parent	Child			
Democrat	Democrat	79.0	65.9	D = .15
Democrat	Independent	7.8	26.8	P = .20
Democrat	Republican	13.2	7.3	
Total %		100.0	100.0	
		N = 38	N = 914	
Republican	Democrat	14.3	12.7	D = .23
Republican	Independent	12.2	36.5	P = .01
Republican	Republican	73.5	50.8	
Total %		100.0	100.0	
		N = 49	N = 495	

* Percent does not equal 100 due to rounding.
† National sample data are compiled from Jennings and Niemi, Paper prepared for delivery at the 1966 annual meeting of the American Political Science Association, Table 2, p. 8.

lack of comparable data, one is unable to ascertain whether this is strictly a subcultural phenomena. It must be suggested, however, that future inquiries differentiate between the cue stimuli of the mother and father.

Since the parent-party identification findings stand in some contrast to those on the role of the parent as a transmitter of information, it is necessary to attempt to reconcile these seemingly contradictory findings.

Table 4.10a
Comparison of Party Identification of Child and Parent: Appalachian Father and Both Parents of National Sample

PARTY IDENTIFICATION		ENTIRE APPALACHIAN SAMPLE	NATIONAL SAMPLE†	SMIRNOV TEST
Parent	Child			
Democrat	Democrat	79.8	65.9	D = .14
Democrat	Independent	8.6	26.8	P = .001
Democrat	Republican	11.6	7.3	
Total %		99.9*	100.0	
		N = 441	N = 914	
Republican	Democrat	8.3	12.7	D = .37
Republican	Independent	4.1	36.5	P = .001
Republican	Republican	87.6	50.8	
Total %		100.0	100.0	
		N = 603	N = 495	

Table 4.10b
Comparison of Party Identification of Child and Parent: Appalachian Father and Both Parents of National Sample

PARTY IDENTIFICATION		APPALACHIAN SENIORS	NATIONAL SAMPLE	SMIRNOV TEST
Parent	Child			
Democrat	Democrat	72.7	65.9	D = .07
Democrat	Independent	18.2	26.8	P = .50
Democrat	Republican	9.1	7.2	
Total %		100.0	100.0	
		N = 44	N = 914	
Republican	Democrat	7.7	12.7	D = .36
Republican	Independent	5.1	36.5	P = .001
Republican	Republican	87.2	50.8	
Total %		100.0	100.0	
		N = 39	N = 495	

* Percent does not equal 100 due to rounding.
† National sample data are compiled from Jennings and Niemi, Paper prepared for delivery at the 1966 annual meeting of the American Political Science Association, Table 2, p. 8.

In regard to information, the parent in Appalachia was not modeled. With party identification he is. The findings are probably subject specific. That is to say that it is entirely possible that the child's preference for his parent's political party identification is not related to the child's receiving information from the parents. Hence, if those who agree with their parent's party identification do not rank the parent higher as an agent of information transmission one could conclude that information transmission is not related to the child's identification with the party of his parents, and that variables other than information transmission are responsible for the identification. It is logical to expect that the close relationship is due to modeling.

Tables 4.11 and 4.12 demonstrate that no matter how the child ranks the parent as an agent of information transmission, there is a significant degree of association between the party identification of parent and child. Even those who rank the parent low as an agent of information continue to identify with the parent's party. To further document the fact that party identification is not based on information transmitted to the child, correlations have been run between the political knowledge index and the

Table 4.11
Gamma Correlations* Between Party of Father and Party of Child Controlling Rank of Father as Information Agent

		GOVERNMENTAL LEVEL		
RANK	Local	State	Federal	International
1	.67	.59	.59	.55
2	.69	.71	.58	.58
3	.59	.70	.48	.55
4	.64	.64	.75	.68
5	.52	.54	.58	.62
6	.64	.62	.57	.62
7	.53	.59	.58	.44
8	.45	.28	.41	.44

* All correlations are significant at .001.

Table 4.12
Gamma Correlations* Between Party of Mother and Party of Child Controlling Rank of Mother as Information Agent

		GOVERNMENTAL LEVEL		
RANK	Local	State	Federal	International
1	.68	.65	.48	.84
2	.66	.58	.56	.54
3	.56	.57	.69	.37
4	.63	.62	.60	.63
5	.69	.69	.62	.64
6	.44	.54	.55	.54
7	.53	.41	.51	.52
8	.54	.38	.58	.43

* All correlations are significant at .001.

Table 4.13
Gamma Correlations* Between
Party of Parent and Party of Child
By Level of Political Information

Information Level		Father	Mother
Low	1	.70	.66
	2	.55	.63
	3	.59	.55
	4	.51	.51
	5	.61	.60
High	6	.65	.67

* All correlations are significant at .001.

party preference of parent and child. The data show that there is a high degree of association at all levels of information (Table 4.13).

The conclusion is inescapable. The child's identification with the party of his parents is not related to the role the parent plays as an agent of information transmission nor to the child's level of political information. The child simply adopts his parents' party.

Children also are reported to consult parental models in other political realms. Greenstein has demonstrated that children not only inherit the political party preference of their parents, but that they are more likely to look to their parents for voting advice.[18] We would expect a similar phenomenon in Appalachia, paralleling the large parental role in party identification patterns just observed.

Hypothesis 4.3: The parent will be the most preferred source of voting advice for the Appalachian child.

Table 4.14 demonstrates that the Appalachian child prefers parents over other sources. This pattern is quite similar to Greenstein's findings on New Haven youth. A direct comparison between the overlapping age groups of the samples, grades five through eight, is reported in Table 4.15.

Table 4.14
Children's Preferred Source of
Voting Advice

Source of Advice	N	%
A friend your own age	207	10
Brother or sister	71	4
Parents	1390	70
Teacher	169	9
Someone else	137	7
Total	1974	100

Table 4.15
**Comparison of Appalachian and New Haven Samples: Parents
as a Preferred Source of Voting Advice By School Years**

SCHOOL YEAR	APPALACHIAN SAMPLE	NEW HAVEN SAMPLE*		χ^2 TEST FOR TWO INDEPENDENT SAMPLES
		Upper SES	Lower SES	
	%			Appalachia and Upper SES
5	72	88	74	$\chi^2 = 11.48$ DF $= 3$ P $= .02$
6	72	70	71	
7	72	76	70	Appalachia and Lower SES
8	74	57	63	$\chi^2 = 13.82$ DF $= 3$ P $= .01$
	N $= 1322$	N $= 177$	N $= 371$	

* The data are compiled from: Greenstein, *Children and Politics*, Table 5.4, p. 104. χ^2 test is performed on the raw data.

Keeping in mind that the instruments used in the two studies are not identical (the question asked of the Appalachian sample contained more categories), it is clear that the gross similarities between Appalachia and New Haven are accompanied by an important, probably culturally determined difference.

Where Greenstein found that by grade eight there was a decrease in the percentage of children who prefer their parents as sources of voting advice, the Appalachian sample shows no decrease with age. This difference is significant, moreover, even when the Appalachian sample is compared with the lower SES of the New Haven sample. It would appear, therefore, that there are distinctive cultural variables operative in Appalachia, and these differences may not be related to poverty alone.

Greenstein's data, however, do not distinguish between mother and father. In order to make comparisons we were forced to combine the percentages for both mother and father in the Appalachian data. Yet, analysis reveals that there is a significant difference between the child's preference for the father and mother.

Table 4.16 indicates that the father is the more preferred source of voting advice at all grade levels. Indeed, the mother's influence appears to decline with the age of the child. This relative weakness is emphasized by the fact that older children prefer not only the father but also the teacher over the mother as a source of voting advice.

This finding stands in some contrast to the great dependency of Appalachian youth upon their mother's party identification. There is no matriarchal pattern in seeking voting advice. The discrepancy is probably related to the fact that asking for voting advice is a more overt type of

Table 4.16
Preferred Sources of Voting Advice by School Year

	SCHOOL YEAR							
SOURCE OF ADVICE	5	6	7	8	9	10	11	12
A friend	10.3	10.9	10.0	9.5	14.7	10.5	10.6	6.4
Brother or sister	3.5	2.7	5.0	3.0	2.4	5.2	1.8	4.8
Father	45.6	44.8	48.0	53.6	49.8	54.9	49.6	50.4
Mother	25.9	27.6	24.1	20.1	19.9	15.0	13.3	12.0
Teacher	10.0	9.4	6.6	8.3	4.3	5.9	9.7	16.8
Someone else	4.7	4.5	6.3	5.6	9.0	8.5	15.0	9.6

$\chi^2 = 78.019$ DF $= 35$ P $= .01$

activity than identifying with the parent's party. It was noted earlier that neither of these was related in any way to information transmission nor to level of information. Modeling the party identification is more of an incidental process, while asking for advice is much more formal. Consequently, the child could feel that his father knows more about politics than his mother and hence would seek out the father as a source of voting advice, while holding the mother, with whom there is more contact, as a more esteemed figure and identifying with her party.

This again emphasizes the necessity that future studies of political socialization examine differential cue stimuli offered to the child by the mother and father.

A SOCIAL LEARNING THEORY EXPLANATION

The exceedingly complex nature of the learning process is shown by Bandura. He identifies a number of variables that operate within the modeling process to influence the results of observational learning. These include orientation to stimuli,[19] age, sex, social power, intellectual and vocational status,[20] perceived similarity of the observer with the model,[21] and contiguity of the model.[22] These variables should operate as controls affecting the efficacy of the agents on the three dimensions that have been identified.

Orientation to Stimuli

The modeling process, according to Bandura and Walters, orients one to stimuli.[23] If, therefore, the child perceives that the parent or parents are not oriented to political stimuli, then one suspects that he will not rank them highly as agents, because he will not become so oriented.

Hypothesis 4.4: Those who perceive their parents as being oriented to political stimuli will rank them significantly higher as agents of political socialization than those who perceive the parents as not being oriented to political stimuli.

As measures of perceived parental orientation to political stimuli we shall use two dimensions: the frequency with which the child discusses politics with his family and reported office holding by members of the child's family.

Investigation of the first dimension demonstrates that there is no significant difference between those children who do and those who do not discuss politics with their family. The data show clearly that those who discuss politics with their family do not rank their parents any higher as agents of information transmission than those who do not discuss politics with their family (Tables 4.17, 4.18, 4.19, 4.20).

In only three instances are there significant differences between the rankings of the children of families that have and have not held office. In two of these cases—the mother on the local and international levels—the

Table 4.17
Relationship Between Discussion of Politics with Family and Rank of Parents as Information Agents*

LEVEL OF GOVERNMENT	GAMMA		χ^2†		P	
	Father	Mother	Father	Mother	Father	Mother
Local	− .02	− .02	11.98	21.23	.95	.50
State	− .06	− .08	8.59	19.07	.99	.50
National	− .04	− .09	9.01	23.96	.99	.30
International	− .08	− .09	10.32	12.40	.98	.95

* For this and all other tables in which the raw data are not reported, supplemented tables are available upon request from the author.
†DF = 21.

Table 4.18
Relationship Between Family Members Holding Political Office and Rank of Parents as Information Agents

LEVEL OF GOVERNMENT	χ^2*		P	
	Father	Mother	Father	Mother
Local	15.23	14.91	.05	.05
State	13.70	2.21	.10	.98
National	9.95	7.01	.20	.50
International	6.66	20.10	.50	.01

* DF = 7.

Table 4.19
**Gamma Correlations Between Party of
Parents and Party of Child: By Frequency
of Discussion of Politics with Family**

FREQUENCY OF DISCUSSION	GAMMA*	
	Father	Mother
None	.61	.61
Yes, once or twice a year	.54	.55
Yes, a few times a month	.54	.56
Yes, several times a week	.66	.67

* All correlations are significant at .001.

Table 4.20
**Gamma Correlations Between Party of
Parents and Party of Child: By Family
Member Holding Political Office**

FAMILY MEMBER IN OFFICE	GAMMA*	
	Father	Mother
Yes	.65	.64
No	.60	.61

* All correlations are significant at .001.

difference is not in the hypothesized direction. Children whose family members have held office do not rank the mother higher as an agent, but rank her slightly lower. In only one instance—the ranking of the father on the local level—is there a significant difference in the hypothesized direction.

The findings are similar when one considers the family as a transmitter of party identification.

Tables 4.21 and 4.22 show that the strength of the relationship between the party of the parent and that of the child does not increase when the child perceives the family as being oriented to political stimuli.

In regard to the child's preferred source of voting advice, however, at least one indicator of stimulus orientation is in fact related to differential ratings of the parents.

Table 4.21 demonstrates that those children who discuss politics with their family are more likely to prefer the father as a source of voting advice than those who do not discuss politics. At the same time, however, the preference for the mother decreases among discussers. Though our data do not allow us to demonstrate this, it is likely that discussion is carried

Table 4.21
Relationship Between Child's Preferred Source of Voting Advice and Discussion of Politics with Family

| | FREQUENCY OF DISCUSSION | | | |
SOURCE OF ADVICE	None	1 or 2 a year	Few a month	Several a week
Friend	12	14	6	10
Brother or sister	4	4	3	3
Father	44	50	52	55
Mother	25	19	21	19
Teacher	8	8	11	6
Other	7	5	7	8
Total %	100	100	100	101
	N = 871	N = 225	N = 412	N = 408

$\chi^2 = 36.63$ DF = 15   P = .01

on with fathers.[24] Those children who discuss politics with their family, i.e. who perceive the family as being oriented to political stimuli, are significantly more likely to prefer the father as a source of voting advice.

The same pattern does not exist in regard to the second measure of orientation to stimuli (Table 4.22).

If anything, there is a negative gradient between perceived family orientation to stimuli and ranking of family as an efficacious agent. Those children from families whose members have held office do not prefer the parents more than those from families who have had no members holding office.

On balance, the stimulus orientation hypothesis does not fare well against this data. Indeed, the family's influence, which appears to be strong

Table 4.22
Relationship Between Family Member Holding Political Office and Preferred Source of Voting Advice

| | FAMILY MEMBER HOLDING OFFICE | |
SOURCE OF ADVICE	Yes	No
Friend	11	10
Brother or sister	4	3
Father	45	50
Mother	18	22
Teacher	9	9
Other	13	6
Total	100	100
	N = 176	N = 173

$\chi^2 = 11.97$ DF = 5   P = .05

in some areas, may proceed by other mechanisms. Children who perceive their parents as being oriented to political stimuli do not rank them higher as agents of information transmission.

These findings have some particularly interesting implications for the learning of party identification. Recalling from our earlier observations that the acquisition of party identification from the parents was not associated with the intake of political information, we add the finding that acquisition of party identification is not dependent upon perceived parental orientation to political stimuli. The observed matriarchal pattern taken by learning of this response is thus not an artifact of communication or stimulus factors involved in the perception of the parent's orientation to stimuli, but is more deeply rooted in cultural variables.

Age

Political science has placed great stress upon the relationship between age and political socialization. The major finding being that the salience of the family as an agent of political socialization declines as the child matures.[25]

This finding is basically in agreement with those uncovered by social learning scholars. For example, both Bandura and Maccoby note that the parents become less influential as models as the child grows older.[26] Hypothesis five is, therefore:

Hypothesis 4.5: There will be a negative relationship between the age of the child and his ranking of the parents as agents of political socialization.

Table 4.23 indicates that there is a slight relationship between the child's age and his ranking of the parents as agents of information transmission. This relationship is quite complex. In regard to the transmission of information concerning the children's local community, one notes that the younger child ranks both the mother and father higher than the older child. Regarding the other three levels of government, one finds a similar tendency but to a smaller degree. In all, however, the rankings of both parents on all four levels of government tend to cluster around the fourth, fifth and sixth ranks. Thus, while Gamma is significant, it demonstrates a small percentage of agreement in the child's rankings. The largest amount of variance accounted for by "age" is 19%, which occurs on the mother's ranking as an agent transmitting information concerning the national level of government. Age appears to be important, but perhaps not as important as previously thought.

Table 4.23
Relationship Between Parents' Ranking as Agents of Information Transmission and the Age of the Child

	GAMMA	
LEVEL OF GOVERNMENT	Father	Mother
Local	.09	−.08
State	.13	.16
National	.12	.19
International	.12	.17

The data on age and party identification are especially interesting. They show a pattern quite different than any heretofore discovered (Table 4.24). The youngest child shows no significant relationship with his father's party, but the next four age brackets do demonstrate a significant degree of association. (The exception is the .08 level of significance at age 13.) Next,

Table 4.24
Gamma Correlations Between Party of Parents and Party of Child: By Age of Child

Age of Child	Father	P	Mother	P
10	.17	.30	.92	.0001
11	.39	.05	.91	.001
12	.57	.03	.90	.001
13	.35	.08	.82	.0001
14	.44	.03	.85	.0001
15	.27	.15	.84	.0001
16	.35	.15	.84	.0001
17	.74	.008	.90	.0001
18	−.49	.13	.89	.0001

the 15- and 16-year-olds show no significant relationship with the relationship reappearing at age 17 and demonstrating the most significant degree of association. At age 18 one finds a negative, but not statistically significant Gamma.

One possible interpretation is that the lack of a relationship at ages 15 and 16 indicates teenage rebellion against the parents, and that by age 17 this has tempered. This interpretation is of dubious merit, however, in light of the fact that "researchers have been hard pressed to uncover any significant evidence of adolescent rebellion in the realm of political affairs."[27]

Moreover, the data on the relationship between age and the child's identification with his mother's party hardly support this notion.

One notes immediately the consistently high relationship between the party of the mother and the party of the child at all age levels. Such findings support the proposition that in the Appalachian culture the status and role of the father is ill-defined while that of the mother is quite clear. Hence, the child is consistently more likely to model the mother and identify with her party identification.

In regard, however, to the relationship between age and voting advice, Table 4.16 demonstrated that as the age of the child increased his preference for his mother as a source of advice decreased, while at the same time age had little effect upon the rating of the father. In concluding the discussion of age, therefore, one is left with the fact that the findings are mixed. Age does have a small relationship to information transmission, while it has a profound effect upon the child's identification with his father's party but not on his identification with his mother's party. Regarding voting advice, it was found that children at all age levels would be more likely to ask their fathers for advice. Moreover, there is evidence to indicate that the age of the child has little relationship to the decline in salience of the family as an agent. In fact, the child's identification with the party of his mother does not decline as age increases, while his preference for his father as a source of voting advice similarly suffers no diminution.

These findings further support our earlier findings that the Appalachian child is more likely than children of other cultures to continue to adopt his parents' party identification and to look to his father as a source of voting advice. The traditions of the Appalachian sub-culture place great emphasis upon the family as a unit to the extent that certain areas of the Appalachian region constitute an extended family with relatives populating an entire hollow.[28] This cultural emphasis on the family may be more important than age or (as the next section shows) sex in accounting for the child's continuing identification with the political party of the parents and for the father's continued importance as a source of voting advice even at the upper age brackets. Given the ideal typical conceptualization of political culture proposed by Elazar,[29] these findings are not surprising. He classifies the Appalachian region as a traditionalistic political culture, the main facets of which are social and family ties found "only in a society that retains some of the organic characteristics of the preindustrial social order."[30] If Appalachia is such a society—and it probably is—then discussion of the other variables involved in the learning process should also be mediated by the cultural factor. As mentioned earlier, sex is one variable that is in fact so mediated.

Sex

Research regarding the influence of sex upon the political socialization of the child is complicated. Jennings and Niemi have found that the sex of the parent has little to do with their roles as agents.[31] Greenstein finds that this is not the case. According to him, "children of both sexes were more likely to choose the father than the mother as an appropriate source of voting advice."[32]

Learning theory favors Greenstein. A study by Bandura, Ross and Ross found that children are more likely to imitate the "resource-controller. They identify with the powerful, rather than the envied adult. . . ."[33] These data would lead one to expect that the father would operate as the main agent. However, the Appalachian family does not fit the classic stereotype in which the father is the main resource controller. Though we have no direct measure of who is the most powerful figure in the family, reports concerning this state of affairs in Appalachia identify the mother as being more powerful than the father.[34] As such we would then expect to find that the mother is the main agent of political socialization.

The above interpretation is consistent with the earlier finding that the mother ranks higher as an agent of information transmission and that the child is more likely to agree with his mother's political party. It is not consistent with the finding that the child prefers the father as a source of voting advice.

The discrepancy in the child's preference for the father as a source of voting advice is probably due, as noted earlier, to the fact that asking advice differs from the other two dimensions in that the question was phrased in the conditional, i.e., "If you could vote, who would be best to ask for voting advice?" We are here asking the child to engage in prospective modeling. Perhaps in doing so the child can escape the matriarchal realities of his sub-culture and respond in terms of the dominant norms of the larger society.

Regarding the parent (or model), then, it is probably true that sex is not the key variable, but that "power" and "status" within the family are more important. Given these interpretations, one would find that the parent whom the child is most likely to model would differ from culture to culture as the parent's role within the family differs from culture to culture.

SEX OF CHILD

According to Bandura and Walters, the sex of the observer is not as important a variable as the rewarding power of the model.[35] Moreover, "power inversions on the part of the male and female models produced cross-sex imitation. . . ."[36] Hence, given the matriarchal nature of the Appalachian culture we would expect children of both sexes to be more likely to model the mother than the father. Greenstein, however, has noted that the sex of the child does make some difference in the child's source of voting advice, and that sex differences are important in influencing political behavior.[37] To maintain consistency with our theory we hypothesize the following:

Hypothesis 4.6: There will be no relationship between the sex of the child and his ranking of the agents of socialization.

Table 4.25 indicates that in only two instances—rank of the mother as an agent of information transmission on the "Local" and "International" levels—is there a significant difference between boys and girls in their rankings of the parents as agents of information transmission. In these two cases girls rank the mother higher than do boys. Generally, Greenstein's hypothesis concerning the importance of sex differences does not hold in regard to the role of the parents as agents of information transmission. Sex makes little difference in the child's rankings of the parents as agents of information transmission.

Table 4.25
Relationship Between Sex of Child and Ranking of Parents as Agents of Information Transmission

LEVEL OF GOVERNMENT	χ^2*		P	
	Father	Mother	Father	Mother
Local	8.65	25.20	.30	.001
State	3.96	4.12	.80	.80
National	9.80	12.95	.20	.10
International	3.27	14.97	.90	.05

* DF = 7.

Examination of the extent of agreement between the political party preferred by parent and child further indicates that sex differences are virtually nonexistent in Appalachia (Tables 4.26 and 4.27). Children of both sexes are equally as likely to agree with the party of their parents.

The relationship between the sex of the child and his preferred source of voting advice substantiates the above finding (Table 4.28). Appalachian children, both male and female, are more likely to state that they would ask their father for voting advice.

Table 4.26
Percent of Child's Agreement with Party Identification of Father: By Sex of Child

	PARTY OF FATHER			
SEX OF CHILD	Republican	Independent	Democrat	N
Male	66.8	50.0	68.7	447
Female	78.2	56.9	69.6	530

$\chi^2 = 1.43$ DF $= 2$ P $= .50$

Gamma between male child and father $= .61$ P $= .001$
Gamma between female child and father $= .61$ P $= .001$

Table 4.27
Percent of Child's Agreement with Party Identification of Mother: By Sex of Child

	PARTY OF MOTHER			
SEX OF CHILD	Republican	Independent	Democrat	N
Male	77.5	60.2	70.1	433
Female	78.6	56.5	73.4	546

$\chi^2 = 1.20$ DF $= 2$ P $= .70$

Gamma between male child and mother $= .62$ P $= .001$
Gamma between female child and mother $= .61$ P $= .001$

Table 4.28
Relationship Between Sex of Child and Preferred Source of Voting Advice

	SEX OF CHILD	
SOURCE OF VOTING ADVICE	Male	Female
Friend	10.4	10.5
Brother or Sister	4.4	2.8
Father	52.1	46.1
Mother	17.0	25.5
Teacher	9.0	8.3
Other	7.1	6.7
Total %	100.0	99.9 *

$\chi^2 = 23.275$ DF $= 5$ P $= .001$

* Percent does not equal 100 due to rounding.

Moreover, in both New Haven and Appalachia it was found that "children of both sexes are more likely to choose the father than the mother as an appropriate source of voting advice."[38] Greenstein also found, however, that there was a significant difference between boys and girls in which parent they choose for voting advice.

The present data do not agree (Table 4.29). We find that there is only a statistically significant difference between boys and girls in grades 6, 7 and

Table 4.29
**Parent Chosen as Preferred Source of Voting Advice: By Sex and
School Year**

| | BOYS | | GIRLS | | | |
SCHOOL YEAR	Father	Mother	Father	Mother	χ^2	P
5	47.9	23.2	44.3	28.1	.91	.50
6	52.6	22.4	38.4	31.4	5.27	.05
7	51.6	17.6	44.0	30.2	4.53	.05
8	56.2	15.0	51.9	23.5	2.53	.20
9	53.4	13.6	45.7	25.9	2.84	.10
10	52.6	14.5	58.7	16.0	.05	.90
11	57.8	8.9	44.8	16.4	.80	.80
12	52.2	2.2	48.7	18.4	4.59	.05

$\chi^2 = 13.61$ P $= .10$ $\chi^2 = 15.33$ P $= .05$

12, indicating the presence of a possible culturally related difference. Greenstein also found that "the male differences also are significant at each age level, but at the individual age levels only eighth-grade female differences are significant."[39] From this Greenstein concludes that " . . . in spite of the general tendency to recognize the father as the source of voting advice, sex differences exist. Girls choose the mother more often than do boys."[40]

The Appalachian child is also more likely to choose the father than the mother as the preferred source of voting advice, and girls are generally more likely to choose the mother than boys. The differences, however, are not as significant as those found in the New Haven data.

A comparison with Greenstein's findings demonstrates that as the age of the New Haven male increases he becomes somewhat less likely to choose the father as a preferred source of voting advice. The Appalachian male, however, is likely to continue to look to his father for voting advice. Moreover, the Appalachian male child is more likely to look to his mother as a source of advice than is the New Haven male child. The Appalachian female reveals the same pattern. She is more likely, as her age increases, to continue to look to her father for voting advice than is the New Haven female. There is no statistical difference between females in the two samples in their preference for their mothers.

The above data further support our earlier contention that the Appalachian child is more likely than children of other cultures to continue to adopt his parents' party identification and to look to his parents as sources of voting advice.

Regarding the sex of the child, the data do substantiate the learning theory propositions and the hypothesis. We find that children of both sexes are equally likely to rank their parents on the same levels as agents of information transmission, that both sexes agree with their parents' party preference, and that both male and female children prefer the father over the mother and both parents over any other source of voting advice.

Since the cultural variable looms so large, the task remaining is to focus upon it and attempt to further ascertain its influence on the parent's role as an agent.

CULTURE AND SOCIALIZATION

Many of the observations in this chapter vary from those gathered by other political scientists. Moreover, they are not entirely congruent with the expectations of social modeling. A more explicit examination of the "cultural" variables behind these differences, and a delineation of whether they are interpretable in social learning terms, are in order.

Social learning theorists, unlike political scientists, have not been remiss in identifying the influence of culture upon learning. Leonard W. Doob notes that "many of the socializing influences upon the individual are themselves culturally determined."[41] The shape of the family and the parents' role within the family are influenced to a large extent by the cultural context in which they exist. For example, in Appalachia, where the male is

no longer able to be the breadwinner, no longer able to make his own independent way, has lost his traditional reason for living. . . . Frustrated at every turn, the mountaineer has suffered a loss of self, of worth. Once the dominant member of the family, he is now its burden. Forced to sit at home, unemployed, while his family suffers or becomes the object of various forms of relief, he becomes discouraged and beaten . . . the whole image of maleness has suffered.[42]

The woman is becoming the strong one. She makes the decisions. "A matriarchal society is developing. . . ."[43] The effect of a matriarchal culture on the role of the family as an agent of political socialization has never been investigated. Bandura leads us to a number of variables that should affect the learning process and that are probably more prevalent in the Appalachian culture than in middle-class America. These are: unemployment, lower education levels, father absence.

In the "culture of poverty" a more matriarchal focus develops, the father's role in the family becomes ill-defined and his role as chief authority figure diminishes.[44] The mother, consequently, is more likely to be the chief source of influence and the child is much more likely to model the mother. This interpretation, of course, was reflected in data presented earlier showing that the mother ranks higher than the father as an agent of information transmission and that the child is more likely consistently to agree with the political party identification of his mother no matter what the child's age or sex. The investigation will now examine the intellectual and vocational status[45] of the parent to ascertain whether they influence the political socialization process. If the matriarchal hypothesis is accurate, then Hypothesis 4.7 should be valid.

Hypothesis 4.7: When the father is unemployed, he will rank significantly lower than the mother as an agent of political socialization.

Table 4.30
Gamma Correlations Between Father's Employment and Child's Ranking of the Parents as Information Agents

Parent and Governmental Level	Gamma
Mother-Local	− .02
Father-Local	− .06
Mother-State	− .04
Father-State	− .03
Mother-Federal	− .04
Father-Federal	− .08
Mother-International	.01
Father-International	− .04

Table 4.30 indicates the complete absence of a relationship between the father's employment and the child's ranking of the parents as agents of information transmission. The relationship between father's employment and the child's identification with the parent's political party is similar.

There is no indication that the child's identification with the party of his father decreases when the father is unemployed, nor is there any sign to show that the child is more likely to identify with his mother's party when the father is unemployed (Table 4.31).

Moreover, as Table 4.32 demonstrates, the employment status of the father does not seem to bring about a statistically significant difference in the child's preferred sources of voting advice.

While there is no relationship between the vocational status of the model and his role as an agent of socialization, there still remain two additional variables, related to the sub-cultural or matriarchal nature of the area, that may influence the process of modeling.

The intellectual status of the model has been found to be an important variable in the learning process. If the theoretical notions are valid, then

Table 4.31
Gamma Correlations Between Party Identification
of Parents and Child: By Employment Status of
Father

EMPLOYMENT STATUS OF FATHER	GAMMA* Father and Child	Mother and Child
Unemployed	.58	.56
Farmer	.66	.59
Education, professional	.24	.73
Laborer	.66	.63
Miner	.60	.54
Clerk	.57	.55
Business man	.69	.74
Disabled	.67	.60
Skilled labor	.57	.58

* All correlations are significant at .001.

Table 4.32
Relationship Between Employment Status of
Father and Child's Preference for Parents as
Sources of Voting Advice

EMPLOYMENT OF FATHER	SOURCE OF ADVICE Father	Mother
Unemployed	41.7	30.6
Farmer	45.4	21.0
Education, professional	49.1	21.9
Laborer	58.1	19.9
Miner	51.0	19.9
Clerk	56.9	20.7
Business man	55.6	24.1
Total	N = 845	N = 361

$\chi^2 = 4.77$ DF = 6 P = .70

one would expect the child to model the parent whose education is high. Hence:

Hypothesis 4.8: There will be a positive relationship between the educational level of the parents and their ranking as agents.

The data are presented in Tables 4.33–4.35.

These data do not substantiate the hypothesis. As the parent's education increases, the strength of the relationship between the child's party identification and that of his parents does not increase. The child even identifies with the party of a poorly educated parent.[46]

Table 4.33
Gamma Correlations Between Parents' Education and the Child's Ranking of the Parents as Information Agents

PARENT AND GOVERNMENTAL LEVEL	GAMMA	
	Father's Education	Mother's Education
Mother-Local	− .02	− .02
Father-Local	− .09	− .06
Mother-State	− .05	− .04
Father-State	− .09	− .03
Mother-Federal	.01	− .03
Father-Federal	− .10	− .08
Mother-International	.02	.00
Father-International	− .10	− .04

Table 4.34
Gamma Correlations Between Party Identification of Parent and Child: By Father's Education

EDUCATION OF FATHER	GAMMA*	
	Father and Child	Mother and Child
No school	.50	.55
Grade school (1–6)	.61	.60
Junior high (7–9)	.62	.64
Some high school (10–11)	.64	.64
Completed high school	.68	.69
Some college	.37	.45
Completed college	.75	.71

* All correlations are significant at .001.

Table 4.35
Gamma Correlations Between Party Identification of Parent and Child: By Mother's Education

EDUCATION OF MOTHER	GAMMA*	
	Father and Child	Mother and Child
No school	.71	.77
Grade school (1–6)	.58	.57
Junior high (7–9)	.60	.60
Some high school (10–11)	.57	.65
Completed high school	.63	.62
Some college	.70	.70
Completed college	.59	.57

* All correlations are significant at .001.

Our hypothesis does find some minimal support, however, in the area of parental voting advice.

Tables 4.36 and 4.37 show that a statistically significant relationship does exist between the father's educational status and the child's preferred

Table 4.36
Relationship Between Education of Father and
Child's Preferred Source of Voting Advice

	SOURCE OF ADVICE	
FATHER'S EDUCATION	Father	Mother
No school	40.0	27.7
Grade school	46.9	22.5
Junior high	54.4	18.5
Some high school	56.6	19.0
Completed high school	56.2	18.5
Some college	58.7	13.7
Completed college	64.9	10.8
Total	N = 827	N = 317

$\chi^2 = 18.71$ DF = 6   P = .01

Table 4.37
Relationship Between Education of Mother and
Child's Preferred Source of Voting Advice

	SOURCE OF ADVICE	
MOTHER'S EDUCATION	Father	Mother
No school	41.7	30.6
Grade school	45.4	21.0
Junior high	49.1	21.9
Some high school	58.1	19.9
Completed high school	51.0	19.9
Some college	56.9	20.7
Completed college	55.6	24.1
Total	N = 845	N = 361

$\chi^2 = 4.57$ DF = 6   P = .70

source of voting advice. As the father's education increases, the child is more likely to look to the father as a source of voting advice and less likely to the mother. The educational status of the mother, on the other hand, does not display the same relationship.

In general, Hypothesis 4.8 was not substantiated. The educational status of the parents had little overall effect upon their role as agents of political socialization.

A variable that may be of particular importance in the Appalachian culture[47] and which has been identified as being involved in the learning process is the contiguity between model and observer.[48]

Berkowitz notes that a child may not only fail to model his father if the mother is the main authority figure in the family, but also if the father is absent.[49]

Hypothesis 4.9: When the father is absent from the home he will rank significantly lower than the mother as an agent of political socialization.

The results indicated by the data are striking (Table 4.38). Father absence has no effect upon the child's ranking of the mother as an agent of information transmission, but has a profound effect upon the child's ranking of the father. There is an extremely large statistical difference between children in father-present and father-absent homes in how they rank the father as an agent of information transmission. Children whose father is present are much more likely to rank him high, while children whose father is absent rank him significantly lower. These findings tend

Table 4.38
Comparison of Child's Ranking of the Parents as Information Agents: By Absence or Presence of the Father

RANK	LOCAL FATHER PRESENT		FATHER ABSENT	
	Mother	*Father*	*Mother*	*Father*
1	12.5	11.9	12.5	3.4
2	17.1	15.6	12.5	6.4
3	14.1	14.9	17.9	6.0
4	18.6	15.2	17.3	12.4
5	20.0	18.1	20.4	20.5
6	10.7	16.4	13.7	17.1
7	5.9	5.9	4.5	17.1
8	1.2	2.0	1.3	17.1
Total %	100.0	100.0	100.0	100.0
N =	1323	1339	313	234
	G = .06 P = .01		G = .51 P = .0001	

RANK	STATE FATHER PRESENT		FATHER ABSENT	
	Mother	*Father*	*Mother*	*Father*
1	6.5	7.1	6.4	3.0
2	10.6	10.3	9.1	6.0
3	10.2	10.5	10.4	6.5
4	19.8	18.5	21.9	8.6
5	26.6	24.2	27.9	22.0
6	16.4	19.9	14.1	22.8
7	8.0	7.4	8.1	14.7
8	1.9	2.2	2.0	16.4
Total %	100.0	100.0	99.9*	100.0
N =	1289	1300	297	232
	G = .02 P = .28		G = .41 P = .0001	

* Percent does not equal 100 due to rounding.

Table 4.38—continued

RANK	NATIONAL FATHER PRESENT		FATHER ABSENT	
	Mother	Father	Mother	Father
1	4.1	3.7	4.2	2.7
2	5.5	5.1	4.9	2.7
3	5.9	6.1	7.7	6.3
4	19.4	20.6	18.9	13.8
5	34.2	30.8	35.3	17.9
6	18.9	23.3	16.8	27.7
7	9.3	8.2	8.7	12.1
8	2.8	2.2	3.5	17.0
Total %	100.0	100.0	100.0	100.0
N =	1253	1264	286	224
	$G = .01$ $P = .35$		$G = .33$ $P = .0001$	

RANK	INTERNATIONAL FATHER PRESENT		FATHER ABSENT	
	Mother	Father	Mother	Father
1	4.2	3.3	3.7	1.8
2	5.2	5.9	3.3	6.0
3	5.7	6.1	7.3	6.0
4	17.5	18.3	17.6	12.4
5	33.9	28.5	32.2	22.0
6	20.1	26.9	22.7	22.0
7	8.9	8.9	7.3	13.8
8	4.5	2.0	5.9	16.1
Total %	100.0	99.9*	100.0	100.1*
N =	1220	1228	273	218
	$G = .09$ $P = .0003$		$G = .22$ $P = .0002$	

* Percent does not equal 100 due to rounding.

to partially substantiate the hypothesis and demonstrate that model contiguity is extremely important.

The preceding also demonstrates that the father's contiguity in the home accounts for a great deal of the variance in the rankings of the parents as agents of information transmission. When the father is absent the child is more likely to rank the mother higher than the father as an agent of information transmission.

Does a similar pattern exist in the two additional dimensions of agent performance? The data are in Table 4.39.

Table 4.39 indicates that when the father is absent there is a smaller, but still significant, relationship between the party identification of the father and child. This tendency is not as pronounced for the mother. The following data (Tables 4.40–4.41) show further that when the father is absent

Table 4.39
Relationship Between Absence of the Father and Party Identification of Father and Child

STATUS OF FATHER			GAMMA	
	Father and Child		Mother and Child	
	G	P	G	P
Father Present	.65	.001	.63	.001
Father Absent	.41	.001	.57	.001

Table 4.40
Percent of Child's Agreement with Party Identification of Father: By Father-Absence

FATHER	PARTY OF FATHER			
	Republican	Independent	Democrat	N
Present	81.3	56.0	71.9	858
Absent	64.6	47.8	71.4	122

$\chi^2 = 10.40$ DF $= 2$ P $= .01$

Table 4.41
Percent of Child's Agreement with Party Identification of Mother: By Father-Absence

FATHER	PARTY OF MOTHER			
	Republican	Independent	Democrat	N
Present	79.2	57.0	72.8	792
Absent	74.2	62.1	71.7	186

$\chi^2 = 6.01$ DF $= 2$ P $= .05$

Table 4.42
Relationship Between Absence of the Father and Parents as a Preferred Source of Voting Advice

Source of Advice	Father-Present	Father-Absent
Friend	10.4	11.0
Brother or Sister	3.2	4.7
Father	55.4	25.7
Mother	16.8	38.0
Teacher	7.9	11.2
Other	6.2	9.2
Total %	100.0	99.8*
	N = 1100	N = 255

$\chi^2 = 134.282$ DF $= 5$ P $= .001$

* Percent does not equal 100 due to rounding.

the child is less likely to agree with his party identification than when the father is present. Moreover, there is a slight tendency, when the father is absent, for the child to agree with the mother's identification if she is an independent.

Regarding the effect of father absence upon the child's preferred source of voting, one notes an even more striking difference between father-present and father-absent children (Table 4.42).

Again the data substantiate that there is a highly significant difference between father-absent and father-present children. In this case, the child whose father is absent is more likely to look to his mother rather than to his father as a source of voting advice. This is quite interesting in light of our earlier findings, which indicated that the father was the overwhelming preference as a source of voting advice and that the mother continually ran second.

Hypothesis 4.9 has been substantiated. When the father is absent from the home: (1) the child ranks him lower as an agent of information transmission; (2) the child is less likely to agree with the party identification of the father, and (3) the mother appears as the child's most preferred source of voting advice.

It is now possible to account for the earlier findings that the mother ranks higher than the father as an agent of information transmission and that the child is consistently more likely to agree with the political party preference of the mother. Father absence is a key factor. When the father is present, the rankings of the two parents are the same; when he is absent, the mother ranks significantly higher. Indeed, father-absence appears to be the most important reason for the child's ranking the mother higher than the father as an agent of socialization. A model that normally produces cues is absent and the child must turn to another.

Thus, there is nothing in the foregoing to substantiate the psychoanalytically based hypothesis that when the father is absent the child idealizes the father and places more emphasis upon him.[50] Absence of the father for the Appalachian child does not lead the child to seek out a father image, but causes the child to turn to his mother as an agent of political socialization. (For data and remarks on the relationship between model contiguity and attitudes see Appendix A.)

SUMMARY

The purpose of the present chapter has been to increase our knowledge of the role of the family, especially the parents, as agents of political socialization. Both social learning theory and prior studies of political socialization lead one to believe that the family should be the foremost model for the child. Learning theorists have noted that the roles played by respective models are influenced by cultural variables. The present findings substantiate this notion.

It was discovered that the family was not the highest ranking agent of information transmission, but that the rankings, relative to those of the other agents, were lower, with the mother only slightly higher than the father. These findings stand in some contrast to the discovery by other scholars of the family's great influence, and is probably due to the particular sub-cultural nature of Appalachia.

Further confirmation of the importance of the cultural variable is given by the findings regarding party identification. The Appalachian child is more likely to model the mother's party than the father's. This relationship is consistent at all age levels and demonstrates the static nature of political maturation in the Appalachian cultural milieu. The influence of the matriarchal sub-culture is further amplified by the data on model contiguity. Father-absence is culturally related, being more prevalent in Appalachia, and was found to exercise a profound affect upon the modeling behavior of the child. When the father is absent, the child looks to the mother as a replacement for the missing political model and, consequently, ranks the mother higher than the father as an agent of information transmission and tends to identify with her political party rather than the father's. Culture seems to be an extremely important variable effecting a wide range of socialization experiences.

Although it is not possible to explore these dramatic cultural differences in all of what follows, we have successfully raised the specter of cultural influence upon the process of political socialization. When possible we shall continue to explore these differences. Much of what follows is, however, exploratory in nature and will be devoted to (1) ascertaining what role the other hypothesized agents play, and (2) discovering what agents, if any, replace the family in the Appalachian culture.

Notes

Chapter 4

[1] Hess and Torney, p. 185. For other studies dealing with the inheritance of party identification see footnote 33, chapter 1. On the parent as a source of voting advice see: Greenstein, *Children and Politics,* pp. 103 and 109.

[2] Hess and Torney, p. 165.

[3] Bandura and Walters, p. 84.

[4] Bandura, "Vicarious Processes," p. 32.

[5] Bandura and Walters, p. 64. The study from which this finding is cited is: Albert Bandura, *Relationship of Family Patterns to Child Behavior Disorders.* Progress Report, U.S.P.H. Research Grant M-1734. Stanford University, 1960.

[6] Bandura and Walters, p. 66.

[7] *Ibid.,* p. 70; and S. Fleck, "Family Dynamics and Origin of Schizophrenia," *Psychosomatic Medicine,* 22 (1960), pp. 333–344.

[8] *Ibid.,* pp. 70–72.

[9] Leonard Berkowtiz, *The Development of Motives and Values in the Child* (New York: Basic Books, Inc., 1964), p. 19 and pp. 82–86.

[10] Dale B. Harris, Harrison G. Gough, and William E. Martin, "Children's Ethnic Attitudes: II. Relationship to Parental Beliefs Concerning Child Training." *Child Development,* 21, 3 (September, 1950), p. 169.

[11] M. Kent Jennings, "Pre-Adult Orientations to Multiple Systems of Government," *Midwest Journal of Political Science,* XI (August, 1967), pp. 291–317.

[12] For a similar conceptualization of sources of information using Appalachian adults rather than children see: Lewis Donohew and B. K. Singh, *Poverty "Types" and Their Sources of Information About New Practices.* Paper presented before the International Communication Division, Association for Education in Journalism, Boulder, Colorado, August, 1967.

[13] Hess and Torney, pp. 182–184.

[14] *Ibid.*

[15] On the agents of socialization see: Easton and Hess, "Youth and the Political System," p. 251; Greenstein, *Children and Politics*, pp. 9–15; and by the same author, *International Encyclopedia*, p. 6; Froman, *Journal of Politics*, pp. 341–352; Mitchell, *The American Polity*, pp. 145–178; and Hess and Torney, pp. 182–228.

[16] On the inheritance of party identification see footnote 33, Chap. 1. In particular see: Jennings and Niemi, p. 2 and pp. 6–8; and Hyman, *Political Socialization*, pp. 69–82.

[17] Jennings and Niemi, p. 173.

[18] Greenstein, *Children and Politics*, pp. 193–204.

[19] Bandura and Walters, p. 32.

[20] Bandura, "Vicarious Processes," p. 29.

[21] Bandura and Walters.

[22] Bandura, "Behavior Modifications," p. 328.

[23] Bandura and Walters, p. 32.

[24] Analyzing the pattern of responses for father and mother alone more pointedly demonstrates the effect of discussion ($\chi^2 = 12.41$, DF $= 3$, P $= .01$).

[25] Hyman, *Political Socialization*, p. 98. Jennings and Niemi. For the effect of age on adolescent's concept of the political community see: Joseph Adelson and Robert P. O'Neil, "Growth of Political Ideas in Adolescence: The Sense of Community," *Journal of Personality and Social Psychology*, 4, 3 (1966), pp. 295–306.

[26] Bandura, "Behavior Modifications," p. 314; and Eleanor E. Maccoby, "Role Taking in Childhood and Its Consequences for Social Learning," *Child Development*, 30 (1959), p. 246.

[27] Jennings and Niemi, p. 4. Also see Robert E. Lane, "Fathers and Sons: Foundations of Political Belief," American Sociological Review, 24 (August, 1959), pp. 502–11; Eleanor E. Maccoby, Richard E. Matthews, and Anton S. Morton, "Youth and Political Change," *Public Opinion Quarterly*, 18 (Spring, 1954), pp. 23–39; and Russell Middleton and Snell Putney, "Political Expression of Adolescent Rebellion," *American Journal of Sociology*, 68 (March, 1963), pp. 527–35.

While rebellion is probably not the answer, social learning theory does lead one to expect that the status of the parent as an agent or model is affected by intra-familial relationships. Brim notes that ". . . the degree to which there is a highly effective relationship between parent and child, in contrast with one of low effectivity . . ." affects learning (Brim and Wheeler, p. 26). More specifically, according to Berkowitz, boys who have warm and affectionate fathers are more likely to model their fathers (*Development of Motives and Values*, p. 73). Thus, we might expect that boys whose relationship with their father is positive would be more likely to model their fathers, while the child whose relationship with his father is negative would look to the mother for political cues.

Evidence gathered by political science regarding the effect of family relationships on political socialization is mixed. Hess and Torney (pp. 187 and 240) claim it is important while Jennings and Niemi (p. 20) say it accounts for little variation.

The present data demonstrate that there is no statistically significant relationship between the child's age and his relationship with his father (G $= .013$), thereby giving an indication of the lack of any rebellion against the father. Even the child whose relationship with his father is poor continues to identify with his father's political party.

[28] John Fetterman, *Stinking Creek: The Portrait of a Small Mountain Community* (New York: E. P. Dutton & Co., Inc., 1967).

[29] Daniel J. Elazar, *American Federalism: A View from the States* (New York: Thomas Y. Crowell Company, 1966), pp. 85–140.

[30] *Ibid.,* pp. 92–3.

[31] Jennings and Niemi, p. 180.

[32] Greenstein, *Journal of Politics,* p. 364.

[33] Berkowitz, *The Development of Motives and Values in the Child,* p. 75. For the original study see: Albert Bandura, Dorothea and Sheila Ross, "A Comparative Test of the Status Envy, Social Power, and Secondary Reinforcement Theories of Identificatory Learning," *Journal of Abnormal and Social Psychology,* LXVLL, 6 (December, 1963), pp. 527–534.

[34] Jack E. Weller, *Yesterday's People: Life in Contemporary Appalachia* (Lexington, Kentucky: University of Kentucky Press, 1965), pp. 76–77.

[35] Bandura and Walters, p. 99.

[36] *Ibid.*

[37] Greenstein, *Children and Politics,* pp. 107–127, and by the same author, *Journal of Politics,* pp. 353–71.

[38] Greenstein, *Journal of Politics,* p. 364.

[39] Greenstein, *Children and Politics,* Table 6.2, p. 119.

[40] *Ibid.*

[41] Leonard W. Doob, *Propaganda: Its Psychology and Technique* (New York: Henry Holt, 1935), p. 52.

[42] Weller, pp. 76–77.

[43] *Ibid.,* p. 77.

[44] Davies, p. 16; and E. Wight Bakke, *Citizens Without Work* (New Haven: Yale University Press, 1940), Chapter 6.

[45] Bandura, "Vicarious Processes," p. 29.

[46] In order to verify this somewhat surprising finding we have put the data into a different form. The two tables below show the percentage of the child's agreement with the party preference of his parents by the parents' education. The data substantiates the fact that the child continues to agree with the party of his parents no matter what the parents' education status happens to be.

Table A

Percent of Children's Agreement with Party of Father: by Father's Education

	PARTY OF FATHER	
EDUCATION	*Republican*	*Democrat*
No school	67	46
Grade school	84	67
Junior high	78	73
Some high school	81	66
Completed high school	76	68
Some college	68	68
Completed college	75	63
Total	N = 454	N = 296

$\chi^2 = 11.75$ DF = 6   P = .10

Table B

**Percent of Children's Agreement with Party of
Mother: by Mother's Education**

	PARTY OF MOTHER	
EDUCATION	Republican	Democrat
No school	77	100
Grade school	81	67
Junior high	79	63
Some high school	70	70
Completed high school	78	86
Some college	74	75
Completed college	64	72
Total	N = 490	N = 298

$\chi^2 = 10.18$ DF = 6   P = .20

[47] Father absence is more prevalent than in Hess and Torney's sample. They found (p. 193) "12 per cent of the children came from homes without fathers." For the Appalachian sample the comparable figure is 20 per cent.

[48] Bandura, "Behavior Modifications," p. 29.

[49] Berkowitz, *Aggression: A Social Psychological Analysis* (New York: McGraw-Hill, 1962), p. 296; and Sewell, pp. 168–169.

[50] For an elaboration of this position see: David Easton and Robert D. Hess, "The Child's Political World," *Midwest Journal of Political Science,* VI, 3 (August, 1962), pp. 229, 246.

5
Interpersonal Agents of Political Socialization:
PEERS AND PEER GROUPS

The role of the peer group, a second "interpersonal" agent of political socialization, has not been adequately investigated. In virtually the only available inquiry Langton notes that in small group literature one of the "better documented generalizations" is "the influence of the group upon the perceptions and expressed opinions of an individual...."[1] He says that the peer group also transmits the culture of the larger society of which it is a part.[2] Langton, however, says little concerning variables that may be influential in the operation of peer groups as agents of socialization. This is the place where variables identified by social learning theory become valuable. Our primary concern is, of course, whether peers take the place of the impaired family models.

According to Bandura and Walters, "innovation of social behavior may also occur, as the child gets older, through increasing contact with models provided by the peer groups...."[3] In adolescence, peer groups give the child his first actual contact with relationships in which adult authority figures may play only peripheral roles.[4] As the child matures, therefore, peers may begin to replace the parents as the important agents of socialization. Intuitively, one might expect the peer group to generate fewer cues for the younger child since he has presumably greater contact with his

Notes to Chapter 5 will be found on p. 92.

parents, but a greater number of cues to the older child as his contact with the family decreases. This should not be taken to mean that the influence of the parents drops out of sight. On the contrary, the fact that they are replaced as models does not lessen the fact that they may have already influenced the child. Replacement, then, does not imply that the effect of previous models has been terminated.

We hypothesize:

Hypothesis 5.1: As the child increases in age, the peer group will replace parents as agents of socialization.

It will be well to recall that the overall ranking of peers as agents of information transmission was somewhat lower than that of the parents, except that peers ranked highly as agents transmitting information concerning the local community. Below is the overall ranking of the peer group (Table 5.1).

Table 5.1
Rank of Peers as Agents of Information Transmission on Four Levels of Government

LEVEL OF GOVERNMENT	RANK								Total%	N
	1	2	3	4	5	6	7	8		
Local	18	9	14	11	14	16	15	3	100	1725
State	3	4	9	10	15	22	32	5	100	1595
National	2	2	5	8	14	25	39	5	100	1554
International	2	3	5	8	13	21	42	6	100	1511

$G = .32$ $P = .001$

Two operations are necessary to test this hypothesis directly. First, we must note the relationship between age and the ranking of peers as agents of information transmission; second, we must correlate the rank of parents with that of the peers while controlling age.

The effect of age on the ranking of peers is presented in Table 5.2.

On three of the four levels there is a significant difference between the child's rankings of his peers as agents, but in only one case is this in the hypothesized direction. The relationships in the opposite direction are, however, quite small. Only on the local level does the importance of the peer groups increase as the age of the child increases. It is not likely, therefore, that the peer group will replace the parents as agents of information transmission on any but the local level of government. A comparison of Table 5.2 with the tables in the previous chapter substantiates the fact

Table 5.2
Relationship Between Age and Rank of Peers as Information Agents

LOCAL

AGE	RANK								Total %	N
	1	2	3	4	5	6	7	8		
10	7	5	15	6	14	29	21	3	100	133
11	12	4	15	10	15	23	17	4	100	210
12	18	8	11	13	16	14	16	3	99*	298
13	17	8	15	12	16	11	18	3	100	285
14	17	12	10	10	16	15	17	3	100	267
15	17	14	16	11	9	18	11	3	99*	174
16	30	7	16	14	9	7	15	1	99*	134
17	29	14	14	13	9	10	8	2	99*	120
18	24	12	18	22	10	8	6	0	100	50

$G = -.17$ $P = .001$ $\chi^2 = 143.496$ $DF = 63$ $P = .001$

STATE

AGE	RANK								Total %	N
	1	2	3	4	5	6	7	8		
10	4	1	9	9	11	27	32	7	100	130
11	3	3	10	9	10	26	32	7	100	191
12	3	4	11	13	16	21	25	7	100	272
13	4	3	8	9	17	19	35	6	101*	274
14	2	3	7	11	16	21	35	6	101*	243
15	3	6	9	10	18	20	31	2	99*	158
16	4	3	6	10	13	24	37	3	100	127
17	6	5	7	12	20	20	29	1	100	112
18	0	0	13	12	16	27	38	4	100	45

$G = -.02$ $\chi^2 = 65.81$ $DF = 63$ $P = .37$

NATIONAL

AGE	RANK								Total %	N
	1	2	3	4	5	6	7	8		
10	1	0	6	12	6	33	36	7	101*	120
11	2	3	5	9	16	23	35	7	100	189
12	2	5	6	6	11	29	32	9	100	262
13	1	1	6	6	15	27	37	7	100	259
14	1	2	5	9	11	26	43	3	100	240
15	2	2	4	11	16	19	44	2	100	158
16	2	1	3	6	17	20	44	6	99*	126
17	3	1	2	8	18	18	48	3	101*	112
18	0	0	2	2	16	29	48	2	99*	44

$G = .03$ $\chi^2 = 86.10$ $DF = 63$ $P = .02$

Table 5.2—continued

AGE	RANK INTERNATIONAL									
	1	2	3	4	5	6	7	8	Total %	N
10	2	3	5	5	7	30	40	8	100	116
11	4	2	7	11	8	20	38	10	100	191
12	2	5	7	6	19	23	31	8	101*	258
13	1	3	5	11	12	19	39	9	99*	248
14	0	2	4	11	11	18	50	3	99*	234
15	1	2	4	8	16	21	44	4	100	155
16	1	4	5	4	13	20	51	2	100	121
17	2	1	5	10	14	19	47	3	101*	107
18	0	2	7	7	12	22	46	2	98*	41

$G = .02$ $\chi^2 = 97.08$ $DF = 63$ $P = .003$

* Percent does not equal 100 due to rounding.

that the hypothesis could only be valid on the local level. Table 5.3 below presents the data. In it the rankings of peer and parent are compared over the age of the child. As the child's age increases, the peer group does not rank higher than the parent as the most salient agent of information transmission.

Table 5.3
Gamma Correlations Between Rank of Peers and Parents as Information Agents: By Age of Child

AGE	LOCAL PEERS AND MOTHER		PEERS AND FATHER	
	G	P	G	P
10	.15	.02	.04	.28
11	.20	.001	.23	.001
12	.19	.001	.14	.004
13	.14	.005	.18	.001
14	.08	.08	.03	.28
15	.14	.02	.11	.06
16	.23	.002	.11	.07
17	.15	.04	.06	.23

AGE	STATE PEERS AND MOTHER		PEERS AND FATHER	
	G	P	G	P
10	.24	.001	.13	.05
11	.31	.001	.29	.001
12	.16	.001	.18	.001
13	.11	.02	.18	.001
14	.21	.001	.17	.004
15	.08	.14	.07	.18
16	.16	.03	.14	.09
17	.12	.08	− .02	.43

Table 5.3—continued

AGE	NATIONAL PEERS AND MOTHER		PEERS AND FATHER	
	G	P	G	P
10	.22	.009	.13	.07
11	.14	.06	.17	.05
12	.21	.001	.23	.05
13	.17	.002	.19	.05
14	− .003	.48	− .04	.26
15	− .09	.14	− .09	.15
16	− .01	.45	− .01	.45
17	− .09	.19	− .28	.005

AGE	INTERNATIONAL PEERS AND MOTHER		PEERS AND FATHER	
	G	P	G	P
10	.02	.30	.13	.05
11	.17	.002	.28	.001
12	.15	.02	.15	.02
13	.08	.08	.16	.02
14	.004	.50	.003	.50
15	− .16	.05	− .05	.25
16	− .01	.45	.17	.05
17	− .20	.05	− .25	.005

If peers had replaced parents as agents we would expect to find large negative gammas at the upper age levels. Yet, when the correlations become negative it demonstrates not that peers rank higher than parents but that the disagreement in the rankings is due to parents ranking higher than peers. This interpretation emerges from examination of the original data matrices, and indicates that Hypothesis 5.1 has not been substantiated.

Table 5.4
Relationship Between Political Party of
Peers and Political Party of Respondent

RESPONDENT'S PARTY	PEER'S PARTY Republican	Democrat
Republican	34.3	39.2
Independent	16.8	8.8
Democrat	25.1	24.5
Will not vote	5.4	5.9
Don't know	18.4	21.5
Total %	100.0	99.9 *
	N = 728	N = 1077

$G = - .04$ $\chi^2 = 27.46$ $DF = 4$ $P = .001$

* Percent does not equal 100 due to rounding.

On the other two measures of agent-performance, a similar finding is evident. The Appalachian child is not at all likely to agree with the political party preference of his peers (Table 5.4).

It is also evident that in the Appalachian sub-culture the child is much more likely to agree with the party of his parents rather than his peers. Nor does partisan agreement with peers increase with age (Table 5.5).

Table 5.5
Relationship Between Party Identification of Peers and Party of Respondent: By Age of Respondent

AGE OF RESPONDENT	PERCENT OF RESPONDENTS AGREE WITH PEER'S PARTY WHEN PEER IS:			
	Republican	*Democrat*	*Gamma*	*P*
10	67.4	69.6	.47	.001
11	81.7	69.0	.51	.001
12	72.3	47.2	.42	.001
13	68.8	60.3	.49	.001
14	67.0	69.6	.51	.001
15	65.5	68.3	.34	.001
16	75.0	67.5	.52	.001
17	74.1	47.8	.42	.001

The strength of the relationship between the party of peers and that of the child is similar at all age levels—it does not increase as age increases. Since the peers' party was identified by the respondent's perception, it is possible that the strength of the relationship is accentuated by the respondent selectively perceiving that his friends have the same political party affiliation that he has. The same problem may, of course, have been operative in the relationship between the respondent's party and that of his parents. Comparing the results, however, yields an interesting pattern (Table 5.6).

The Appalachian child shows a stronger affinity for the political party of his peers than his father, and even a stronger relation to his mother's party.

The data indicate, therefore, that (1) peers do not increase in impact as the child grows older, and (2) the parents (mainly the mother) do not decrease in impact with age. These points tend to lead one to reject the peer hypothesis and to confirm the cultural argument put forth earlier.

This cultural effect tends to depress the father's role as an agent of socialization, and allows the child's peers to have more influence upon his party identification. At the same time, the hypothesis that peers replace parents as agents as the child's age increases is not borne out because peers rank higher than father at all ages and the correlation between mother and

Table 5.6
Comparison of Gamma Correlations Between Party of Respondent and Party of Peers and Party of Respondent and Party of Parents: By Age of Respondent

AGE	RESPONDENT AND FATHER		RESPONDENT AND PEER		RESPONDENT AND MOTHER	
	G	P	G	P	G	P
10	.17	.30	.47	.001	.92	.0001
11	.39	.05	.51	.001	.91	.0001
12	.57	.03	.42	.001	.90	.0001
13	.35	.08	.49	.001	.82	.0001
14	.44	.03	.51	.001	.85	.0001
15	.27	.15	.34	.001	.84	.0001
16	.35	.15	.52	.001	.84	.0001
17	.74	.008	.42	.001	.90	.0001

child is consistently higher than that for peer and child. The matriarchal sub-culture would appear to have a profound affect upon the child's source of party identification.

Concerning voting advice, a glance back at Table 4.16 indicates that as the child grows older the peers do not replace the parents as preferred sources of advice. On the contrary, the parents continue to be the primary source of advice at all age levels.

As noted earlier, this continued emphasis on the parents as sources of voting advice may be related to the traditionalistic structure of the Appalachian sub-culture. It was demonstrated that there is a statistically significant difference between New Haven and Appalachian children in their preferences for the parents as sources of voting advice. Unfortunately, we cannot determine whether or not a similar difference exists between the Appalachian and New Haven samples in their preference for their peers as sources of voting advice. Although Greenstein did include peers as a possible response-category, he does not give the pattern of responses. Therefore, we cannot reach any conclusion concerning cultural differences. For the time being, then, we can reject the hypothesis that peers replace parents as agents as the age of the child increases.

Sex

Research concerning the influence of sex differences upon the role of the peers as agents of political socialization is sketchy at best. Bandura notes, however, that sex differences account for some variation in the child's response to models. He found, for example, that boys were more likely than girls to imitate aggressive models and that girls displayed more "prosocial" and less "contrasocial" aggression than boys.[5] These findings were interpreted as being related to cultural norms in that it is more appropriate for boys to display physical aggression. It has also been suggested that boys are more politically oriented than girls.[6] If the modeling dynamic extends into the realm of political behavior we should observe sex differences in the imitation of political models.

Hypothesis 5.2: There will be a relationship between the sex of the child and the role of peers as agents of political socialization.

Table 5.7
Relationship Between Sex of Child and Rank of Peers as Information Agents: By Sex of Child

	LEVEL OF GOVERNMENT							
RANK	LOCAL		STATE		NATIONAL		INTERNATIONAL	
	Male	Female	Male	Female	Male	Female	Male	Female
1	17	19	3	3	2	2	2	2
2	10	9	4	4	2	2	3	3
3	14	14	10	8	6	5	5	6
4	11	12	10	11	8	7	10	8
5	13	15	14	17	14	13	12	13
6	17	15	22	22	27	24	22	20
7	16	15	32	31	36	41	41	43
8	3	3	6	5	6	5	6	6
Total %	100	100	100	100	100	100	100	100
N =	734	967	678	899	667	871	645	849

$\chi^2 = 5.09$ $\chi^2 = 7.32$ $\chi^2 = 5.97$ $\chi^2 = 5.92$
DF = 7   DF = 7   DF = 7   DF = 7
P = .70   P = .50   P = .70   P = .70

Table 5.7 shows that with respect to peers as political information transmitters there are no statistically significant differences between male and female subjects. Regarding party identification and voting advice one finds no differences that can be attributed to sex.

The relationship between party identification of peers and that of the respondent is the same for both males and females (Table 5.8) and the same percentage of males and females state that they would prefer peers as sources of voting advice (males = 10.4%; females = 10.5%).

Hypothesis 5.2 has not been validated. There is no observable relationship between the sex of the child and his perception of the peers role as agents of political socialization. The Appalachian male is not more likely to be oriented to political models than the female.

Table 5.8
Gamma Correlations
Between Party
Identification of Peers
and Respondent: By
Sex of Respondent

Sex	Gamma	P
Male	.48	.001
Female	.45	.001

Orientation to Stimuli

It has already been found that the child's perception of parental orientation to political stimuli has little relationship to the role the parents play as agents of political socialization. The task ahead is to find out what role it plays in the child's perception of his peers as agents.

Hypothesis 5.3: Children who perceive their peers as being oriented to political stimuli will rank them higher as agents than those who perceive them as not being so oriented.

The measure of peers orientation to political stimuli is more direct than those used in the discussion of the parents. It consists of a direct question asking whether or not the child perceives his friends as being interested in politics. Those who do perceive their peers as being interested in politics should rank them higher as agents (Table 5.9).

Table 5.9
Relationship Between Child's Perception
of Peers' Orientation to Political Stimuli
and Rank of Peers as Information Agents

RANK	LOCAL FRIENDS INTERESTED IN POLITICS?	
	Yes	No
1	17.8	17.9
2	9.6	7.6
3	13.0	14.4
4	10.6	11.5
5	13.5	13.1
6	15.4	17.3
7	16.1	16.4
8	4.0	1.8
Total %	100.0	100.0
	N = 747	N = 764

$\chi^2 = 9.77$ DF = 7   P = .30

Table 5.9—continued

RANK	STATE FRIENDS INTERESTED IN POLITICS?	
	Yes	No
1	3.2	3.3
2	3.8	3.8
3	7.6	9.7
4	8.2	11.0
5	17.1	13.4
6	21.5	21.8
7	33.9	30.8
8	4.7	6.3
Total %	100.0	100.0
	N = 708	N = 702

$\chi^2 = 10.48$ DF = 7 P = .20

RANK	NATIONAL FRIENDS INTERESTED IN POLITICS?	
	Yes	No
1	1.4	1.9
2	1.8	2.2
3	3.7	6.2
4	6.8	9.0
5	13.5	12.6
6	26.7	25.3
7	40.6	36.7
8	5.5	5.9
Total %	100.0	99.8*
	N = 705	N = 675

$\chi^2 = 9.27$ DF = 7 P = .30

* Percent does not equal 100 due to rounding.

RANK	INTERNATIONAL FRIENDS INTERESTED IN POLITICS?	
	Yes	No
1	1.4	1.8
2	3.0	2.8
3	3.8	7.8
4	7.7	9.3
5	12.9	11.8
6	22.7	19.4
7	41.5	41.6
8	7.1	5.5
Total %	100.0	100.0
	N = 692	N = 654

$\chi^2 = 14.46$ DF = 7 P = .05

On only one level of government (international) is there a significant difference in the child's ranking of the peers as agents of information transmission and this difference is both small and not in the hypothesized direction. Children who perceive their peers as being oriented to political stimuli do not rank them higher than those who do not perceive them as being so oriented. This pattern is duplicated for party identification and voting advice.

Table 5.10
Gamma Correlations
Between Party
Identification of
Respondent and Party
of Peers: By Peers'
Interest in Politics

Friends Interested in Politics?	Gamma
Yes	.41
No	.51

Table 5.11
Relationship Between Preferred Source of Voting Advice and Peers' Interest in Politics

PREFERRED SOURCE OF ADVICE	PEERS INTERESTED IN POLITICS?	
	Yes	No
Friend	10.5	10.8
Brother or Sister	3.5	3.7
Father	49.4	48.3
Mother	20.3	22.4
Teacher	8.5	9.0
Other	7.8	5.8
Total %	100.0	100.0
	N = 885	N = 976

$\chi^2 = 3.93$ DF = 5   P = .70

Table 5.10 demonstrates that the relationship between the party identification of respondent and peers is not stronger when the peers are perceived as being oriented to political stimuli (both correlations are significant at .001), while Table 5.11 demonstrates that there is no statistically significant difference in the preferred source of voting advice of those respondents who perceive their peers as being oriented or not oriented to political stimuli. Even when the peers are perceived as being so oriented they do not rank higher and the parents do not rank lower.

Hypothesis 5.3, then, must be rejected. As was found for the parents, perception of the agents' orientation to political stimuli does not seem to be a particularly salient variable in the process of political learning.

Intrafamilial Relationships and Peers as Agents of Political Socialization

Intrafamilial relationships have been found to influence the modeling process. In the previous chapter it was noted that the child's relationship with his father had little affect upon the role of the parents as agents of political socialization. However, we saw that when the child's relationship with the father is extremely poor the child is more likely to look to the mother as an agent of information transmission. We also noted that affectivity within the family affects the learning process in that boys who have a positive relationship with their fathers are more likely to model their fathers.[7]

We might expect, therefore, that when the father's position as a model is impaired, the peers may assume this role (even though mother has already been shown to fill the gap to some extent). These propositions lead to the following hypothesis:

Hypothesis 5.4: When the child's relationship with his father is poor, the peer group will rank higher than the father as an agent of political socialization.

Table 5.12
Gamma Correlations Between
Child's Relationship-With-
Father Score and Ranking of
Peers as Information Agents

Peer and Level of Government	Gamma
Local	.01
State	− .02
National	.004
International	.02

The data for Hypothesis 5.4 are presented in Tables 5.12 through 5.14.

These data disprove Hypothesis 5.4. There is no relationship between the child's relationship with his father and the rank of peers as agents of information transmission, the relationship between the party identification of the peer and the child does not increase (if anything it declines slightly) as the child's relationship with his father decreases, and finally, while the

Table 5.13
Gamma Correlations Between Party
Identification of Peers and Party of
Respondent: By Respondent's
Relationship-With-Father Score

Relation With Father Score		Gamma	P
Good	6	.94	.001
	7	.63	.002
	8	.41	.007
	9	.38	.008
	10	.57	.001
	11	.71	.001
	12	.54	.001
	13	.44	.001
	14	.43	.001
	15	.44	.001
	16	.29	.001
	17	.44	.001
	18	.56	.001
	19	.39	.001
	20	.57	.001
	21	.45	.005
Poor	22	.44	.008

peer does become more important as a source of voting advice as the relationship with the father deteriorates, the father similarly becomes more important!

Contiguity of the Family Model

Bandura and Walters note that model contiguity exercises a pronounced effect upon the process of modelling.[8] The previous chapter demonstrated that the contiguity of the father model was the most successful variable that discriminated between the roles of the respective parents as socializing agents. It has also been theorized that peers are likely to play a more important role as agents when family ties are loosened.[9] Extrapolating this phenomenon to the peers, it is logical to expect the absence of the father model to cause the peer models to become more salient.

Hypothesis 5.5: In father-absent families, peers will rank higher as agents of political socialization than in father-present families.

Table 5.14 does indeed demonstrate that children from father-absent homes rank the peers significantly higher as agents of information transmission than children from father-present homes. A similar pattern is

Interpersonal Agents of Political Socialization:
Peers and Peer Groups

Table 5.14
Relationship Between Child's Preferred Source of Voting Advice and Relationship with Father

RELATION WITH FATHER		Friend	Brother or Sister	Father	Mother	Teacher	Other
				SOURCE OF ADVICE			
Good	6	0	1	3	2	2	2
	7	1	1	2	1	1	0
	8	3	6	3	3	3	3
	9	2	9	3	1	1	4
	10	5	7	4	3	3	4
	11	5	9	4	1	1	4
	12	8	3	4	3	3	3
	13	6	6	6	3	3	10
	14	7	3	6	2	3	7
	15	7	16	10	9	9	7
	16	10	10	15	14	14	12
	17	12	10	15	17	17	11
	18	14	3	12	10	10	16
	19	5	4	7	11	11	6
	20	6	4	5	8	8	5
	21	2	3	2	7	7	3
	22	3	2	1	2	2	2
Total %		97*	97*	99*	97*	97*	99*
N =		204	70	958	424	168	135
G = .12							

* Percent does not equal 100 due to rounding and to small percentage in category 3.

observed in the relative rankings of peers and parents. While father-absence has little affect upon the relationship between the child's ranking of the peers and the mother as agents of information transmission (Table 5.15), it has a quite profound affect upon the relationship between the respective rankings of the peers and the father. When the father is absent from the home the child tends to rank his peers higher than his father as agents of information transmission. It will be remembered that this was the pattern father-absence produced in the comparative rankings of the mother and father. However, while father-absence is extremely important in who the child looks to as an agent of information transmission, it is not nearly so important regarding the political party identification. In the previous chapter it was found that father-absence caused the relationship between the father's party and child's party to diminish and that there was a significant difference between father-absent and father-present children in their agreement with the party of their fathers. Regarding the peers one finds that there is no diminution in the strength of the relationship between

Table 5.15
Relationship Between Absence of the
Father and Rank of Peers as
Information Agents

Rank of Peers	LOCAL Father-Present	Father-Absent
1	17.1	20.2
2	9.4	8.3
3	14.9	10.4
4	10.5	14.7
5	13.0	16.8
6	16.4	12.8
7	15.7	14.7
8	3.0	2.1
Total %	100.0	100.0
	N = 1358	N = 327

$\chi^2 = 15.33$ DF = 7   P = .05

Rank	STATE Father-Present	Father-Absent
1	2.9	4.0
2	3.5	4.4
3	9.7	4.7
4	9.8	11.8
5	14.0	19.9
6	21.1	24.6
7	33.2	26.6
8	5.8	4.0
Total %	100.0	100.0
	N = 1267	N = 297

$\chi^2 = 20.65$ DF = 7   P = .01

Rank	NATIONAL Father-Present	Father-Absent
1	1.7	1.1
2	1.9	2.5
3	5.5	3.9
4	7.4	9.9
5	11.8	21.6
6	25.8	25.4
7	40.7	31.4
8	6.0	4.2
Total %	100.8*	100.0
	N = 1242	N = 283

$\chi^2 = 26.58$ DF = 7   P = .001

* Percent does not equal 100 due to rounding.

Table 5.15—continued

| | INTERNATIONAL | |
Rank	Father-Present	Father-Absent
1	1.6	1.1
2	2.7	3.0
3	5.9	3.7
4	8.1	12.5
5	11.0	18.8
6	19.7	25.5
7	44.3	31.0
8	6.6	4.4
Total %	99.9*	100.0
	N = 1211	N = 271

$\chi^2 = 32.88$ DF = 7   P = .001

* Percent does not equal 100 due to rounding.

Table 5.16

Gamma Correlations Between Ranking of Peers and Parents as Information Agents: By Father-Absence (F-A) or Father-Presence (F-P)

PEER AND PARENT	LEVEL OF GOVERNMENT							
	Local		State		National		International	
	F-A	F-P	F-A	F-P	F-A	F-P	F-A	F-P
Peers & Mother	.16a	.14a	.13a	.18a	.06*	.12*	.06*	.05d
Peers & Father	−.06*	.13a	−.10b	.20a	−.13c	.14a	.09*	.14a

a. Significant at .001
b. Significant at .01
c. Significant at .02
d. Significant at .05
* Not significant at .05

the party of the respondent and the party of the peers and that there is no significant difference between the extent of agreement (Tables 5.17 and 5.18).

Thus, father-absence does not have as much of an effect upon the child's identification with the party of his peers as it does on his identification with that of his parents. The same finding is true regarding the respondent's preference for his peers as sources of voting advice. While the father-absent child chose the mother over the father as a preferred source of voting advice, the difference between father-absent and father-present children in their choice of their peers is miniscule—10.4% of the father-present children chose their peers or friends while 11% of the father-absent children did so.

Table 5.17
Relationship Between
Father-Absence and Party
Identification of Respondent
and Peers

Status of Father	Gamma	P
Father-Present	.47	.001
Father-Absent	.43	.001

Table 5.18
Percent of Respondent's Agreement
with Party Identification of Peers By
Father-Absence

FATHER	PARTY OF PEERS		
	Republican	Democrat	N
Present	72.1	60.4	468
Absent	67.3	65.9	126

$\chi^2 = 3.49$ DF $= 2$ P $= .20$

Thus, while it might seem as though this section tested the obvious—that if the model is not contiguous, it cannot be modeled—the above findings indicate that at least one variable that is important in influencing the process of social learning is also involved in the process of political learning. Where fathers are absent, peers clearly enjoy an enhanced position as agents of information transmission. Moreover, it is important to note that this variable is related to sub-cultural differences, for father-absence is present to a greater degree in Appalachia.

However, while it is true that father-absence does have some relationship to the ranking of the peers as agents of information transmission, it has little bearing on the child's agreement with his peers' party or with their choice as preferred sources of voting advice. The evidence regarding Hypothesis 5.5 is mixed, but it can be stated that father-absence is not as important in influencing the peers' role as agents of political socialization as in influencing the parents' role. Generally, peers do not appear to be as salient as parents. Even when the age of the child increases, when the peers are perceived as oriented to stimuli, and when the father is absent, peers do not rank extremely high.

Well-Structured Peer Groups as Agents of Political Socialization

Peers might possibly be thought to act as agents in a capacity other than direct contact with one's friends. Children, even in the Appalachian sub-culture, belong to institutionalized and well-structured groups that might act in a manner similar to the school. Hence, contact with peers may come about not only in face-to-face situations, but in the more impersonal atmosphere of well-structured peer groups where adults are often present and where a well-defined hierarchy of authority exists. Thus, the child may be influenced by this authority structure. In order to examine this aspect and to more fully document the peers' role as socializing agents it is necessary to change dependent variables.

Thus, Hess and Torney note that the peer groups may act as agents not only through interpersonal interaction with individual friends, but also through three types of group membership: "Children's service organizations (YMCA, Scouts, Campfire Girls, etc.); school-sponsored clubs (band, sports, etc.); and positions of leadership (holding office, etc.) in these groups."[10] These organizations operate to socialize certain attitudes and orientations. Mitchell states that "each of these organizations inculcates ideal notions of citizenship...."[11] They tend to reinforce the status quo, to isolate the child from political conflict, and to de-emphasize political expression.[12] Not only substantive attitudes, but norms concerning political activity may be transmitted through these groups. Hence, students who join groups express more interest in political affairs, are more actively involved in conversations about politics and current events, and defend their opinions on those issues.[13] These propositions lead to the framing of several hypotheses.

Table 5.19
Relationship Between Membership in Youth Organizations and Desire to Maintain Status Quo

MAINTAIN STATUS QUO*	ORGANIZATION							
	BOY SCOUTS		GIRL SCOUTS		FFA		4-H	
	Member	Non-Member	Member	Non-Member	Member	Non-Member	Member	Non-Member
Yes	39	44	56	46	40	44	49	45
No	61	56	44	54	60	56	51	55
Total %	100	100	100	100	100	100	100	100
N =	98	740	59	887	90	695	276	1499
	$\chi^2 = .79$		$\chi^2 = 2.35$		$\chi^2 = .49$		$\chi^2 = 1.57$	
	DF = 1		DF = 1		DF = 1		DF = 1	
	P = .50		P = .20		P = .50		P = .30	

* Question read: "Do you believe that people have the right to change the government if they don't like what it is doing, or do you think the government should be kept like it is?"
1.——People have the right to change the government.
2.——The government should be kept as it is.
Response one equals no, i.e., do not want to maintain status quo.

Hypothesis 5.6: Membership in youth organizations will be related to a desire to maintain the status quo.

Hypothesis 5.6 is rejected. There is no significant difference between members and non-members in their desire to maintain the status quo (Table 5.19). Moreover, membership seems to have little relationship to interest in or discussion of politics (Tables 5.20 and 5.21).

Hypothesis 5.7: Membership in youth organizations will be related to interest in politics.

Table 5.20
Relationship Between Membership in Youth Organizations and Interest in Politics

INTERESTED IN POLITICS?	ORGANIZATION							
	BOY SCOUTS		GIRL SCOUTS		FFA		4-H	
	Member	Non-Member	Member	Non-Member	Member	Non-Member	Member	Non-Member
Yes	29	40	36	40	40	35	40	37
No	71	60	64	60	60	65	60	63
Total %	100	100	100	100	100	100	100	100
N =	24	966	61	948	92	709	289	1557
	$\chi^2 = 1.14$		$\chi^2 = .41$		$\chi^2 = 1.03$		$\chi^2 = .79$	
	DF = 1		DF = 1		DF = 1		DF = 1	
	P = .30		P = .70		P = .50		P = .50	

Table 5.21
Relationship Between Membership in Youth Organizations and Discussion of Politics

DISCUSS POLITICS?*	ORGANIZATION							
	BOY SCOUTS		GIRL SCOUTS		FFA		4-H	
	Member	Non-Member	Member	Non-Member	Member	Non-Member	Member	Non-Member
Yes	25	30	40	28	30	29	30	29
No	75	70	60	72	70	71	70	71
Total %	100	100	100	100	100	100	100	100
N =	102	732	57	914	91	689	277	1515
	$\chi^2 = .70$		$\chi^2 = 4.23$		$\chi^2 = .005$		$\chi^2 = .16$	
	DF = 1		DF = 1		DF = 1		DF = 1	
	P = .50		P = .05		P = .95		P = .70	

* Question read: "In discussions of public affairs, I think I would prefer to say nothing at all than to say something that will make people angry with me."
 1.——Agree.
 2.——Disagree.
"Disagree" equals a *yes*.

Hypothesis 5.8: Membership in youth organizations will be related to discussion of politics.

Hypotheses 5.7 and 5.8 are both rejected. In no case is there a statistically significant difference between members and non-members in regard to their interest in politics, and in only one organization is there a statistically significant difference between members and non-members in discussion of politics. This occurs for the Girl Scouts, but even though the difference is significant it remains that even a majority of those members are unlikely to engage in discussions of politics.

SUMMARY

The purpose of this chapter has been to compare the role of peers and parents as agents of socialization. Both social learning theory and prior studies of political socialization lead one to expect the peers to play a fairly important role as socializing agents, and to further expect their salience as agents to increase as the child matures and "leaves the nest." The findings do not substantiate these notions.

It was discovered that peers generally ranked rather low as agents of political socialization. As agents of information transmission, peers were most salient at the local level of government, but generally clustered in ranks 6 and 7. This generally low ranking was not mediated by the child's age. As age progresses, peers do not replace parents as agents of information transmission.

The Appalachian child's agreement with the party identification of his peers is also lower than the general agreement with his parents. When age is controlled, the child shows a consistently stronger relationship with the party of his peers than with that of his father, but not as strong as the relationship between his party identification and that of his mother. There is, consequently, some documentary evidence that peers might replace the father as an agent, but not the mother. This finding is further documentation of the sub-culture hypothesis. Oscar Lewis notes that one of the characteristics of the "culture of poverty" is a "trend toward mother-centered families. . . ."[14] This trend exists in Appalachia even to the extent that the mother is the most salient agent whom the child looks to for his political party identification. Peers are nowhere near as salient as the mother.

Furthermore, the influence of the cultural variable is again bolstered by the finding regarding model contiguity. As was true with the family, father-absence again showed some relationship to the peers role as agents.

This relationship occurred only in regard to the peers rankings as agents of information transmission. When the father is absent, peers tend to rank somewhat higher. The differences are, however, not as substantial as those noted for the parents, and father-absence has no relationship to identification with the political party of the peers, nor to the child's preference for the peers as sources of voting advice.

Generally speaking, peers, at least in Appalachia, are not a particularly salient agent of political socialization.

Notes

Chapter 5

[1] Kenneth P. Langton, "Peer Groups and School and the Political Socialization Process," *The American Political Science Review,* LXI, 3 (September, 1967), p. 752.

[2] *Ibid.*

[3] Bandura and Walters, p. 99; Bandura "Vicarious Processes," pp. 25–26; Sewell, p. 174. On adolescent culture see: James S. Coleman, *The Adolescent Society* (Glencoe: The Free Press, 1962); Richard L. Simpson, "The School, the Peer Groups, and Adolescent Development," *Journal of Educational Psychology*, Vol. 32 (September, 1958), pp. 37–41; Robert D. Hess, "The Adolescent: His Society," *Review of Educational Research*, Vol. 30 (February, 1960), pp. 5–12; Robert R. Bell, "The Adolescent Sub-Culture," in Robert R. Bell (ed.), *The Sociology of Education* (Homewood, Ill.: The Dorsey Press, 1962), pp. 106–109; Ernest A. Smith, *American Youth Culture: Group Life in Teen Age Society* (Glencoe: The Free Press, 1962); and Friedenberg, *The Vanishing Adolescent.*

[4] Frederick Elkin, *The Child and Society* (New York: Random House, 1960), pp. 62–63.

[5] Bandura and Walters, p. 105.

[6] Greenstein, *Children and Politics*, pp. 107–127.

[7] Brim and Wheeler, p. 36; and Berkowitz, *The Development of Motives and Values in the Child*, p. 73.

[8] Bandura and Walters, pp. 56–59.

[9] Almond and Powell, p. 68.

[10] Hess and Torney, p. 222; also see, Mitchell, pp. 165–166.

[11] Mitchell, p. 166.

[12] *Ibid.*, pp. 166–167.

[13] Hess and Torney, p. 222.

[14] Oscar Lewis, *The Children of Sanchez* (New York: Random House, 1961), p. xxvi.

6
Interpersonal Agents of Political Socialization:
THE SCHOOL

Research into political education has a long and venerable history. As Friedenberg notes, the school is the

chief formal institution bearing on the adolescent. . . . The school is the official agent—the contemporary secular arm—by which society deals with adolescents. As such, the school is peculiarly representative of social forces and demands.[1]

Unlike membership in youth organizations, school is an institution in which membership is involuntary. The school environment presents to the child another possible source of objects for modeling. The exact role the school plays as an agent of political socialization is, however, unclear. There is disagreement, in fact, over whether or not it is even an important agent.

Greenstein regards the family as the most important agent, while Hess and Torney feel that "the public school is the most important and effective instrument of political socialization in the United States."[2] This blunt statement, in turn, does not entirely accord with data from a national study of high school seniors. Langton and Jennings find that the school has little or no relationship to the political socialization of the middle class portion of their sample, but has rather profound implications for a Negro sub-sample.[3]

Notes to Chapter 6 will be found on pp. 116–117.

Evidence concerning the role of the school is, therefore, rather mixed. Intuitively, one would expect the Appalachian sub-culture to manifest a result similar to that which Langton and Jennings found for the Negro sub-sample. One could logically expect this since both groups would represent low SES sub-cultures and since the Negro sub-sample used by Langton and Jennings is composed mostly of southern Negroes. We will proceed, then, with the following hypothesis.

Hypothesis 6.1: The school will rank higher than the parents or peers as an agent of information transmission.

This general hypothesis will, of course, be broken into more specific sub-hypotheses as variables are tested to ascertain why the school ranks as it does. Before proceeding to this task, however, it is necessary to look at the general overall ranking of the school.

Table 6.1 indicates that the rankings of the school tend to cluster in rank 4. The school does seem to be an important agent of information transmission about the local level, but it decreases as the level of government becomes more remote.

Table 6.1
Child's Ranking of the School as an Agent of Information Transmission on Four Levels of Government

| | | LEVEL OF GOVERNMENT | | |
RANK	Local	State	National	International
1	10	4	2	3
2	11	5	5	3
3	17	14	9	8
4	26	29	38	41
5	9	11	9	10
6	13	18	16	16
7	10	14	15	13
8	4	5	6	6
Total %	100	100	100	100
N =	1674	1615	1595	1545

G = .14   P = .001

Since the modal ranking of the school is in the fourth category, while the modal rankings of the parents and peers are in the lower categories, the school does rank higher than parents and peers as an agent of information transmission. (The comparative rankings are found in Tables 4.1–4.4, pp. 35–36.)

The school, consequently, does not appear to be as important an agent as conventional wisdom might indicate, but the comparative picture is one of moderate influence. Hypothesis 6.1 has been substantiated, for the school does indeed rank higher than parents and peers.

There may be occasions, however, when the school could increase in salience. The opportunities for modeling school-associated cue givers clearly increases with age. Curricula become progressively more specific in political content. It may be that there is a great impact in later childhood, an impact that is concealed in the aggregate data. Controlling for age, therefore, is called for.

It has been noted that the salience of the family as an agent does not decrease as age increases and that the importance of peers as agents does not increase as the child grows older. These findings run contrary to theoretical propositions of both social learning theory and political socialization studies from which the hypotheses of the present study are derived. Since this body of literature posits that the family is supposed to decrease in importance as age of the child increases,[4] the hypotheses will be stated in that direction.

Hypothesis 6.2: As the age of the child increases, the school will increase in rank as an agent of political socialization.

On all four levels of government we note a significant increase in the child's ranking of the school as an agent of information transmission (Table 6.2). Most of the age groups consistently rank the school fourth. In the fourth ranking there is a consistent increase with age, but this is not the case for rankings 1, 2 and 3. It is likely, therefore, that the school will rank higher than either parents or peers on all levels of government. Gamma correlations are presented in Table 6.3.

Where there is a significant negative relationship it indicates that there is no general agreement in the ranks and that one of the agents ranks significantly higher than the other. When the relationship is positive it indicates general agreement. For example, the positive Gamma on the local level between school and peers indicates that when the school is ranked sixth, so are the peers. Thus, there is general agreement. A small positive or negative Gamma that is insignificant indicates the absence of any overall pattern.

Hence, the significant negative Gamma's between parents and the school indicate that there is no overall agreement in the comparative rankings. The finding noted earlier holds when age is controlled. The

Table 6.2
Relationship Between Age of Child and Rank of School as an Information Agent

LOCAL
RANK

AGE	1	2	3	4	5	6	7	8	Total %	N
10	5	5	12	23	11	20	19	5	100	132
11	5	6	11	28	9	14	19	6	98 *	202
12	11	8	14	24	10	16	11	6	100	279
13	7	11	20	28	9	13	6	5	99 *	278
14	13	13	18	25	7	14	8	3	101 *	259
15	18	13	17	24	8	11	9	0	100	179
16	9	20	18	24	10	10	7	2	100	132
17	9	17	21	28	10	8	6	1	100	116
18	13	11	20	36	7	7	4	2	100	45

$G = -.16$ $\chi^2 = 136.07$ $DF = 63$ $P = .001$

* Percent does not equal 100 due to rounding.

STATE
RANK

AGE	1	2	3	4	5	6	7	8	Total %	N
10	5	5	6	24	15	24	16	5	100	127
11	5	3	14	25	11	17	18	8	101 *	191
12	4	5	9	27	12	18	17	8	100	281
13	4	3	17	27	11	19	11	8	100	272
14	4	6	17	26	13	16	15	4	101 *	253
15	3	4	16	38	9	16	10	4	100	162
16	5	9	13	33	9	14	15	2	100	129
17	3	7	15	35	9	20	11	0	100	111
18	4	7	11	42	7	22	7	0	100	45

$G = -.11$ $\chi^2 = 103.58$ $DF = 63$ $P = .001$

* Percent does not equal 100 due to rounding.

NATIONAL
RANK

AGE	1	2	3	4	5	6	7	8	Total %	N
10	2	2	6	26	12	19	25	7	99 *	123
11	2	3	12	25	7	18	23	9	99 *	189
12	2	6	8	36	12	12	14	9	99 *	266
13	3	8	10	36	7	15	14	7	100	273
14	3	6	10	32	13	18	12	5	99 *	251
15	3	3	9	43	7	15	15	4	99 *	162
16	1	4	9	53	5	16	8	4	100	127
17	1	2	3	62	4	17	10	1	100	114
18	2	0	4	63	6	15	9	0	99 *	46

$G = -.12$ $\chi^2 = 157.78$ $DF = 63$ $P = .001$

* Percent does not equal 100 due to rounding.

Table 6.2—continued

INTERNATIONAL

AGE	RANK 1	2	3	4	5	6	7	8	Total %	N
10	2	1	9	27	8	22	21	9	99*	118
11	2	5	10	29	10	16	18	9	99*	182
12	4	5	7	33	11	16	17	7	100*	263
13	3	3	9	36	10	20	14	6	101*	255
14	3	2	8	43	10	21	8	5	100	244
15	4	2	8	52	7	9	13	4	99*	160
16	1	3	2	59	12	11	6	5	99*	126
17	0	2	4	59	10	13	12	1	101*	111
18	0	0	2	71	7	10	10	0	100	42

$G = -.12$ $\chi^2 = 144.15$ $DF = 63$ $P = .001$

* Percent does not equal 100 due to rounding.

Table 6.3
Gamma Correlations Between Rank of School and Peers, and School and Parents as Information Agents: By Age of Child

LOCAL

AGE	SCHOOL AND PEERS Gamma	P	SCHOOL AND MOTHER Gamma	P	SCHOOL AND FATHER Gamma	P
10	.17	.01	−.18	.009	−.12	.05
11	−.01	.43	−.17	.009	−.23	.001
12	.02	.34	−.21	.001	−.13	.01
13	.08	.06	−.22	.001	−.20	.001
14	.18	.01	−.26	.001	−.19	.001
15	.14	.05	−.11	.06	−.03	.27
16	.13	.05	−.20	.001	−.11	.09
17	.20	.01	−.15	.01	−.42	.001

STATE

AGE	SCHOOL AND PEERS Gamma	P	SCHOOL AND MOTHER Gamma	P	SCHOOL AND FATHER Gamma	P
10	−.22	.07	−.21	.001	−.13	.01
11	−.22	.001	−.24	.001	−.32	.001
12	−.12	.07	−.22	.001	−.24	.001
13	.04	.25	−.24	.001	−.26	.001
14	−.07	.14	−.21	.001	−.28	.001
15	.02	.30	−.24	.001	−.30	.001
16	−.08	.13	−.20	.001	−.21	.001
17	.12	.05	−.28	.001	−.21	.001

Table 6.3—continued

NATIONAL

AGE	SCHOOL AND PEERS		SCHOOL AND MOTHER		SCHOOL AND FATHER	
	Gamma	P	Gamma	P	Gamma	P
10	− .24	.001	− .23	.001	− .29	.001
11	− .16	.01	− .28	.001	− .29	.001
12	− .21	.001	− .24	.001	− .29	.001
13	− .04	.27	− .32	.001	− .29	.001
14	.01	.40	− .26	.001	− .40	.001
15	− .18	.009	− .30	.001	− .35	.001
16	− .07	.14	− .40	.001	− .26	.001
17	− .19	.001	− .33	.001	− .35	.001

INTERNATIONAL

AGE	SCHOOL AND PEERS		SCHOOL AND MOTHER		SCHOOL AND FATHER	
	Gamma	P	Gamma	P	Gamma	P
10	− .32	.001	− .31	.001	− .37	.001
11	− .22	.001	− .22	.001	− .37	.001
12	− .13	.01	− .28	.001	− .31	.001
13	.03	.40	− .16	.01	− .28	.001
14	− .13	.01	− .16	.01	− .44	.001
15	− .07	.14	− .31	.001	− .29	.001
16	− .24	.001	− .41	.001	− .47	.001
17	− .31	.001	− .21	.001	− .27	.001

great majority of the sample ranks the school fourth, the mother fifth, and the father sixth.

An interesting observation is that the overall pattern is mediated by age. At all age levels, rankings are not the same. Hence, the hypothesis can be accepted. Age does have some relationship to the ranking of the school.

Findings on the other measures of agent performance are mixed. We, unfortunately, have little data regarding the relationship between the school's role as an agent and the party identification of the child. It has been noted that the school tells the child little or nothing about the workings of politics, but stresses "the structure rather than the dynamics of government."[5] One could expect, therefore, that the role the school plays as an agent of information transmission will have no relationship to the child's preference for a political party.

Table 6.4 indicates that there is no relationship between the child's preference for a political party and the rank of the school as an agent of information transmission.

These data, of course, tell us nothing concerning the role of the teacher as an agent passing on party identification to the child. We do, however, have a measure of the teacher's role as a source of voting advice.

Table 6.4
Gamma Correlations
Between Party Preference
of Child and Rank of the
School as an Information
Agent

Level of Government	Gamma
Local	.003
State	− .04
National	.01
International	− .04

Generally, the teacher is not a more preferred source of voting advice than either the parents or the peers (see Table 4.14, p. 44). When grade in school is controlled, however, as demonstrated by Table 4.16, p. 46, the finding becomes similar to that on the school's role as an agent of information transmission. As the child's age increases, especially at the uppermost level, the child chooses the teacher as the second most preferred source of advice after the father. Yet at grade 11, the child chooses the teacher as the fourth most preferred source after the peers. Consequently, it is only at the very top age levels that the teacher becomes a more preferred source of advice than mother or peers.

Age does have some relationship to the school's role as an agent. Hypothesis 6.2 cannot, therefore, be rejected. As the child's age increases, the school does seem to become a more salient source of advice. There is, moreover, some evidence to indicate that the preference for the teacher as a source of voting advice is also influenced by the cultural variable.

Thus, the position of both family and teacher as agents appears to be a function of distinctive Appalachian culture patterns (Table 6.5). Appalachian children differ radically from Greenstein's New Haven subjects in their preference for the teacher as a source of voting advice. The youngest Appalachian child is much more likely than the upper SES New Haven child to choose the teacher as a source of voting advice, while the older upper SES New Haven child is more likely to prefer the teacher. The differences between the Appalachian sample and the lower SES portion of the New Haven sample are not as large, but are significant at the .02 level. There appears to be, therefore, something in the role of the teacher—perhaps his position as a bridge between the broad middle class culture and the specific sub-culture—that causes him to be a more salient agent for children of poverty sub-cultures, including those in New Haven.

Table 6.5
Comparison of Appalachian and New Haven Samples:
Teacher as a Source of Voting Advice

SCHOOL YEAR	APPALACHIAN	NEW HAVEN* Upper SES	NEW HAVEN* Lower SES	χ² TEST FOR TWO INDEPENDENT SAMPLES
5	10	2	8	Appalachian and Upper SES
6	9	0	16	χ² = 11.38, DF = 3, P = .01
7	7	0	14	Appalachian and Lower SES
8	8	11	15	χ² = 11.01,† DF = 3, P = .02
	N = 113	N = 5	N = 51	

* New Haven data compiled from Greenstein, *Children and Politics,* p. 104.
† χ² test is performed on the raw data.

Sex

The second control variable used in this study is sex. As stated previously, Bandura and Walters note that sex differences are influential in the modeling process in that boys are more likely to model and display aggression than girls.[6] Greenstein notes that boys are "more political" than girls, but he presents no data on how this difference relates to the roles of the different agents.[7] Hess and Torney, however, assert that girls perform better in school than boys, but the literature implies that this performance is not related to the acquisition of political attitudes. They then go on to demonstrate that there are in fact differences in the political attitudes of boys and girls.[8] Given, therefore, that girls react more favorably to the school environment, we would expect the school to be a more salient agent for females than for males. Such expectations follow logically from the findings noted above.

Hypothesis 6.3: There will be a statistically significant difference between males and females in their ranking of the school as an agent of political socialization.

Table 6.6 demonstrates that there are no statistically significant differences between the sexes in their rankings of the school as an agent of information transmission, nor is there any difference between males and females in their choices of the teacher as a source of voting advice (9% males prefer teacher and 8.3% of the females). Hypothesis 6.3 cannot be accepted, for there is no evident relationship between the sex of the child and the role of the school as an agent of political socialization. This finding is in agreement with the findings for parents and peers. Sex is not a very salient variable in the child's perception of the role played by the respective agents.

Table 6.6
Relationship Between Sex of Child and Rank of School as an Information Agent

	LEVEL OF GOVERNMENT							
RANK	LOCAL		STATE		NATIONAL		INTERNATIONAL	
	Male	Female	Male	Female	Male	Female	Male	Female
1	10	10	5	3	3	2	3	2
2	11	12	5	5	6	4	2	4
3	16	17	12	15	8	10	8	8
4	26	25	27	30	39	37	41	41
5	11	8	10	12	9	9	9	10
6	11	15	19	17	15	16	16	16
7	10	10	14	14	13	16	14	14
8	5	3	7	4	7	5	7	5
Total %	100	100	99*	100	100	99*	100	100
N =	712	939	686	907	681	895	658	868
	$\chi^2 = 12.27$		$\chi^2 = 10.56$		$\chi^2 = 6.33$		$\chi^2 = 9.35$	
	DF = 7		DF = 7		DF = 7		DF = 7	
	P = .10		P = .20		P = .50		P = .30	

* Percent does not equal 100 due to rounding.

Orientation to Stimuli

The child's perception of whether or not the model is oriented to political stimuli has proven to be of little importance in this paper in ascertaining the process by which the child learns about politics from the parents and peers. Yet Bandura and Walters maintain that the modeling process orients one to stimuli.[9] Given this, if the child perceives the teacher as being oriented to political stimuli, he should be more likely to look to the teacher for political cues. Following the theoretical framework, we postulate

Hypothesis 6.4: Children who perceive their teachers as being oriented to political stimuli will rank them higher as agents than those who perceive them as not being so oriented.

As measures of the teachers' orientation to stimuli, two items were used: (1) the teacher's talking about politics and government in the school, and (2) do teachers ever say anything about which political candidate the child's parents should vote for.

Given the earlier results, which demonstrated that orientation to political stimuli on the parts of peers and parents does not influence the child's ranking of them as agents of information transmission, Table 6.7 is impressive. It demonstrates that on the local and international level there

Table 6.7
Relationship Between Child's Perception of Teacher's Orientation to Political Stimuli and Rank of School as an Information Agent

| | | | | LEVEL OF GOVERNMENT | | | | |
| RANK | LOCAL | | STATE | | NATIONAL | | INTERNATIONAL | |
	Yes	No	Yes	No	Yes	No	Yes	No
1	11	8	4	4	2	3	3	4
2	12	8	5	5	5	5	3	4
3	17	16	14	12	9	9	8	6
4	27	22	30	25	39	33	45	32
5	8	11	11	11	9	10	10	9
6	12	17	18	18	16	16	14	21
7	9	13	12	18	13	18	12	17
8	4	5	5	6	6	6	5	8
Total	100	100	99*	99*	99*	100	100	101*
N =	1140	416	1109	400	1096	398	1064	384

$\chi^2 = 25.42$	$\chi^2 = 12.77$	$\chi^2 = 8.99$	$\chi^2 = 34.13$
DF = 7	DF = 7	DF = 7	DF = 7
P = .001	P = .10	P = .30	P = .001

* Percent does not equal 100 due to rounding.
"Yes" response indicates that child *does* perceive teacher as being oriented to political stimuli.

Table 6.8
Relationship Between Teacher's Orientation to Political Stimuli and Preferred Source of Voting Advice

| | TEACHER ORIENTED TO STIMULI? | |
SOURCE OF ADVICE	Yes	No
Friend	10	11
Brother or Sister	3	4
Father	51	46
Mother	19	27
Teacher	10	6
Other	8	6
Total %	101*	100
	N = 1353	N = 584

$\chi^2 = 22.39$ DF = 5   P = .001

* Percent does not equal 100 due to rounding.

is in fact a relationship between the teacher's orientation to political stimuli and the ranking of the school. Those children who perceive their teachers as being oriented to political stimuli do rank the school significantly higher than those children who do not perceive the teacher as being so oriented. This finding is further substantiated by the fact that children who perceive their teachers as being oriented to political stimuli also prefer them as a source of voting advice more often than those who do not perceive the teacher as being oriented to political stimuli (Table 6.8).

The above relationships are quite complex. Merely talking about politics and government in the school is not exactly what one could consider overt and active participation. It is, moreover, probably quite common in most schools, especially in a general sense. On the other hand, when the question is raised concerning whether or not the teacher ever says anything about which candidate the child's parents should vote for, one finds that the relationship disappears. There is no statistically significant difference. Discussion of particular candidates as an overt participatory act is likely to be frowned upon by school administrators,[10] while general discussion of politics and government is more likely to be a commonplace activity. Since the child has probably assimilated this orientation, he too would probably perceive overt discussions of candidates (concerning who his parents should vote for) as being incongruent with the teacher's proper role. Consequently, the child is not affected by such discussion; it does not cause him to rank the school higher as an agent of information transmission, or to prefer the teacher as a source of voting advice (Tables 6.9 and 6.10).

Future students of political socialization would do well to inquire into the child's perception of the teacher's role and what influence, if any, it

Table 6.9
Relationship Between Teacher's Discussion of Candidates and
Rank of School as an Information Agent

RANK	LOCAL		STATE		NATIONAL		INTERNATIONAL	
	Yes	No	Yes	No	Yes	No	Yes	No
1	12	10	5	4	4	2	4	3
2	7	11	9	5	5	5	3	3
3	22	16	15	14	13	9	12	7
4	22	26	25	29	34	38	37	42
5	10	9	14	10	10	9	9	10
6	13	13	15	18	15	16	18	16
7	10	10	14	14	12	15	12	13
8	3	4	4	5	8	6	5	6
Total %	99*	99*	101*	99*	101*	100	100	100
N =	106	1481	103	1432	103	1421	104	1369

$\chi^2 = 4.76$ $\chi^2 = 4.85$ $\chi^2 = 3.96$ $\chi^2 = 4.81$
DF = 7   DF = 7   DF = 7   DF = 7
P = .70   P = .70   P = .80   P = .70

* Percent does not equal 100 due to rounding.

Table 6.10
Relationship Between Discussion of Candidates
and Preferred Source of Voting Advice

	TEACHER DISCUSSES CANDIDATES?	
SOURCE OF ADVICE	Yes	No
Friend	17	10
Brother or Sister	7	3
Father	50	49
Mother	15	22
Teacher	7	9
Other	5	7
Total %	101 *	101 *
	N = 151	N = 1811

$\chi^2 = 14.31$ DF = 5 P = .02

* Percent does not equal 100 due to rounding.

has upon the child's perception of the school as an agent of political socialization.

Hypothesis 6.4 can be accepted, but only when orientation to stimuli on the part of the teacher-model is perceived as a proper one.

Thus far we have been discussing the child's perception of the teacher's orientation to political stimuli. It is equally important to inquire into the school's role in orienting the child to political stimuli, for it is, after all, this manifestation that Bandura and Walters refer to when they note that the model orients one to stimuli.

As a measure of the school's role in orienting the child to stimuli we shall employ the attendance or non-attendance of the child in a civics course. Naturally, if the child is not exposed in some form to political stimuli and their attendant cues in the school, then the school will not rank highly as an agent of political socialization. Once one is cognizant of the role the child perceives the school to play, it is necessary to inquire into the methods by which the orientation takes place. Almond and Powell state that the school operates as both a manifest and a latent agent.[11] It operates manifestly through classroom instruction and patriotic rituals and latently by socializing role behavior within the school that may be transferred to behavior outside the school.[12] The question of latency involves an extrapolation by the child of school authority structure to the political. The latency dimension is most difficult to measure because it entails some means of measuring children's orientations toward the school itself. The present study is only able to measure directly the manifest aspects of the school's role as an agent.

Regarding this manifest aspect, Brown notes that those who have had a civics class tend to pay more attention to news than those who have not.[13] Jennings and Langton, on the other hand, found that taking or not taking civics courses only affected the socialization of their Negro sub-sample.[14] Since the Appalachian group is probably closer in socioeconomic status and family patterns to the Negro portions of the Jennings and Langton sample, the present hypothesis will posit that the Appalachian child will be affected by his presence in a civics course. The child will probably assimilate the norm that it is a "good" idea to be informed. Thus, the school will orient the child to political cues.

Hypothesis 6.5: Children who have had a civics class will rank the school higher as an agent of information transmission than those who have not had a civics course.

On three of the four governmental levels, those who have had a civics course rank the school significantly higher as an agent of information transmission than those who have not (Table 6.11). There does seem to be some communication of information from the school to the child. Thus, to further corroborate this point, if the school is to have a substantial effect it would have to encourage the child to seek out political information on his own.

Hypothesis 6.6: Children who have had a civics class will be significantly more likely to seek out news in the media than those who have not had such a class.

Table 6.11
Relationship Between
Attendance in a Civics
Course and Rank of School
as an Information Agent

RANK	LOCAL CIVICS COURSE	
	Yes	No
1	11	9
2	11	11
3	19	12
4	27	22
5	9	10
6	12	15
7	8	13
8	2	7
Total %	99*	99*
	N = 1112	N = 518

$\chi^2 = 45.22$ DF $= 7$ P $= .001$

* Percent does not equal 100 due to rounding.

Table 6.11—continued

	STATE	
RANK	COURSE	
	Yes	*No*
1	4	5
2	5	5
3	15	11
4	30	26
5	12	10
6	17	20
7	13	16
8	5	6
Total %	101 *	99 *
	N = 1090	N = 490

$\chi^2 = 11.03$ DF = 7   P = .20

	NATIONAL	
RANK	COURSE	
	Yes	*No*
1	27	4
2	5	4
3	9	8
4	39	36
5	10	8
6	15	16
7	14	16
8	5	8
Total %	99 *	100
	N = 1083	N = 481

$\chi^2 = 14.66$ DF = 7   P = .05

	INTERNATIONAL	
RANK	COURSE	
	Yes	*No*
1	2	4
2	3	3
3	8	6
4	46	32
5	9	12
6	16	15
7	11	18
8	4	10
Total %	99 *	100
	N = 1048	N = 468

$\chi^2 = 49.80$ DF = 7   P = .001

* Percent does not equal 100 due to rounding.

Table 6.12
Relationship Between Attendance in a Civics Course and Attention Paid to News in the Media

ATTENTION TO NEWS IN:	CIVICS COURSE?	
	Yes	No
Television	4	2
Radio	5	4
Newspaper	12	13
Total %	21	19
	N = 247	N = 130

$\chi^2 = 3.00$ DF $= 2$ P $= .30$

Table 6.13
Relationship Between Attendance in a Civics Course and Reading a Newspaper

"DO YOU READ ANY NEWSPAPERS REGULARLY?"	CIVICS COURSE?	
	Yes	No
Yes	62	46
No	38	54
Total %	100	100
	N = 1467	N = 875

$\chi^2 = 51.82$ DF $= 2$ P $= .001$

Table 6.14
Relationship Between Attendance in a Civics Course and Interest in Politics

INTERESTED IN POLITICS?	CIVICS COURSE?	
	Yes	No
Yes	44	27
No	56	73
Total %	100	100
	N = 1431	N = 845

$\chi^2 = 66.14$ DF $= 1$ P $= .001$

It does not appear that attending a civics course has any relationship to seeking out news in the media (Table 6.12). There are data that indicate, however, that those children who have had such a course are significantly more likely to read a newspaper than those who have not (Table 6.13).

Overall, the school does appear to communicate to the child the norm of being an informed citizen and to orient him to political stimuli. The question that remains is: "Does attendance in such a course have any relationship to the child's interest in politics and his level of political information?" In other words, how much orientation takes place?

The data (Tables 6.14 and 6.15) tend to substantiate the hypothesis. Those children who have had a civics course are more likely to read a newspaper, to be more interested in politics, and to have a higher level of political knowledge than those who have not attended such a course. The school does orient the child to political stimuli. This finding is similar to that for the sub-sample used by Jennings and Langton. They found that "Civics courses have little effect on the absolute political knowledge level of Whites (beta = .08). The number of courses taken by Negroes, on the other hand, is significantly associated with their political knowledge score (beta = .30)."[15]

The Appalachian sample is overwhelmingly Caucasian—only 50 Negroes—but displays a socialization pattern in regard to the school that is much more similar to the Negro sub-sample of a national random sample. It is likely, therefore, that the school will have a more pronounced effect in orienting the child to political stimuli if the child is a member of a minority sub-culture.

Additional Means of Stimulus Orientation

Since the school is so important we shall look into some additional factors involved in its operation to ascertain more fully its role as a socializing agent.

While it has been demonstrated that the school acts manifestly in influencing the child to read newspapers and to have a higher level of political knowledge, it has little relationship to the more dynamic aspects of the system. This finding is parallel to an earlier one.

Table 6.15
Relationship Between Attendance in a Civics Course and Political Knowledge

		CIVICS COURSE	
POLITICAL KNOWLEDGE SCORE		Yes	No
Low	1	7	10
	2	13	16
	3	19	17
	4	16	18
	5	14	14
High	6	31	25
Total %		100	100
		N = 1367	N = 791

$\chi^2 = 16.96$ DF $= 5$ P $= .01$

When the child perceived the teacher as being oriented to political stimuli as measured by general discussion of politics and government, the child ranked the school higher as an agent of information transmission. However, when the question referred to a discussion of candidates to vote for, the relationship dropped out. Overt discussion of political dynamics was much less common and had a much smaller relationship to the child's ranking of the school as an agent of information transmission.

If the school does not have much of a role as an agent regarding the dynamic aspects of politics, how does it orient the child to stimuli? Numerous studies have noted that the school teaches a "glorification of the country in question and its general or specific superiorities over all others."[16] In other words, it inculcates chauvinism. If this is the case, then cues emanating from the school should have some relationship to the child's score on the political chauvinism scale. One means of orientation that might be meaningful in this connection is the subjection of the child to patriotic rituals within the context of the school. As measures of exposure, we merely asked the child whether or not he had been subjected to four rituals. The following relationship is hypothesized.

Hypothesis 6.7: Exposure to patriotic rituals will be positively related to political chauvinism.

Hypothesis 6.7 cannot be accepted. Exposure to patriotic rituals has no relationship to political chauvinism (Table 6.16). In the one case where the chi square is statistically significant, the difference is not in the hypothesized direction. The difference occurs at the medium and low levels of chauvinism and demonstrated that those who have been compelled to memorize the Preamble to the Constitution are more likely to display medium chauvinism and less likely to display low chauvinism. Exposure

Table 6.16
Relationship Between Exposure to Patriotic Rituals and Political Chauvinism

CHAUVINISM SCORE	PLEDGE TO FLAG	
	Yes	No
Low	39	36
Medium	46	50
High	15	14
Total %	100	100
	N = 361	N = 1092

$\chi^2 = 1.48$ DF $= 2$ P $= .50$

Table 6.16—continued

CHAUVINISM SCORE	MEMORIZE OR RECITE DECLARATION OF INDEPENDENCE	
	Yes	No
Low	36	37
Medium	53	48
High	11	15
Total %	100	100
	N = 464	N = 916

$\chi^2 = 3.60$ DF = 2   P = .20

CHAUVINISM SCORE	MEMORIZE OR RECITE PREAMBLE TO THE UNITED STATES CONSTITUTION	
	Yes	No
Low	32	41
Medium	54	46
High	14	13
Total %	100	100
	N = 627	N = 770

$\chi^2 = 12.63$ DF = 2   P = .01

CHAUVINISM SCORE	MEMORIZE OR RECITE GETTYSBURG ADDRESS	
	Yes	No
Low	35	37
Medium	52	48
High	13	15
Total %	100	100
	N = 623	N = 786

$\chi^2 = 2.71$ DF = 2   P = .30

to the patriotic rituals tested does not, therefore, relate to an increase in chauvinism.

The final element to be tested regarding the school's role in orienting the child to political stimuli has to do with the idealization of democratic norms.

Dollard and his colleagues have noted that the school not only teaches about the ideals of the regime, but gives the children a feeling ". . . that even while immature they are able to put these ideas into practice."[17] The school should, therefore, give the children a feeling of efficaciousness. (The data are presented in Table 6.17.)

Table 6.17
**Relationship Between Attendance in a Civics Course
and Political Efficacy**

EFFICACY	CIVICS COURSE	
	Yes	No
Low	5	8
Medium	51	48
High	44	44
Total %	100	100
	N = 1187	N = 633

$\chi^2 = 6.44$ DF $= 2$ P $= .05$

There is a statistically significant difference between those who have and those who have not attended civics courses. The difference is found at the low and medium levels. Those who have had such a course are not as low in efficacy as those who have not. Yet those who have had a course are not higher in efficacy than those who have not.

Efforts to isolate further means of stimulus orientation have come to naught. While it is clear that attendance in a civics course does orient the child to seek out information and does raise his level of political knowledge, it does not relate to political efficacy, and subjection to patriotic rituals does not relate to other attitudinal dimensions. Orientation to political stimuli by the school, therefore, stops at the edge of influencing attitudes, but does have a consistent impact upon other dimensions.

Intrafamilial Relationships and the School as an Agent

Up to this point it has been found that the child's relationship with his father has little relationship to the ranking of either parents or peers as agents of political socialization. Despite this, the theoretical framework maintains that a poor relationship with one's father leads to the child ranking other agents higher than the parents.

Hypothesis 6.8: As the child's relationship with his father becomes poorer, the school will increase in rank as an agent of information transmission.

Table 6.18 shows that there is absolutely no relationship between the child's ranking of the school as an agent of information transmission and the child's relationship with his father. Table 5.14 (p. 84) does indicate, however, that when the child's relationship with his father deteriorates, the teacher does become more important as a source of voting advice. The same

Table 6.18
Gamma Correlations
Between Relationship-
With-Father Score and
Rank of School as
Information Agent

Level of Goverment	Gamma
Local	.02
State	− .03
National	− .01
International	− .03

is true, however, for the other agents, including the father. Hypothesis 6.8 is therefore rejected.

Family Model Contiguity and the School as an Agent

The earlier chapters have demonstrated that the most salient variable influencing the rankings of the respective agents is the absence or presence of the father. When the father is absent, the mother plays an increasingly important role as an agent and so, moreover, do the peers. Thus, not only social learning theory but past results lead us to believe the same will be true of the school.

Hypothesis 6.9: In father-absent families the school will rank higher as an agent than in father-present families.

Table 6.19 indicates that father-absence does have some relationship to the rank of the school as an agent. Children in father-absent homes tend to rank the school higher as an agent of information transmission than children from father-present homes. Turning to the question of whether or not father-absence has any relationship to the comparative rankings of the parents and the school, a comparison of Table 4.38 with Table 6.19 indicates that father-absence does not have as much of a relationship to the school's rank as it does to the parents.

Table 6.20 indicates that when the father is absent, the strength of the negative Gamma does not increase, demonstrating that the disagreement in the ranks does not increase when the father is absent.

Table 4.42 demonstrates that father-absence does seem to have some effect upon the teacher as source of voting advice (8% of father-present children and 11% of father-absent children prefer the teacher). While there is a highly significant difference between the preferences of father-present and father-absent children, the great discrepancy comes in at the

Table 6.19
Relationship Between Father-Absence and Rank of School as an Information Agent

| | LEVELS OF GOVERNMENT | | | | | | | |
| | LOCAL | | STATE | | NATIONAL | | INTERNATIONAL | |
RANK	F-P	F-A	F-P	F-A	F-P	F-A	F-P	F-A
1	10	10	4	5	2	4	2	5
2	10	14	5	4	5	5	3	3
3	16	18	13	15	8	12	7	9
4	25	28	28	34	37	42	40	45
5	9	12	11	14	8	11	9	13
6	14	10	18	15	16	14	17	13
7	11	5	16	8	16	9	15	9
8	4	3	6	4	7	3	6	3
Total %	99*	100	101*	99*	99*	100	99*	100
N =	1315	320	1284	297	1263	302	1226	289

$\chi^2 = 20.01$ $\chi^2 = 17.72$ $\chi^2 = 23.57$ $\chi^2 = 18.83$
DF = 7   DF = 7   DF = 7   DF = 7
P = .01   P = .02   P = .01   P = .01

* Percent does not equal 100 due to rounding.

Table 6.20
Gamma Correlations Between Rankings of Peers, Parents, and School as Information Agents: By Father-Absence (F-A) or Father-Presence (F-P)

| SCHOOL | LEVELS OF GOVERNMENT | | | | | | | |
| | LOCAL | | STATE | | NATIONAL | | INTERNATIONAL | |
AND:	F-A	F-P	F-A	F-P	F-A	F-P	F-A	F-P
Peer	.21a	.12a	− .03d	− .07b	− .11c	− .14a	− .19a	− .14a
Father	− .10c	− .19a	− .22a	− .27a	− .25a	− .33a	− .27a	− .36a
Mother	− .09c	− .22a	− .18a	− .26a	− .30a	− .29a	− .24a	− .25a

a. Significant at .001.
b. Significant at .01.
c. Significant at .05.
d. Not significant at .05.

choice of the parents where the mother becomes the most preferred source of voting advice.

The father-absent child is likely to rank the school higher than the father-present child as an agent of information transmission.

Consequently, the hypothesis has been partially substantiated. Even though the differences between father-present and father-absent children are not dramatic, they do appear and give further confirmation of the importance that family-model contiguity plays in the Appalachian sub-culture.

SUMMARY

The school is a fairly salient agent of political socialization in Appalachia. Generally, it is ranked in fourth place as an agent of information transmission. The school ranks higher than peers at the state, national and international levels, but lower than the peers on the local level. There is some increase in the rank of the school as the child's age increases. The school ranks higher than the parents at all age levels. Regarding voting advice, it was also discovered that the salience of the school increased with age. There is also a distinct cultural difference evident in the teacher's role as a source of voting advice. Generally, the Appalachian child is more likely than the upper SES New Haven child to choose the teacher. Culture plays as important a part in the child's perception of the school as an agent as it does in regard to the parents.

As was true of parents and peers, sex differences have no relationship to the school's ranking. The child's perception of the teacher's orientation to political stimuli does, however, relate to the school's ranking. When the teacher is perceived as being so oriented, the Appalachian child tends to rank the school higher as an agent of information transmission and as a source of voting advice. As of now, it is not possible to explain why the child's perception of the teacher's orientation to stimuli has a relationship to the school's ranking, while the perception of the peers and parents orientation to political stimuli is not related to their respective rankings. It is possible that perceived orientation to stimuli is more influential in non-primary groups, while in agents who operate more personally and with whom the child has more prolonged contact, orientation to stimuli is not particularly salient. Such an interpretation is plausible in light of the fact that intrafamilial relationships and contiguity of the model do not have as profound a relationship to the ranking of the school as they do on the parents. Thus, models with whom the child has greater contact are more likely to be modeled regardless of whether they are oriented to political stimuli, while models with whom the contact is occasional and impersonal are only salient to the child when the child perceives them as being oriented to the stimuli in question.

Regarding further aspects of stimuli orientation, which relate to the more manifest aspects of the socialization process, it was found that those children who had attended a civics course were more likely to rank the school higher than those who had not. They were also more likely to seek out news, to express an interest in politics, and to have a higher level of political knowledge. The school did not have a significant relationship to the more dynamic aspects of politics nor to the expression of certain political attitudes. The school operates, therefore, as a manifest agent teaching what might be called rote or textbook knowledge.

Knowledge concerning the overall effect of the school upon the socialization process is sketchy at best. The above findings shed additional light upon this important subject and further emphasize the need for additional research.

Notes

Chapter 6

[1] Edgar Z. Friedenberg, *The Vanishing Adolescent* (Boston: Beacon Press, 1959), p. 37. Also see: Francis J. Brown, *The Sociology of Childhood* (New York: Prentice-Hall, 1939).

[2] Hess and Torney, p. 200.

[3] Kenneth P. Langton and M. Kent Jennings, "Political Socialization and The High School Civics Curriculum in the United States," *American Political Science Review,* (Sept., 1968), 852–867.

[4] Hyman, *Political Socialization*, p. 98; Jennings and Niemi; Adelson and O'Neil; Bandura, "Behavior Modifications," p. 314; and Maccoby, "Role Taking in Childhood and Its Consequences for Social Learning," p. 246.

[5] Greenstein, *International Encyclopedia*, p. 6; and Hess and Torney, p. 202.

[6] Bandura and Walters, p. 105.

[7] Fred I. Greenstein, "Sex-Related Political Differences in Childhood," *Journal of Politics,* 23, 2 (May, 1961), p. 360.

[8] Hess and Torney, pp. 175–194.

[9] Bandura and Walters, p. 32.

[10] Harmon Zeigler, *The Political Life of American Teachers* (Englewood Cliffs, N. J.: Prentice-Hall, 1967), p. 97, 101, and pp. 121–143.

[11] Almond and Powell, pp. 65–66.

[12] Hess and Torney, p. 200; Greenstein, *International Encyclopedia,* p. 6; Mitchell, p. 161.

[13] Brown, p. 329.

[14] Jennings and Langton.

[15] *Ibid.,* p. 16.

[16] Charles E. Merriam, *The Making of Citizens: A Comparative Study of Civic Training* (Chicago: University of Chicago Press, 1931), p. 338; George A. Coe, *The Sovereign State as Ruler and as Teacher* (New York: Charles Scribners Sons, 1932), p. 64. For more recent studies hypothesizing the same thing see: Hess and Torney, p. 202; also see: DeGrazia, p. 36; Hess and Easton, *The School Review,* p. 257; and Mitchell, p. 161.

[17] Dollard *et al.,* p. 145.

7
Impersonal Agents of Political Socialization:
THE MASS MEDIA AS SYMBOLIC MODELS

Political scientists have largely ignored the mass media as possible agents of political socialization. Greenstein notes that they are important, but presents no data other than the number of hours children spend in front of the television set.[1] It is necessary, therefore, to turn primarily to learning theory and to communications theory as sources of hypotheses concerning the probable effect of the media as agents of socialization.

The largest group of models Bandura identifies are symbolic.[2] Symbolic models include: pictorially presented or audio-visual stimuli such as provided in films and television, audio stimuli such as radio, and visual stimuli such as newspapers.[3] Though such models clearly induce rather specific kinds of behavior, like performing aggressive acts,[4] their increasing availability may have broader implications. Symbolic models may

play a major part in shaping behavior and in modifying social norms and thus exert a strong influence on the behavior of children and adolescents. Consequently, parents are in danger of becoming less influential as role models. . . .[5]

Indeed, the findings on information transmission reported in Chapter 4 seem to confirm these suggestions. For local objects of government, both radio and television rank higher than the parents. On the state level, all

Notes to Chapter 7 will be found on p. 136.

118

Table 7.1
Child's Ranking of the Media as Agents of Information Transmission on Four Levels of Government

RADIO
LEVEL OF GOVERNMENT

RANK	Local	State	National	International
1	39	47	25	23
2	18	24	39	40
3	12	12	23	23
4	9	6	4	5
5	9	5	3	3
6	6	3	2	2
7	4	2	2	2
8	2	1	1	1
Total %	99*	100	99*	99*
N =	1805	1817	1772	1733

$G = .11$ $P = .001$

TELEVISION
LEVEL OF GOVERNMENT

RANK	Local	State	National	International
1	17	31	63	66
2	16	23	20	18
3	9	15	6	5
4	7	8	2	2
5	8	5	2	2
6	12	6	2	2
7	20	7	1	1
8	10	4	3	3
Total %	99*	99*	99*	99*
N =	1623	1755	1874	1850

$G = .58$ $P = .001$

NEWSPAPER
LEVEL OF GOVERNMENT

RANK	Local	State	National	International
1	10	15	9	8
2	19	26	25	25
3	20	30	45	47
4	10	7	7	6
5	15	7	4	5
6	12	5	3	3
7	10	6	4	4
8	3	3	2	2
Total %	99*	99*	99*	100
N =	1667	1703	1694	1660

$G = -.36$ $P = .001$

* Percent does not equal 100 due to rounding.

three media—radio, television, and newspapers—rank higher than parents. Similar patterns are visible for the national and international levels. One cannot escape the conclusion that the media are generally more salient agents of information transmission than the parents, peers, or school.

The media, however, do not rank the same as transmitters of information regarding all levels of government. This is not unexpected, for the radio is almost completely dominated by local programming while television programming is controlled by the national network and is less parochial in scope and content. Thus, radio is more salient an agent on the state and local levels than on the national and international, while television is more salient on the national and international than on the state and local. Newspapers generally rank about the same on all levels—usually clustering in the third position. Such a demonstration that different agents are salient transmitters of information about different levels of government reinforces the notion that governmental level is in fact an important variable that future scholars must consider. The data are presented in Table 7.1.

Age and the Role of the Media as Agents of Information Transmission

Since the media are generally the highest ranking agents of information transmission, and since age has been shown to have little effect upon the rankings of the other agents, it is not likely that age will relate positively to the rankings of the media. Hence:

Hypothesis 7.1: There will be no relationship between age and the rank of the media as agents of information transmission.

If age is not so related to the media's ranking, then the conclusion must be that the media are generally pervasive in their own right.

Hypothesis 7.1 is accepted. As Tables 7.2, 7.3 and 7.4 show, age accounts for little variation in the ranking of the media. Radio's ranking does not increase as the age of the child increases. On only two levels, the national and international, are differences in the rankings statistically significant. However, they are not in the expected direction. The same is true of television. Newspapers do show some tendency to increase their ranking as the respondent's age increases, but this occurs only on the state and national levels. Generally, as age increases, the ranking of the media remains the same.

When compared with the rankings of the other agents with age controlled, the strong negative Gamma at all age levels indicates that the

Table 7.2
Relationship Between Rank of Radio as an Information Agent and Age of Child

Level of Government	Gamma	χ^2	DF	P
Local	.06	78.23	63	.08
State	.05	65.73	63	.36
National	.07	110.02	63	.001
International	.05	107.10	63	.001

Table 7.3
Relationship Between Rank of Television as an Information Agent and Age of Child

Level of Government	Gamma	χ^2	DF	P
Local	.17	145.45	63	.001
State	.06	74.36	63	.15
National	−.12	81.54	63	.05
International	−.08	73.93	63	.15

Table 7.4
Relationship Between Rank of Newspaper as an Information Agent and Age of Child

Level of Government	Gamma	χ^2	DF	P
Local	.05	91.77	63	.01
State	−.13	91.91	63	.01
National	−.10	86.81	63	.02
International	−.10	74.49	63	.15

overall negative relationship between the ranking of the media and the other agents generally holds true. (The negative gamma indicates disagreement in the rankings and is associated with higher rankings for the media.) Age has little relationship to the general ranking of the agents. The media simply are the prominent agents.

There are no means whereby one can test hypotheses for the media parallel to those tested for the three previous groups of agents. For example, there is no way to determine media orientation to political stimuli. One might have reason to expect that sex, intrafamilial relationships, or contiguity of familial models would have some relationship to the ranking of the media. Given, however, that the media are generally ranked higher than the other agents, this may not be the case.

Sex

We have noted previously that Bandura finds that the sex of the child influences the models he imitates.[6] There are also data that demonstrate

Table 7.5
Relationship Between the Sex of the Child and Rank of Radio as an
Information Agent

RANK	LOCAL		STATE		NATIONAL		INTERNATIONAL	
	Male	*Female*	*Male*	*Female*	*Male*	*Female*	*Male*	*Female*
1	42	36	48	45	26	24	23	23
2	21	17	24	24	41	38	41	40
3	11	13	11	13	21	25	22	24
4	9	10	6	5	3	4	4	5
5	7	11	5	4	4	3	3	3
6	5	7	2	4	1	2	1	2
7	4	4	2	2	3	2	3	1
8	2	2	2	1	1	1	1	1
Total %	101*	100	100	98*	100	99*	98*	99*
N =	777	999	777	1013	760	988	735	975

Heading spanning the four level columns: LEVEL OF GOVERNMENT

$$\chi^2 = 20.57 \qquad \chi^2 = 6.41 \qquad \chi^2 = 11.79 \qquad \chi^2 = 9.67$$
$$DF = 7 \qquad\qquad DF = 7 \qquad\qquad DF = 7 \qquad\qquad DF = 7$$
$$P = .01 \qquad\qquad P = .50 \qquad\qquad P = .20 \qquad\qquad P = .30$$

* Percent does not equal 100 due to rounding.

the existence of sex differences in media exposure. For example, both Greenstein[7] and Brown[8] find that boys are more likely than girls to expose themselves to news content in the media. It is therefore logical to expect that the media will be more salient agents for males. Hence

Hypothesis 7.2: There will be a significant difference between males and females in their ranking of the media as agents of information transmission.

Tables 7.5, 7.6, and 7.7 indicate that the data are inconclusive. More research is needed before the hypothesis can be accepted or rejected. There is a significant difference between males and females in their rankings of all three media as agents on the local level. Males rank the media higher than girls. While there are no differences by sex in the rankings of the peers and the school, girls do rank the mother significantly higher than boys on the local level. Therefore, if the media are compared with the mother on the local level, girls should rank the mother higher than the media, while boys should rank the media higher. Without making the comparison and merely by comparing Table 4.1 (p. 35), with the above tables, one can see that such an occurrence is likely only when television and newspapers are compared with the mother because radio is ranked, on the local level, much higher than the mother by both males and females.

Comparing the rankings of the mother as seen in Table 4.5 (p. 37)

Table 7.6
Relationship Between Sex of Child and Rank of Television as an Information Agent

RANK	LOCAL		STATE		NATIONAL		INTERNATIONAL	
	Male	Female	Male	Female	Male	Female	Male	Female
1	20	14	34	27	65	61	67	65
2	17	14	23	23	20	20	18	19
3	10	9	14	16	6	7	4	6
4	6	8	7	8	2	3	2	2
5	7	10	5	6	1	2	2	2
6	11	14	6	7	2	2	2	3
7	18	22	5	9	1	2	1	2
8	11	8	5	4	3	3	3	2
Total %	100	99*	99*	100	100	100	99*	101*
N =	702	901	765	960	822	1022	809	1014

$\chi^2 = 25.86$ $\chi^2 = 17.68$ $\chi^2 = 11.17$ $\chi^2 = 5.06$
DF = 7 DF = 7 DF = 7 DF = 7
P = .001 P = .02 P = .20 P = .70

* Percent does not equal 100 due to rounding.

Table 7.7
Relationship Between Sex of Child and Rank of Newspaper as an Information Agent

RANK	LOCAL		STATE		NATIONAL		INTERNATIONAL	
	Male	Female	Male	Female	Male	Female	Male	Female
1	11	9	14	17	9	10	7	8
2	20	18	26	26	22	27	24	26
3	22	18	32	29	48	42	48	46
4	11	10	7	8	7	7	6	5
5	13	16	6	7	3	5	4	5
6	12	13	5	5	3	4	4	3
7	8	13	7	5	5	3	3	4
8	3	3	3	3	2	2	2	2
Total %	100	100	100	100	99*	100	98*	99*
N =	713	932	733	952	724	952	710	931

$\chi^2 = 19.73$ $\chi^2 = 6.80$ $\chi^2 = 15.19$ $\chi^2 = 3.98$
DF = 7 DF = 7 DF = 7 DF = 7
P = .01 P = .50 P = .05 P = .80

* Percent does not equal 100 due to rounding.

and running Gamma correlations between the rankings (Table 7.8), one can see that girls do not rank the mother higher than the media. The negative Gamma is significant, indicating that both sexes rank the media higher than the mother. The correlations indicate that males and females in Appalachia do not seem to differ in attention to the media. To examine the

Table 7.8
Gamma Correlations Between Rank of Media
and Rank of Mother as Agents of Information
Transmission on Local Level of Government:
By Sex of Respondent

AGENTS	MALE		FEMALE	
	Gamma	P	Gamma	P
Radio-Mother	− .21	.001	− .32	.001
TV-Mother	− .17	.001	− .24	.001
Newspaper-Mother	− .31	.001	− .33	.001

Table 7.9
Relationship Between Sex of Respondent and
Attention Paid to News in the Media

MEDIA	PERCENT WHO PAY ATTENTION TO NEWS	
	Male	Female
TV	18	15
Radio	27	19
Newspaper	55	66
Total %	100	100
	N = 194	N = 213

$\chi^2 = 5.08$ DF = 2   P = .10

extent of this relationship fully, it is necessary to find out whether, as Brown observed, males pay more attention to news in the media (Table 7.9).

The above data show that there are no significant differences between the sexes in attention paid to news in the media. One might have expected that if the newspaper category were left out, the differences between the sexes in regard to television and radio would have been significant. This is not in fact the case. Chi-square with newspaper extracted remains insignificant. Numerous scholars have suggested that the male role is more concerned with politics than the female.[9] For example, Greenstein, after surveying a number of studies of media exposure and political information, notes that "these media studies and the political information data . . . indicate that boys exceed girls in two dimensions: interest in and information about matters of relevance to politics."[10] There is, moreover, data that indicates that the adult male is more interested in politics than the adult female. If all this evidence is accurate, then the culture content of Appalachia tends to alter political sex roles even in childhood. The Appalachian male child is not more likely than his female counterpart to pay attention to

Table 7.10
Relationship Between Sex and Frequency of
Reading a News Story on Front Page of
Newspaper

FREQUENCY	SEX	
	Male	Female
Yesterday or today	33	32
In the last week	28	36
Last month	19	17
Never	20	15
Total %	100	100
	N = 1016	N = 1221

$\chi^2 = 18.41$ DF = 3   P = .001

news in the media. Hence, in Appalachia the male role as the most politically oriented does not occur.

There are additional confirming data. If we examine the relationship between sex and the frequency with which news stories are read by the Appalachian child, we observe that females read such material significantly more frequently than males (Table 7.10).

These findings are consistent with those noted in Chapter 4 where it was found that the mother ranks higher than the father as an agent of information transmission and that the child is more likely to agree with the political party preference of the mother. The increasing importance of the female as an agent of political socialization appears to have its roots in childhood, where the female is somewhat more likely to be oriented to political stimuli than the male.

This cultural phenomenon, like others reported here, is understandable in terms of social learning theory. The child is most likely to imitate that model which has the most to offer him in terms of resource mediation. In Appalachia this model is more likely to be the mother than in other areas. Accordingly, it is not surprising that girls, in emulation of the female parent, should very early exhibit a more acute political consciousness. Hypothesis 7.2 is accepted. Sex differences are in fact influential.

Intrafamilial Relationships and the Media
as Agents of Information Transmission

Learning theorists have noted that the status of the parent as an agent or model is affected by intrafamilial relationships. According to Brim ". . . the degree to which there is a highly affective relationship between

Table 7.11
Gamma Correlations
Between Child's
Relationship-With-Father
Score and Ranking of the
Media as Information
Agents

RADIO

Level of Government	Gamma
Local	− .001
State	− .007
National	.04
International	.02

TELEVISION

Level of Government	Gamma
Local	− .01
State	.04
National	− .003
International	− .004

NEWSPAPER

Level of Government	Gamma
Local	.02
State	− .007
National	.006
International	.008

parent and child, in contrast with one of low affectivity . . ." affects learning.[11] More specifically, according to Berkowitz, if the father is warm and affectionate the child is more likely to model him,[12] whereas if the child's relationship with his father is poor, he will look to other sources for his political cues.

Hypothesis 7.3: As the child's relationship with his father becomes poorer, the media increase in rank.

Hence, if the hypothesis were valid, one would expect to find significant negative gammas between the "relationship with father score" and the ranking of the respective media. Table 7.11 shows that this is not the case.

The relationship between the child's "relationship with father-score" and the rank of the media is miniscule. The hypothesis cannot be accepted. A possible explanation may lie in the earlier finding that demonstrated that when the child's relationship with his father declines, he is more likely to look to the mother for political cues. That is, if the child's relationship with his father is poor, he will probably look for a parent substitute and the media cannot fulfill this function.

Family Model Contiguity and the Rank of the Media

Previous chapters have demonstrated that father-absence is the prominent variable relating to the rankings of the respective agents. When the

Table 7.12
Relationship Between Father-Absence (F-A) or Father-Presence (F-P) and Rank of Media as Information Agents

RADIO

LEVEL OF GOVERNMENT

RANK	LOCAL		STATE		NATIONAL		INTERNATIONAL	
	F-P	F-A	F-P	F-A	F-P	F-A	F-P	F-A
1	37	44	46	50	25	28	22	26
2	18	19	24	24	39	39	41	40
3	12	13	12	14	24	21	23	20
4	10	9	6	4	3	5	5	4
5	10	7	5	2	4	2	3	3
6	7	3	3	2	2	1	2	1
7	4	3	2	2	2	1	2	2
8	2	2	1	2	1	2	1	3
Total %	100	100	99*	100	100	99*	99*	99*
N =	1395	363	1405	366	1383	349	1353	341

$\chi^2 = 16.53$ $\chi^2 = 12.03$ $\chi^2 = 11.83$ $\chi^2 = 11.28$
DF = 7   DF = 7   DF = 7   DF = 7
P = .05   P = .10   P = .20   P = .20

TELEVISION

LEVEL OF GOVERNMENT

RANK	LOCAL		STATE		NATIONAL		INTERNATIONAL	
	F-P	F-A	F-P	F-A	F-P	F-A	F-P	F-A
1	17	15	29	35	63	64	66	65
2	14	22	23	26	20	20	18	21
3	9	13	15	16	6	7	5	5
4	8	6	8	6	3	2	2	1
5	9	8	6	5	2	2	2	1
6	11	18	7	6	2	2	2	2
7	22	12	8	4	1	2	1	2
8	11	6	5	2	3	2	3	3
Total %	101*	100	101*	100	100	101*	99*	100
N =	1287	303	1376	338	1466	365	1445	364

$\chi^2 = 44.83$ $\chi^2 = 17.19$ $\chi^2 = 4.62$ $\chi^2 = 9.22$
DF = 7   DF = 7   DF = 7   DF = 7
P = .001   P = .02   P = .80   P = .30

Table 7.12—continued

	NEWSPAPER							
	LEVEL OF GOVERNMENT							
RANK	*LOCAL*		*STATE*		*NATIONAL*		*INTERNATIONAL*	
	F-P	*F-A*	*F-P*	*F-A*	*F-P*	*F-A*	*F-P*	*F-A*
1	9	12	16	13	9	11	8	7
2	18	23	25	28	24	26	25	25
3	20	20	30	32	45	42	47	49
4	10	11	7	10	6	9	5	7
5	15	12	7	6	4	4	5	2
6	13	10	6	3	4	3	4	3
7	11	8	6	6	4	4	4	3
8	3	3	3	2	2	1	2	3
Total %	99*	99*	100	100	98*	100	100	99*
N =	1309	320	1338	329	1329	331	1306	322
	$\chi^2 = 11.95$		$\chi^2 = 13.40$		$\chi^2 = 6.37$		$\chi^2 = 8.30$	
	DF = 7		DF = 7		DF = 7		DF = 7	
	P = .20		P = .10		P = .50		P = .50	

* Percent doe not equal 100 due to rounding.

father is absent, the alternative agents are ranked more highly. The same should hold for the media.

> *Hypothesis 7.4*: There will be a significant difference between father-absent and father-present children in their ranking of the media as an agent of information transmission.

Table 7.12 indicates that though the rankings of the media are universally high, father-absence does produce significant differences on the local level for radio and on the local and national for television. Father-absent children rank radio and television higher than their father-present counterparts, though not dramatically so.

There can be little doubt that the media, regardless of other variables, are the foremost agents of information transmission for the Appalachian child. Clearly, a foremost priority is to attempt to discover how the media operate.

Before proceeding to this concern it is necessary to note that this chapter contains no discussion of party identification and voting advice. The reason is simple. It did not seem logical to expect the media to express a party identification of their own with which the child could identify. The question on voting advice, on the other hand, was taken from Greenstein, and in order to maintain comparability was not altered.

The Operation of the Media as Agents
in the Process of Political Learning

Up to this point our primary concern has been to explain what child is most likely to look to the media as a political model. This section represents a subtle departure in that we now turn our attention to more direct measures of media behavior, our concern being to ascertain how the child's exposure to the media affects his ranking of the media as agents.

Hyman has hypothesized that the media act as agents of political socialization and that they do so in a highly complex manner.[13] According to him, the media operate both manifestly and latently. They are manifest when specifically political views are presented; they are latent when, as Elkin notes, they present a view of the world and portray aspects of the popular culture. Elkin refers to this dimension and states that even though the media do not involve personal interaction they are a "significant agency of socialization,"[14] the learning from which is largely incidental learning.[15] By incidental learning Elkin means that there is no close personal interaction between the model and the observer. "The media in themselves do not punish, reward, love, hate, necessitate day-to-day adjustments, or respond to feelings and actions."[16] This is similar to Bandura and Walter's conceptualization of observational learning and they do note that incidental learning is of prime importance in the acquisition of role behavior.[17]

Studies of media by communication theorists tend to reinforce the above. Schramm agrees that ". . . very little of the information learned from television comes from seeking. Much of it is incidental learning. . . ."[18] The question of incidental learning is integrally related to the manifest-latent dimensions of media operation. Thus, if the media operate manifestly, learning will probably be less of the incidental type for there should be a significant relationship between the content to which the child is exposed and the outcomes. On the other hand, if the media operate latently and the learning process is incidental, there should be no significant relationship between exposure content and outcomes. There may, however, be a relationship between the amount of exposure and the outcomes if the media operate latently. Actually, the manifest-latent dimensions are questions primarily of content of exposure, for length of exposure could conceivably relate to either means of operation.

The hypotheses to be tested are

Hypothesis 7.5: As the number of hours per week the child is exposed to the media increases, the rank of the media will also increase.

Hypothesis 7.6: Those children who pay attention to news in the media will rank the media significantly higher than those who do not.

Hypothesis 7.5 is accepted. On all levels—with the exception of television on the local level—the greater the exposure to the media the higher the rank of the media as agents of information transmission (Tables 7.13 through 7.16). The negative Gammas indicate a lack of agreement in the rankings while the significant chi squares indicate a significant difference. If the media operate manifestly, however, the significant differences should also be evident when the content of the respondents exposure differs.

Table 7.13
Relationship Between Rate of Exposure to Television and Rank of Television as an Information Agent

Level of Government	Gamma	χ^2	DF	P
Local	− .03	28.59	35	.50
State	− .06	50.90	35	.03
National	− .18	112.29	35	.001
International	− .19	109.17	35	.001

Table 7.14
Relationship Between Rate of Exposure to Radio and Rank of Radio as an Information Agent

Level of Government	Gamma	χ^2	DF	P
Local	− .03	52.61	35	.02
State	− .12	51.89	35	.02
National	− .11	68.70	35	.002
International	− .09	52.56	35	.02

Hypothesis 7.6 cannot be accepted. Those children who say they pay attention to news in the media—and they are few in number—do not rank the media higher than those who do not (Tables 7.17, 7.18, 7.19). Hence, the media probably operate more latently than manifestly. Regarding the specified input conditions, we find that the rate of exposure does relate to the rank of the media, while the distribution or content of this exposure does not. This indicates that it is not the content of what the child is exposed to, but the quantity of his exposure that is important.

If the media do in fact operate latently, this mode of operation should theoretically have some influence upon the inculcation of political knowledge. While it is true that one probably does not acquire knowledge directly through modeling, it is also true that the acquisition of knowledge

Table 7.15
Relationship Between Reading a Newspaper and Rank of Newspaper as an Information Agent

	DO YOU READ A NEWSPAPER REGULARLY?							
RANK	LOCAL		STATE		NATIONAL		INTERNATIONAL	
	Yes	No	Yes	No	Yes	No	Yes	No
1	12	7	19	10	11	7	9	6
2	21	16	28	24	27	21	28	21
3	20	19	29	32	46	43	47	47
4	11	10	7	7	6	7	4	8
5	16	13	6	8	3	6	4	5
6	10	15	5	5	3	4	3	4
7	8	15	4	9	3	7	3	5
8	2	5	2	4	1	4	1	4
Total %	100	100	100	99*	100	99*	99*	100
N =	987	648	1014	661	1004	664	982	651
	$\chi^2 = 61.61$		$\chi^2 = 61.07$		$\chi^2 = 60.04$		$\chi^2 = 45.38$	
	DF = 7		DF = 7		DF = 7		DF = 7	
	P = .001		P = .001		P = .001		P = .001	

* Percent does not equal 100 due to rounding.

Table 7.16
Relationship Between Frequency of Reading a News Story and Rank of Newspaper as an Information Agent

Level of Government	Gamma	χ^2	DF	P
Local	.15	118.79	21	.001
State	.18	114.04	21	.001
National	.23	137.36	21	.001
International	.25	148.44	21	.001

is enhanced by favorable modeling experiences. Thus, since we have found that the media operate latently, we hypothesize the following:

Hypothesis 7.7: There will be a relationship between rate of exposure and political knowledge.

Chi-square is significant, indicating that there is a relationship between the differential rates of exposure to the media and political knowledge (Table 7.20). Those who do watch television and listen to radio are slightly higher in knowledge than those who do not. But it is when the newspapers are examined that the relationship between knowledge and exposure becomes striking. Those who read newspapers are significantly higher on political knowledge than those who do not; and those who read news stories in the paper most often are higher than those who read them less. Hypothesis 7.7 is confirmed. While one might argue that factors such

Table 7.17
Relationship Between Content Exposed to
on Television and Rank of Television as
an Information Agent

Level of Government	χ^2	DF	P
Local	14.21	7	.05
State	5.06	7	.70
National	5.96	7	.70
International	10.71	7	.20

Table 7.18
Relationship Between Content Exposed to
on Radio and Rank of Radio as an Information
Agent

Level of Government	χ^2	DF	P
Local	10.12	7	.20
State	4.44	7	.80
National	3.47	7	.90
International	6.74	7	.50

Table 7.19
Relationship Between Section of Newspaper
Usually Read and Rank of Newspaper as an
Information Agent

Level of Government	χ^2	DF	P
Local	25.18	28	.70
State	66.63	28	.001
National	35.25	28	.30
International	55.41	28	.01

as income should be controlled, the sample did not contain enough high income respondents to distort the relationship. Most respondents (72%) did not, in fact, know their father's income. Age has been controlled and does not cause the relationship to vary.

The above finding is parallel to the finding regarding the overall operation of the media as a latent agent of socialization. Application of the earlier finding to the question of content and knowledge leads to the following hypothesis.

Hypothesis 7.8: There will be no relationship between content exposed to and political knowledge.

Table 7.21 substantiates the finding that the content of exposure has no relationship to political knowledge. In the one case (radio) where a

Table 7.20
Relationship Between Rate of Exposure to Media and Political Knowledge

TELEVISION

KNOWLEDGE		RATE OF EXPOSURE					
		None	1–5	6–10	11–15	16–20	21 +
Low	1	11	10	9	5	6	9
	2	18	14	11	12	16	17
	3	21	18	20	19	15	18
	4	14	17	13	14	21	18
	5	17	13	15	15	13	14
High	6	19	29	32	34	29	24
Total %		100	101*	100	99*	100	100
N =		97	394	461	298	318	602

$\chi^2 = 44.13$ DF = 25   P = .02

RADIO

KNOWLEDGE		RATE OF EXPOSURE					
		None	1–5	6–10	11–15	16–20	21 +
Low	1	12	10	5	7	5	8
	2	21	14	15	9	17	13
	3	22	19	18	13	19	19
	4	10	17	16	19	17	16
	5	9	14	15	18	13	15
High	6	25	25	31	33	28	30
Total %		99*	99*	100	99*	99*	101*
N =		108	1045	477	215	120	205

$\chi^2 = 43.68$ DF = 25   P = .02

NEWSPAPERS

KNOWLEDGE		"DO YOU READ ANY NEWSPAPERS REGULARLY?"	
		Yes	No
Low	1	6	12
	2	13	16
	3	17	20
	4	18	15
	5	14	14
High	6	32	23
Total %		100	100
		N = 1262	N = 924

$\chi^2 = 43.20$ DF = 5   P = .001
* Percent does not equal 100 due to rounding.

Table 7.20—continued

NEWSPAPERS

KNOWLEDGE		LAST TIME READ NEWS STORY ON FRONT PAGE			
		Yesterday or Today	Last Week	Last Month	Never
Low	1	6	6	9	17
	2	14	13	14	17
	3	18	15	20	21
	4	16	19	17	13
	5	14	16	13	11
High	6	31	31	26	21
Total %		99*	100	99*	100
N =		682	675	379	325

$\chi^2 = 67.41$ DF = 15   P = .001

* Percent does not equal 100 due to rounding.

Table 7.21
Relationship Between Content Exposed to in Media and Political Knowledge

	TELEVISION		RADIO		NEWSPAPER	
KNOWLEDGE	News	Other	News	Other	News	Other
Low 1	12	8	19	8	9	8
2	18	14	15	14	11	15
3	16	19	21	18	18	18
4	9	17	11	16	16	17
5	17	14	14	14	13	13
High 6	28	28	20	29	33	29
Total %	100	100	100	99*	100	100
N =	57	1829	80	1856	233	1430
	$\chi^2 = 4.04$		$\chi^2 = 13.43$		$\chi^2 = 5.01$	
	DF = 5		DF = 5		DF = 5	
	P = .70		P = .02		P = .50	

* Percent does not equal 100 due to rounding.

relationship exists it is not in the expected direction. Those who are exposed to news are lower in political knowledge than those who are not exposed to news. The present evidence leads us to posit that the media probably operate more latently than manifestly. Since rate of exposure does have a relationship to knowledge and content does not, then, merely being exposed to the media is the most salient variable. (For data regarding the media and attitude formation, see Appendix A.)

SUMMARY

The purpose of this chapter has been to outline the role played by the media as agents of information transmission. While political scientists have largely ignored the media as socialization agents, social learning theorists have noted that the media act as symbolic models and constitute the largest group of models to which the child is exposed. As such they present to the child numerous stimuli and induce certain specific kinds of behavior. Our data corroborate the findings of social learning theorists.

The main finding of the present chapter is the considerable importance of the media as agents of information transmission. Radio, television, and newspapers are the three top ranked agents of information transmission, and these high rankings are not affected by the respondent's age or by the status of the intrafamilial relationships in his primary environment. Model contiguity of the father did have some influence upon the rankings. When the father was absent, the media increased slightly in rank. Of all the control variables, the findings regarding sex were the most interesting. The relationship between the child's sex and the role of the media as agents did not follow the usual pattern. In Appalachia, males do not pay more attention to news in the media than females, nor do they expose themselves to the media more often than females. This finding is further evidence for cultural differentiation in socialization experiences, and is congruent with our earlier finding that the Appalachian child is more likely to consistently identify with the party of his mother rather than that of his father, and that the mother ranks higher as an agent of information transmission than the father. All this evidence leads to the conclusion that sex roles in Appalachia, especially regarding political stimuli, are different from those revealed by other studies undertaken in more homogeneous middle class cultures. The Appalachian female child is more likely to be oriented to political stimuli than the Appalachian male child.

Turning to the output side, it was found that the media seem to operate as latent rather than manifest agents. The media content to which the child is exposed had no relationship to the media's performance as an agent, while the hours of exposure did. Thus, rate of exposure was a more salient variable than content.

Hence, the basic general conclusions are that the media are the most important agents of information transmission to the Appalachian child and that they operate latently in transmitting this information.

Notes

Chapter 7

[1] Greenstein, *International Encyclopedia*, p. 6.

[2] Bandura and Walters, p. 49.

[3] *Ibid.*

[4] *Ibid.*, pp. 61–63; pp. 73–76; p. 82; p. 117; and Berkowitz, *Aggression*, Chapter 9, pp. 229–255. Symbolic models also act as models for sexual behavior. See: Bandura and Walters, p. 65 and pp. 148–152.

[5] Bandura and Walters, p. 49.

[6] Bandura and Walters, pp. 57–60 and 97–100, and p. 105.

[7] Greenstein, *Children and Politics,* pp. 117–118.

[8] Brown, p. 328.

[9] Elkin, p. 53; and Greenstein, *Children and Politics,* pp. 107–127.

[10] Greenstein, *Journal of Politics,* p. 359.

[11] Brim and Wheeler, p. 36.

[12] Berkowitz, *The Development of Motives and Values in the Child,* p. 73.

[13] Herbert H. Hyman, "Mass Media and Political Socialization: The Role of Patterns of Communication," in Lucian Pye (ed.), *Communications and Political Development* (Princeton: Princeton University Press, 1963), pp. 128–148.

[14] Elkin, p. 74.

[15] *Ibid.* pp. 70–76.

[16] *Ibid.,* p. 74.

[17] Bandura and Walters, pp. 90–91 and 95–96.

[18] Schramm, *et al.,* p. 67.

8
Conclusion

Political socialization research has been criticized as being "static" and "culture bound." Scholars have emphasized the study of content rather than process. Yet the balance is beginning to shift. More studies of sub-cultural and cross-national populations are being undertaken. These new directions raise the problem of subsuming this diverse knowledge under a general theoretical framework, which may be applied to explain the process of socialization across cultures and sub-cultures. Social learning theory helps bridge the gap. It provides a basic psychological framework substantiated by sophisticated laboratory experimentation that leads the political scientist to an explanation of the agents of political socialization. Social learning theory stresses the importance of modeling and posits the influence of certain variables that affect the process of observational learning. These variables include many of the same ones that political scientists have been investigating, without the benefit of a theoretical framework to tell them why, but also includes additional variables. One of the most important of these is culture.

For this reason the present study was undertaken in a very distinct poverty sub-culture. Logically, if we can demonstrate that social learning theory is viable and useful in explaining the child's choice of models or

Notes to Chapter 8 will be found on p. 143.

agents in a sub-culture, then it should be applicable to a broader national sample. The use of a distinct sub-culture provides a more rigorous test of the theory.

The present study has concentrated upon a number of different stimuli—identified by social learning theory, acting as inputs, or giving cues—to the child. These stimuli emanate from "agents" of different types, i.e., individuals with whom the child has interpersonal contact, from individuals acting within institutionalized settings, and from impersonal sources such as the media. Hence the family and peers are individuals whose inputs flow through interpersonal contact. The school and the peer groups are more institutionalized agents who operate on a more cognitive level by providing information and inculcating "civic virtues." The media portray a culture and act as symbolic models. Finally, all of these input cue stimuli are influenced by the systemic level in which the child functions, i.e., culture, which influences the content of what is fed to the child by the above mechanisms and which, consequently, influences the output or attitudes expressed by the child.

The basic organization of the study revolves around the four hypothesized agents of political socialization, i.e., family, peers, school, and media. They have been found to operate in two distinct ways: through interpersonal interaction and through more impersonal means. The agents have each been analyzed in regard to the process by which they provide political cues to the Appalachian child. Involved in this are three areas in which the agents could operate. The family and peers were hypothesized to act as agents of (1) information transmission, (2) party identification, and (3) voting advice. The school was tested regarding (1) and (3) and the media regarding (1) only.

Following this basic examination, variables identified by social learning theory were entered into the analysis in an attempt to explain the basic processes. Rather than repeat each individual hypothesis, this summary will proceed by generally indicating some of the main findings in each of the above identified areas.

Regarding the four basic agents and the three areas of agent performance, it was found that the three media—radio, television, and newspapers—were the highest ranking agents of information transmission. They were followed in importance by the school, the parents, and the peers. These relationships, however, were further complicated by identification of the agent's salience on four governmental levels. Each agent did not rank equally high on each level. Thus, radio was the most important agent on the local and state levels, while television ranked highest on the national and international levels. The lower ranking agents also varied from level to level. For example, peers were ranked second on the local level and declined in ranking on each successive level.

The importance of these basic findings lies in the fact that the differentials in the rankings indicate that different cue stimuli are presented to the child on each governmental level. This quite basic hypothesis has also been noted by Jennings, who hypothesized that the child is exposed to

stimuli having to do with multiple levels of government and politics. These levels are most commonly derived from the tripartite divisions of American federalism—local, state and national levels—plus the fourth level of international politics. It will be observed that this step-like graduation encompasses a dimension of scope or domain. Each level envelops successively wider domains of geopolitical space.[1]

The present study provides further documentation for this hypothesis.

The second dimension of agent performance related to the political party identification of the child. In this case, the child was most likely consistently to identify with the party of his mother. The father was not ranked as high as previous studies have shown him to be. In fact, when model contiguity was controlled, it was discovered that the relationship between the party of the peers and that of the child was stronger than the relationship between the party of the father and the child. Hence, the mother was the main agent of party identification, with peers second, and father third. As noted in the study, the variable of model contiguity is probably culturally related and contributes to the matriarchal structure of the Appalachian family.

On the third measure of agent performance—sources of voting advice—the father was the preeminent choice. The father maintained his role as the prime political cue giver only in the case of voting advice, and even this was mediated by his absence or presence in the home. Speculation concerning this curious state of affairs was indulged earlier. What seems important is that propositions drawn from other socialization studies lead one to expect the father to be the main source of political cues. When these propositions are not validated, two possibilities arise. First, there may be something wrong with the techniques through which the propositions were arrived at. For example, the failure of prior scholars to differentiate between the cues given by the father and mother. Second, the possibility, or perhaps probability, that the laws of socialization are, as Argyle and Delin suggest, non-universal.[2] This means that the primary agent of political socialization quite probably differs from sub-culture to sub-culture, and, moreover, that the content of what is socialized also differs. It is extremely important to note, however, that the process by which learning occurs would be the same. Nevertheless, it is possible that the variables identified by social learning theory would also vary in importance from sub-culture to sub-culture. This leads into a discussion of the effect the learning variables had upon the basic relationship outlined above.

The basic learning variables used in the present study were: model's orientation to political stimuli, age, sex, social power, intellectual and vocational status of the model, and contiguity of the model.

Generally speaking, the child's perception of the model's orientation to political stimuli had no relation to the salience of the agent. The same finding held for the intellectual and vocational status of the model.

While it was found that age had little influence on the agents, i.e., as the child matured, his choice of agents did not alter significantly, it is important to note the stability in modeling over all age levels. The media are the primary agents of information transmission for all age groups, the father is the primary source of voting advice for all age groups, and the mother is the primary source of party identification for all age groups. These findings are in contrast to the previously hypothesized relationship between age and agent performance. In the Appalachian sub-culture the child's choice of political models is much more stable than in other areas.

Sex differences were likewise important in a culturally related manner. The Appalachian female appears to be more politically oriented than the Appalachian male. Again, this stands in contradiction to earlier socialization studies which had posited that the male sex role is more politically directed than the female. In Appalachia the dominance of a matriarchal sub-culture drastically alters this situation.

The most important learning variable was also culturally related. Model contiguity, in this case father absence, had a profound effect upon the role of the agents. When the father is absent from the home, the mother, peers and media all increase in rank as agents of information transmission and, furthermore, when the father is absent the child is more likely to identify with the political party of his mother and his peers. Contiguity even mediated the strong showing of the father as a source of voting advice. When the father was absent, the mother became the most preferred source of advice.

All these findings are congruent with expectations derived from social learning theory, which leads us to look for cultural differences. This implies that when the efficacy of one model is impaired, the child will look to alternative models who can provide him with the cues or resource which he is seeking. Hence, as noted previously, we expect the salience of models to differ from culture to culture.

It is important to note that cultural influences upon learning are well documented. Bandura and Walters note that there are cultural differences in the learning of all of the following[3]: ability to postpone reinforcement and self control,[4] achievement,[5] resistance to deviation from the norm,[6] aggression,[7] alcoholism and attitudes toward work,[8] sex behavior,[9] sexually attractive characteristics,[10] and on the very basic role that models play in observational learning.[11] The present study has further documented the importance of the cultural variable in political learning.

The use of a different theoretical framework raises a question that has become somewhat of a standard: "Have you proven or disproven a theory?" The usual answer is, of course, "no," and this author gives the usual answer, but not necessarily for the usual reason. Social learning theory does not require proof. It requires further refinement and extension into new areas of endeavor such as political socialization. The case for observational learning has been fairly well documented. It seems quite evident that one of the ways man acquires his responses to social stimuli is through modeling. The task undertaken by the present study is to find out how this process of social learning applies to political socialization. In doing so, one must reiterate the necessity to distinguish the process of learning from the content of what is learned.

Regarding the process, one of the ways man learns is through modeling. This study has demonstrated that all of the variables identified by social learning theorists do not operate at the same time in Appalachia. Political learning in Appalachia is affected by the cultural variable influencing presence or absence of models. For example, the importance of father-absence means that one of the chief models upon whom the child depends for political cues has been removed from the child's environment. When this occurs, the salience of other agents increases as the child searches for models to replace the absent father.

What is called for is further application of social learning theory to the study of political socialization.

The present study is not intended as the definitive application. In a field study using human subjects one cannot control or measure all the elements of the learning process. As Bandura and Walters state, in "real life . . . situations" where one is not able to easily manipulate variables, "it is advantageous to start with field studies that are essentially correlational in nature."[12] This is exactly what the present study has done, and if it serves as a catalyst for future work it will have fulfilled a vital function.

Notes

Conclusion

[1] Jennings, *Midwest Journal of Political Science,* p. 294.

[2] Michael Argyle and Peter Delin, "Non-Universal Laws of Socialization," *Human Relations,* XVIII (February, 1965), pp. 77–86.

[3] See Bandura and Walters and the studies cited therein.

[4] *Ibid.,* pp. 171–2.

[5] *Ibid.,* p. 175.

[6] *Ibid.,* p. 176.

[7] *Ibid.,* p. 68.

[8] *Ibid.,* p. 36 and p. 174.

[9] *Ibid.,* pp. 48–49 and 65–66.

[10] *Ibid.,* pp. 26–27.

[11] *Ibid.,* pp. 46–49, 65–66, 172–175.

[12] *Ibid.,* p. 39.

Appendix A

POLITICAL SOCIALIZATION AND POLITICAL ATTITUDES

SECTION 1

Father-Absence and Political Attitudes

The additional effects of father-absence is still a fairly open question. The quest for answers leads one to consider the relationship between father-absence and political attitudes. Such an inquiry would round out a rough systemic paradigm by leading one to the output side. The main body of this text has concentrated on the input side, i.e., what variables affect the child's choice of political models. This section gives us the opportunity to consider briefly what eliciting effects this choice of models has upon the child's political attitudes.

We have already found that father-absence has a profound effect upon the role of the respective agents. If it can now be established that father-absence affects the child's political attitudes we shall have succeeded in further documenting the influence of an extremely important variable in the process of political learning.

To the present, scholars of political socialization have found that the effect of father-absence upon attitudes has been mixed. Hess and Torney found no differences between children in father-present and father-absent homes in their attitudes toward authority.[1] Jaros, Hirsch, and Fleron found that father-absence did make some difference in the attitudinal dimension of political cynicism and attitudes toward the President of the United States.[2]

However, since father-absence does seem to affect the child's personality,[3]

Notes to Appendices will be found on p. 152.

144

and since Bandura notes that the contiguity of the model may lead to the acquisition of imitative responses,[4] it is hypothesized:

Hypothesis 1: There will be a statistically significant difference in the political attitudes and knowledge of father-present and father-absent children.

Table 1
Differences Between Father-Present and Father-Absent Children on Political Attitudes and Knowledge

Attitude	χ^2	DF	P
Political cynicism	12.62	12	.50
Political efficacy	2.48	2	.30
Civil rights	9.42	9	.50
Chauvinism	16.03	15	.50
Political knowledge	11.31	5	.05

Out of the five dimensions of "attitudes and knowledge" the data demonstrate that there is a significant difference between father-absent and father-present children only in political knowledge.

Table 2
Relationship Between Father-Present and Father-Absent Children and Political Knowledge

Political Knowledge		Father-Present	Father-Absent
Low	1	8.5	8.0
	2	13.7	16.1
	3	17.4	21.8
	4	16.5	17.9
	5	14.6	13.3
High	6	29.3	22.8
Total %		100.0	99.9 *
		N = 1735	N = 435

$\chi^2 = 11.31$ DF = 5   P = .05

* Percent does not equal 100 due to rounding.

Father-present children are somewhat more likely to have a higher degree of political knowledge than father-absent children. Taken together, these findings do not demonstrate that father-absence has any affect upon the child's political attitudes.

One could have hypothesized such to be the case, for it was found earlier that the father ranks low as an agent of information transmission. If he does not transmit information, his absence should be relatively unimportant. Thus, while we have no direct measure of the political attitudes of the father which would could be compared with those of the child, we do know that the absence of the father has little or no effect upon the child's political attitudes.

SECTION 2

A Comparison of the Political Attitudes of Appalachian and Non-Appalachian Samples

One question that must now be considered is "Does the Appalachian sample differ significantly in attitudes from other samples ?" If it can be shown that the Appalachian child differs significantly in the content of his political attitudes from his counterparts elsewhere in the country, then there is even greater evidence to demonstrate the importance of cultural differences in socialization.

The two attitudes to be compared are political efficacy and political cynicism.

The Appalachian sample is significantly different from the Easton and Dennis sample. Appalachian children are surprisingly less likely to be low in efficacy than their peers. They cluster in the middle range and are somewhat less likely to be high in efficacy. Given the nature of the Appalachian sub-culture, this cultural difference is surprising in that one might have though that the overwhelming poverty of the region would have caused a general despondency and a sense of low efficacy. The child does not manifest such an orientation. He or she displays a medium or a high sense of efficacy that does not vary with the age of the

Table 1
Comparison of Political Efficacy of Appalachian Sample (A-S) With Easton and Dennis Sample (E-D)† By School Year

EFFICACY				GRADE				
	5		6		7		8	
	A-S	E-D	A-S	E-D	A-S	E-D	A-S	E-D
Low	13	35	10	29	15	23	13	17
Medium	49	29	52	27	48	29	51	29
High	38	36	39	44	38	48	35	54
Total %	100	100	101*	100	101*	100	99*	100
N =	312	1622	294	1602	304	1624	300	1615
	D = .22		D = .19		D = .11		D = .18	
	P = .001		P = .001		P = .01		P = .001	

* Percent does not equal 100 due to rounding.
† The Easton and Dennis data are compiled from David Easton and Jack Dennis, "The Child's Acquisition of Regime Norms: Political Efficacy," The American Political Science Review, LXI, 1 (March 1967), Table 2, p. 33.

child. This is even more surprising given the fact that the Appalachian child is also significantly more cynical than his counterparts in a national sample. Intuitively, one would expect to find a high negative correlation between efficacy and cynicism. Yet, in the Appalachian sample the correlation was positive: $G = .205$, $P = .001$. Examination of the items making up the two

Notes to Section 2 will be found on p. 152.

scales leads one to doubt this intuitive notion. According to Easton and Dennis, the efficacy scale deals with five main elements:

A sense of the direct political potency of the individual; a belief in the responsiveness of the government to the desires of individuals; the idea of the comprehensibility of government; the availability of adequate means of influence; and a general resistance to fatalism about the tractability of government to anyone, ruler or ruled.[5]

Table 2
Comparison of Political Cynicism of Appalachian Sample (A-S) with National Sample (N-S) *

Cynicism Score		A-S (Whole Sample)	A-S (Seniors)	N-S	Smirnov Two-Sample Test
Least	1	2	1	17	A-S (Whole sample)
Cynical	2	6	3	25	and N-S, D = .53,
	3	18	13	37	P = .001
	4	30	26	13	A-S (Seniors) and
Most	5	27	37	3	N-S, D = .62
Cynical	6	16	20	5	P = .001
Total %		99†	100	100	
N =		2347	170	1869	

* National sample data is compiled from Jennings and Niemi, Table 5, p. 15.
† Percent does not equal 100 due to rounding.

The cynicism scale, on the other hand, is aimed more at the perception of corruption, trust, and ignorance on the part of governmental officials. It is entirely possible, therefore, that one could be, in this sense, highly cynical and still highly efficacious. In fact, if one were to perceive that governmental officials were corrupt and ignorant one might feel as though they had more, rather than less, possibility of affecting policy because if governmental officials were honest then they would not be amenable to influence.

Such an interpretation is compatible with the Appalachian's view of politics and government. According to Weller, the

mountaineer's individualism and person-orientation team up to lead him into politics so he can get favors for his own area, people, and reference group. He conceives of government processes in terms of personal relationships. . . . He sees the actions of government . . . in terms of the personal whims of each official. Thus, government agencies are closely identified with the persons who run them. If those in power are not person-oriented, he sees them as enemies or as corrupt in their dealings toward him.[6]

Consequently, a person-oriented conception of politics leads to the inevitable conclusion that one can influence those in office—and thus lead to high efficacy. At the same time a person may see officeholders as ignorant and corrupt. It is possible, moreover, that the results of the scores would be different if the questions were asked about the different governmental levels. The Appalachian child probably would be more efficacious in regard to the local level than on the national. Such a comparison is not possible due to the lack of data.

The Appalachian child may also be manifesting a realistic appraisal of the political situation in Appalachia. One could theoretically be cynical about the corruption of politicians while he controls half the county. Obviously he does not feel inefficacious. Such an interpretation does more than substantiate the finding of extreme cultural differences. It calls for a reinterpretation of the conceptualization of the concepts of efficacy and cynicism.

SECTION 3

Peer Group Organizations and Political Attitudes

Hypothesis 1: There will be a significant difference between the political attitudes of those who do and those who do not belong to youth organizations.

Earlier it was found that the Appalachian child differs significantly from national samples in cynicism and feelings of efficacy. It is possible that these differences are mediated by membership in youth organizations.

Generally, there is no statistically significant difference between the political attitudes of those who do and those who do not belong to youth organizations.

There are a few exceptions, however. For example, those girls who belong to the girl scouts and 4-H clubs are more positive toward civil rights than girls who are not members. Similarly, males who belong to the 4-H club are significantly lower on chauvinism and cynicism than boys who do not belong. At present it is not possible to ascertain the reason that membership in the 4-H clubs reduces cynicism and chauvinism.

Further research on the relationship between political attitudes and membership in youth organizations should inquire into the content of the cue stimuli emitted by the respective groups. Even though this has not been done, the hypothesis cannot be completely rejected since membership in youth organizations does seem to have some relationship to political attitudes. More research is called for to clarify this relationship.

Table 1
Chi-Square Test of Difference Between Membership and Non-Membership in Youth Organizations and Political Attitudes, Interest, and Discussion

	ATTITUDE							
ORGANI-ZATIONS	CHAUVINISM χ^2	P	CYNICISM χ^2	P	EFFICACY χ^2	P	CIVIL RIGHTS χ^2	P
Boy Scouts	9.36	.90	14.59	.30	23.35	.90	16.55	.10
Girl Scouts	12.31	.70	14.19	.30	22.56	.90	24.57	.01
FFA	7.29	.95	13.51	.50	40.25	.20	5.09	.90
4-H								
Male	26.53	.05	22.43	.05	21.57	.90	12.29	.20
Female	13.92	.70	10.25	.70	40.97	.10	19.52	.05

SECTION 4

The School and Political Attitudes

Scholars have hypothesized that the school socializes respect and awe for the system and little or nothing concerning the dynamics by which the system operates. If these notions are valid, then one could expect the school's ranking as an agent of information transmission to be positively related to the attitudes of chauvinism and efficacy. (Data presented in Tables 1 and 2.)

Table 1
Gamma Correlations Between Rank of the School as an Agent of Information Transmission of Four Levels of Government and Child's Score on Political Chauvinism

Level of Government	Political Chauvinism (Gamma)
Local	.07
State	.06
National	.05
International	− .003

Table 2
Gamma Correlations Between Rank of the School as an Agent of Information Transmission on Four Levels of Government and Political Efficacy

Level of Government	Gamma	P
Local	.02	.24
State	.03	.22
National	− .01	.39
International	.03	.21

There is no relationship between the rank of the school as an agent of information transmission and the child's chauvinism or efficacy scores. Thus, we have found that the school does have a relationship to the child's level of political knowledge and to his interest in politics, but not to his political attitudes. Two conclusions are possible. First, that the present attempt has not isolated the correct output dimensions. Possibly if one were to ask what is communicated from the school to the child one might have been better able to ascertain what role the school plays. The second possible interpretation is that there is no relationship between attitudes and the role of the school as an agent. If this is the case, the school merely orients the child to the structure of his government and heightens his interest. It is entirely plausible for one to opt for the latter conclusion.

SECTION 5

Media Exposure and Political Attitudes

Evidence regarding the effect of the media upon political attitudes is both complicated and mixed. Klapper feels that "television exerts an influence only where the views are put over repeatedly, preferably in dramatic form . . ." and "where views are not already firmly fixed, or where it gives information not already obtained from other sources. . . ."[7] Campbell, on the other hand, feels that television "does not appear to have had any appreciable influence on the general level of political interest. . . ."[8] Since it has been noted that the Appalachian child ranks the media highest as an agent of information transmission, one would expect (in line with Klapper) that the child has not obtained the information from other sources and, consequently, the media should be of some importance. Bandura, moreover, observes that symbolic models can influence a number of forms of behavior.

Yet we have noted that the content of this exposure does not seem to have much effect upon knowledge. If similar findings exist for political attitudes, there will be more evidence to indicate the latent nature of the media's operation. Table 1, below, demonstrates that there is no relationship between the content of exposure and political attitudes. In only one case was a significant relationship evident.

Table 1
Relationship Between Exposure to News in Media and Political Attitudes

ATTITUDE	TELEVISION		MEDIA RADIO		NEWSPAPER	
	χ^2	P	χ^2	P	χ^2	P
Cynicism*	7.30	.20	5.26	.50	1.54	.95
Efficacy†	2.84	.30	.30	.90	4.19	.20
Civil Rights	4.08	.20	.28	.90	.97	.70
Chauvinism†	8.54	.02	2.97	.30	2.44	.30

*DF = 5
†DF = 2

The question remaining is whether or not the number of hours exposed to the media related to political attitudes. Table 2 indicates that exposure to television has no significant relationship to attitudes. Exposure to radio does relate to cynicism and civil rights.

Increasing exposure to media is negatively related to cynicism while it is positively related to civil rights. Exposure to newspapers is only significantly related to chauvinism. Greater exposure leads to lower cynicism. Generally speaking, exposure to media is not related to political attitudes.

If the control variables of age[9] and self-esteem[10] are inserted into the analysis, interesting results appear. Self-esteem is significantly related to three of the attitudinal dimensions, while age is related to two attitudes. In the overlapping case the relationship between self-esteem and the attitudes is stronger than that between age and the attitudes. Self-esteem, consequently, would appear to be the most important predictor of political attitudes.

Table 2
Gamma Correlations Between Exposure to Media and Political Attitudes

ATTITUDE	TELEVISION		MEDIA RADIO		NEWSPAPER	
	G	P	G	P	G	P
Cynicism	.01	.37	− .05	.01	.02	.18
Efficacy	.02	.22	.001	.49	.05	.07
Civil Rights	− .01	.31	.08	.003	.04	.08
Chauvinism	.03	.15	− .05	.08	− .09	.005

Table 3
Gamma Correlations Between Self-Esteem and Attitudes

ATTITUDE	SELF-ESTEEM		AGE	
	G	P	G	P
Cynicism	− .08	.006	− .01	.25
Efficacy	.05	.12	.04	.09
Civil Rights	.13	.001	.07	.002
Chauvinism	− .12	.01	− .11	.001

Table 4
Gamma Correlations Between Exposure to Media and Age and Self-Esteem

EXPOSURE TO MEDIA	AGE		SELF-ESTEEM	
	G	P	G	P
Television	.09	.001	− .02	.24
Radio	− .19	.001	− .07	.01
Newspaper	− .09	.001	− .05	.05

The case for using personality variables as intervening variables, made by Greenstein, is confirmed by the present data.[11] There is, moreover, a significant relationship between media (radio and newspapers) and self-esteem and between media and age. Since the media do not relate directly to political attitudes, it would appear that exposure to media is related to the control variables of age and self-esteem.

Media exposure, therefore, is not directly related to attitudes.

Notes

Appendix A

[1] Hess and Torney, p. 193.

[2] Jaros, Hirsch, and Fleron, pp. 572–574.

[3] For the effects of father-absence upon the child see: George R. Bach, "Father-fantasies and Father-typing in Father-separated Children," *Child Development*, XVII (March, 1946), pp. 63–80; Roger V. Burton and John W. Whitting, "The Absent Father and Cross-Sex Identity," *Merrill-Palmer Quarterly*, 7 (April, 1961), pp. 84–95; and David B. Lynn and William L. Sawrey, "The Effects of Father-Absence on Norwegion Boys and Girls," *Journal of Abnormal and Social Psychology*, 59 (September, 1959), pp. 258–262.

[4] Bandura and Walters, p. 57; and Bandura, "Behavior Modification," p. 328.

[5] Easton and Dennis, "The Child's Acquisition of Regime Norms: Political Efficacy," p. 29.

[6] Weller, pp. 115–125.

[7] Joseph Klapper, *The Effects of Mass Communication* (Glencoe: The Free Press, 1960); and Hilda T. Himmelweit, A. N. Oppenheim, and Pamela Vince, *Television and the Child: An Empirical Study of the Effect of Television on the Young* (New York: Oxford University Press, 1958), p. 260.

[8] Angus Campbell, "The Passive Citizen," *Acta Sociologica*, VI (Fascia 1 and 2, 1962), p. 21.

[9] According to Hyman, *Political Socialization*, pp. 32–33; age is related to exposure to media.

[10] Rosenberg, pp. 206–223; states that self-esteem is related to exposure to media.

[11] Greenstein, "The Impact of Personality on Politics," pp. 629–641.

Appendix B

QUESTIONNAIRE

University of Kentucky

OEO-CAP Project

Time 1

November-December, 1966

The University of Kentucky and the Office of Economic Opportunity are conducting a study of Knox County. We are interested in how you feel about a number of things. THIS IS NOT A TEST. No one in this school will ever see any of your answers, and the results will not be put into your records.

Please answer the questions as frankly and quickly as you can. In most cases you only need to place a check mark before the answer that you want. Disregard the numbers beside the answers; these numbers are for tabulating purposes only.

Thank you for your help.

Case number____ ____ ____ ____   Card number __1__
               1   2   3   4   5

6. Have you heard about the community centers operated by the government in Knox County?

    1____No
    2____Yes

7. If yes, what is the closest one to where you live? (check one)

    _____Barbourville
    _____Bethel
    _____Cannon
    _____Flat Lick
    _____Fount
    _____Grays
    _____Grove
    _____Jackson
    _____Kay Jay
    _____Ketchen
    _____Messer
    _____Middle Fork
    _____Rosenwald-Boone
    _____Wilton

8. Approximately how far is your home from the closest center to you? (check one)

    1____Less than ½ mile
    2____Between ½ mile and 1 mile
    3____1 mile to 1½ miles
    4____1½ miles to 2 miles
    5____2 miles to 3 miles
    6____3 miles to 4 miles
    7____4 miles to 5 miles
    8____5 miles to 6 miles
    9____Over 6 miles

154

9) Where do you remember hearing or seeing something about the community centers?

1_____Other persons
2_____Radio
3_____T.V.
4_____Newspaper
5_____Other

10) Do you know anything about the Youth Activities Program for young people that is operated at the community centers?

1_____No
2_____Yes

11) Have you visited the community center in your neighborhood?

1_____No
2_____Yes

12) Have you ever taken part in any activities at the community center?

1_____No
2_____Yes

13) If you _still_ _take_ _part_, what is your opinion of the "Youth Activities Program" in general? (check one only)

1_____no opinion
2_____very poor
3_____poor
4_____average
5_____good
6_____excellent

14) Have you visited with a counselor at a center?

1_____No
2_____Yes

15) If you talked with a counselor at a center, were you interested in discussing or receiving help in :

1_____Problems concerning home
2_____Need for money
3_____Securing a job
4_____School problems
5_____Other (specify)_____

16) Do you read anything at a center?

1_____No
2_____Yes

17) If yes, what do you read?

1_____Books
2_____Magazines
3_____Newspapers
4_____Comic books
5_____Other (specify)_____

If you still take part in the center activities, indicate which ones you participate in and about how often. (For every block you check YES, also check ONE of the "frequency of participation" blocks)

| | 1 | 2 | 19 FREQUENCY OF PARTICIPATION | |
18 Activity	No	Yes	Regularly	Very little
Dances				
Basketball				
Softball				
Volleyball				
Ping Pong				
Guitar Lessons				
Arts and Crafts				
Youth or junior Council				
(Homework Tutoring Help				
Movies				
Swimming				
Scout Meetings				
Reading Club				
Bingo				
Driving Lessons				
Home Ec. Meeting				
4-H Club				
Hootenanny				
Picnics				
Sewing Class				
Acting in Plays				
Work on Float				
Pot Luck Supper				
Career Exploration				
Bowling				
Talent Show				
Pie Supper				
Hay Ride				
Youth or Teen night				
Birthday Party				
Clean Up				
Study				
Children's morning				
Grand Old Opry				
Other				
Other				
Other				
Other				
Other				
Other				

20-21) How old are you?

```
01_____9 years old
02_____10 years old
03_____11 years old
04_____12 years old
05_____13 years old
06_____14 years old
07_____15 years old
08_____16 years old
09_____17 years old
10_____18 years old
11_____19 years old
12_____20 years old
```

22)   What is your sex?

```
1_____Male
2_____Female
```

23)   Were you born in Kentucky?

```
1_____Yes
2_____No
```

24-25) In what part of Knox County do you live?

```
01_____Bethel              07_____Harpe's Fork
02_____Turkey Creek        08_____Golden Creek
03_____Middle Fork         09_____Clate
04_____Messer              10_____Flat Creek
05_____Artemus             11_____Bailey's Switch
06_____Kay Jay             12_____Prichard Branch
                           13_____Barbourville
                           00_____Other
```

26)   Does your Father now live in your home with you?

```
1_____Yes
2_____No
```

27)   How many people other than yourself live in your home with you?

```
1_____1-3
2_____4-6
3_____7-9
4_____10-12
5_____12 or more
```

Do any of the following people live in your home with you?

	1 Yes	2 No
28) Brother		
29) Sister		
30) Step-brother		

31) Step-sister_____   _____
32) Mother_____   _____
33) Father_____   _____
34) Grandmother_____   _____
35) Grandfather_____   _____
36) Uncle_____   _____
37) Aunt_____   _____
38) Cousin_____   _____
39) Brother-in-law_____   _____
40) Sister-in-law_____   _____

41) What church do you go to?

       1_____Methodist
       2_____Baptist
       3_____Lutheran
       4_____Presbyterian
       5_____Church of Christ
       6_____Holiness
       7_____Church of God
       8_____Catholic
       9_____Jewish
       0_____Other

42) How often do you go to church?

       1_____Never
       2_____Once a year or on holidays
       3_____Once a month
       4_____Once a week
       5_____More than once a week

43) What is your race?

       1_____White
       2_____Negro

44) What social class do you think that you belong to?

       1_____Don't understand what "social class" means
       2_____Upper class
       3_____Middle class
       4_____Working class
       5_____Lower class

45) What is your father's (Head of Household's) annual income?

       1_____Under $1,000
       2_____1,000-1,999
       3_____2,000-2,999
       4_____3,000-3,999
       5_____4,000-4,999
       6_____5,000-5,999
       7_____6,000-7,999
       8_____8,000-9,999 or over
       9_____Don't Know

How many brothers and sisters do you have who are now in school or in college?

46) _____ Grade school (write in number)
47) _____ High school
48) _____ College
49) _____ Too young for school

50) What grade in school are you in?

1____5th grade
2____6th grade
3____7th grade
4____8th grade
5____9th grade
6____10th grade
7____11th grade
8____12th grade

How far did your Mother and Father go in school? (check one for each parent)

51) Father   52) Mother

1_____   1_____No school
2_____   2_____Grade school (1-6)
3_____   3_____Junior high school (7-9)
4_____   4_____Some high school (10-11)
5_____   5_____Completed high school
6_____   6_____Some college
7_____   7_____Completed college

What is your Father's job? If he is retired or no longer living. Write this in.
(Be specific and tell exactly what he does)

_____
_____
_____

```
Leave this space blank it is for our Office use only.
Do not write anything here.
53) Occupation code:
1_____unemployed
2_____Farmer
3_____Education, Professional
4_____Laborer
5_____Miner
6_____Clerk
7_____Business man
8_____Disabled
9_____Skilled labor
0_____Deceased
```

Do you have any brothers or sisters who have graduated from.

54) High school   55) College

1____Yes   1____Yes
2____No   2____No

56) For which political party does your father usually vote?

1. _____Republican
2. _____Democrat
3. _____Sometimes one, sometimes other
4. _____Father couldn't vote
5. _____Don't know

57) For which political party does your mother usually vote?

1. _____Republican
2. _____Democrat
3. _____Sometimes one, sometimes other
4. _____Mother couldn't vote
5. _____Don't know

58) If you could vote, for which political party would you vote?

1. _____Republican
2. _____Democrat
3. _____Sometimes one, sometimes other
4. _____Don't know
5. _____Will not vote

59) Which candidate did your father prefer in the 1964 Presidential election?

1. _____Goldwater
2. _____Johnson
3. _____Don't know

60) Which candidate did your mother prefer in the 1964 Presidential election?

1. _____Goldwater
2. _____Johnson
3. _____Don't know

61) If you could have voted in the 1964 Presidential election, for which candidate would you have voted?

1. _____Goldwater
2. _____Johnson
3. _____Don't know

62) To the best of your knowledge, has any member of your family ever held a political or governmental office of any kind?

1_____Yes
2_____No

63) Do you ever hear your parents talk about current events, public affairs, or politics?

1_____Yes
2_____No

64) How much influence do you think you have in decisions that your family makes?

1_____Some influence
2_____No influence
3_____Don't know

65) Have you had any courses in school that required you to pay attention to current events, public affairs, and politics?

1_____Yes
2_____No

66) Have you ever run for an office in school or out of school? (Check one)

1 _____ No, haven't run
2 _____ Yes, both in school and out
3 _____ Yes, in school only
4 _____ Yes, out of school only

Have you ever been a member of any of the following?

67) A school athletic team?
1 _____ Yes
2 _____ No

68) A school band, orchestra, or singing group?
1 _____ Yes
2 _____ No

69) A school debating or speech team?
1 _____ Yes
2 _____ No

70) Have you ever been an officer or committee chairman of a class, club, athletic team or other school organization?
1 _____ Yes
2 _____ No

71) Do you watch television?
1 _____ Yes
2 _____ No

72) About how many hours a week do you watch television?
1 _____ None
2 _____ 1-5
3 _____ 6-10
4 _____ 11-15
5 _____ 16-20
6 _____ 21 or over

73) What type of TV programs do you watch most of the time? (Check one)
1 _____ News
2 _____ Music
3 _____ Cartoons
4 _____ Drama (Includes westerns, police, etc.)
5 _____ Sports
6 _____ All of the above

74) Do you listen to any radio programs?
1 _____ Yes
2 _____ No

75) How many hours a week do you listen to the radio?
1 _____ None
2 _____ 1-5
3 _____ 6-10
4 _____ 11-15
5 _____ 16-20
6 _____ 21 or over

76) What type of radio programs do you listen to most of the time?

1_____Music
2_____Drama
3_____Sports
4_____News
5_____All of the above

77) Do you read any newspapers regularly?

1_____Yes
2_____No

78) Which newspaper do you read?

1_____Courier Journal
2_____Corbin Daily Times
3_____Corbin Daily Tribune
4_____Grit
5_____Knoxville News Sentinel
6_____Mountain Advocate
7_____Other

79) What section of the paper do you read most of the time? (Check one)

1_____Comics   3_____Editorial page   5_____All the paper
2_____Front page   4_____Sports

80) When was the last time that you read a news story on the front page of the newspaper?

1_____Yesterday or today
2_____In the last week
3_____Last month
4_____Never

Do not write in between these lines.
Case number _____ _____ _____ _____   Card number _2_ _____
            1   2   3   4   5   6

Begin here.

7. Do you receive any newspapers regularly in your home?

1_____Yes
2_____No

8. Which papers do you receive?

1_____Courier Journal
2_____Corbin Daily Times
3_____Corbin Daily Tribune
4_____Grit
5_____Knoxville News Sentinel
6_____Mountain Advocate
7_____Other

9. Do you read any magazines?

1_____Yes
2_____No

10. What type of magazines do you read most of the time? (Check one)

1_____Love and romance
2_____Police and detective
3_____Sports and health
4_____News (includes Time, Newsweek, etc.)
5_____Picture and current affairs (includes, Look, Life, etc.)
6_____Womens Magazines (Includes McCalls, Better Homes, etc.)
7_____Junior Scholastic

11. Have you read any books lately?

1_____Yes
2_____No

12. What type of books do you like to read best? (Check one)

1_____None
2_____Adventure
3_____Mystery
4_____Western
5_____Love
6_____Information (historical, etc.)
7_____Animal stories
8_____Sports

13. Is there a bookmobile that comes near your home?

1_____Yes
2_____No

14. If yes, do you use the bookmobile?

1_____Yes
2_____No

15. Do you ever get books from a library that is not connected with a bookmobile?

1_____Yes
2_____No

16. Do you ever go to the movies?

1_____Yes
2_____No

17. How often do you go to the movies?

1_____More than once a week
2_____Once a week
3_____Once a month
4_____A couple of times a year
5_____Once a year
6_____Never

18. Can you think of a news story which interested you? If so, tell what it was about. It can be from the newspaper, radio, or television.

_____

_____

_____

_____

19. Can you think of a news story which made you feel happy?_____

_____

_____

_____

Do not write in this space. Code for questions 18-20.

Story named dealt with:
1. Foreign policy
2. National domestic policy
3. State Politics
4. Local politics
5. Crime
6. Sports
7. Entertainment
8. Did not name a story

20. Can you think of a news story which made you feel angry?_____

_____

_____

_____

21. Are politics and government ever discussed in your church?

1_____Yes
2_____No

22. Does your minister ever say anything about which candidate the members of your church should vote for?

1_____Yes
2_____No

164

Rank in order of importance by placing a number (1-8) in front of each. Where do you get most of your information about what's going on in your home community?

23. _____Radio   27. _____Mother

24. _____TV   28. _____Father

25. _____Newspaper   29. _____Friends

26. _____School   30. _____Other (specify)_____

Rank in order of importance by placing a number (1-8) in front of each. Where do you get most of your information about what's going on in your home state?

31. _____Radio   35. _____Mother

32. _____TV   36. _____Father

33. _____Newspaper   37. _____Friends

34. _____School   38. _____Other (specify)_____

Rank in order of importance by placing a number (1-8) in front of each. Where do you get most of your information about what's going on in the United States?

39. _____Radio   43. _____Mother

40. _____TV   44. _____Father

41. _____Newspaper   45. _____Friends

42. _____School   46. _____Other (specify)_____

Rank in order of importance by placing a number (1-8) in front of each. Where do you get most of your information about what's going on in the world?

47. _____Radio   51. _____Mother

48. _____TV   52. _____Father

49. _____Newspaper   53. _____Friends

50. _____School   54. _____Other (specify)_____

55. How often do you and your parents do things together?

1._____infrequently
2._____frequently
3._____don't know

56. In comparison with spending time in doing things with your friends, to what extent do you enjoy these things with your parents?

1. _____very little
2. _____little
3. _____much
4. _____very much
5. _____undecided

57. In your case, does your family want to have quite a lot to say about your friends and the places you go and so on, or are you pretty much on your own?

1. _____parents have a lot to say
2. _____about average amount to say
3. _____parents leave you on your own

58. Are you interested in politics?

1. _____Yes
2. _____No

Do you ever talk about current events, public affairs, or politics with any of the following people:

59. Members of your family?

1_____No
2_____Yes, once or twice a year
3_____Yes, a few times a month
4_____Yes, several times a week

60. Friends outside of class?

1_____No
2_____Yes, once or twice a year
3_____Yes, a few times a month
4_____Yes, several times a week

61. Adults, other than teachers or members of your family?

1_____No
2_____Yes, once or twice a week
3_____Yes, a few times a month
4_____Yes, several times a week

62. When you were growing up, who appeared to be your father's favorite child?

1_____I did
2_____Older brother
3_____Older sister
4_____Younger brother
5_____Younger sister
6_____Had no favorite as far as I know
7_____Different children at different times

63. When you were growing up, who appeared to be your mother's favorite child?

1_____I did
2_____Older brother
3_____Older sister
4_____Younger brother
5_____Younger sister
6_____Had no favorite as far as I know
7_____Different children at different times

64. During this period, did your father know who most of your friends were?

1_____Knew who all were
2_____Knew who most were
3_____Knew who some were
4_____Knew none, almost none

65. During this period, did your mother know who most of your friends were?

1_____Knew who all were
2_____Knew who most were
3_____Knew who some were
4_____Knew none, almost none

66. Which parent is it easier for you to talk to?

1_____Father
2_____Both about the same
3_____Mother

67. Which parent is more likely to praise you?

1_____Father
2_____Both about the same
3_____Mother

68. Which parent shows you more affection?

1_____Father
2_____Both about the same
3_____Mother

69. When your parents disagree, whose side are you usually on?

1_____Father
2_____Both about the same
3_____Mother

70. I feel that I'm a person of worth, at least on an equal plane with others.

1_____Agree
2_____Disagree

71. I feel that I have a number of good qualities.

1_____Agree
2_____Disagree

72. All in all, I am inclined to feel that I am a failure.

1_____Agree
2_____Disagree

73. I am able to do things as well as most other people.

1_____Agree
2_____Disagree

74. I feel I do not have much to be proud of.

1_____Agree
2_____Disagree

75. I take a positive attitude toward myself.

1_____Agree
2_____Disagree

76. On the whole, I am satisfied with myself.

1_____Agree
2_____Disagree

77. I wish I could have more respect for myself.

1_____Agree
2_____Disagree

78. I certainly feel useless at times.

1_____Agree
2_____Disagree

79. At times I think I am no good at all.

1_____Agreee
2_____Disagree

80. Blank_____

8. No one is going to care much what happens to you, when you get right down to it.

    1____Agree
    2____Disagree

9. Human nature is really cooperative.

    1____Agree
    2____Disagree

10. If you don't watch yourself, people will take advantage of you.

    1____Agree
    2____Disagree

11. Would you say that most people are more inclined to help others or more inclined to look out for themselves?

    1____To help others
    2____To look out for themselves

12. If you were to offer your opinion on some subject of national or international importance, and someone were to laugh at you for it, how would this make you feel?

    1____Deeply hurt and disturbed
    2____Somewhat hurt and distrubed
    3____Wouldn't bother me very much

13. When national or international questions are discussed, I often prefer to say nothing at all than to say something that will make a bad impression.

    1____Agree
    2____Disagree

14. In discussions of public affairs, I think I would prefer to say nothing at all than to say something that will make people angry with me.

    1____Agree
    2____Disagree

15. Who is the President of the United States?

    1. His name is_____
    2. Don't know_____

16. Who is the governor of Kentucky?

    1. His name is_____
    2. Don't know_____

17. Who is the County Judge of Knox County?

    1. His name is_____
    2. Don't know_____

18. Who is the Sheriff of Knox County?

    1. His name is_____
    2. Don't know_____

19. Who is the School Superintendent of Knox County?

    1. His name is_____
    2. Don't know_____

20. Name one United State Senator from Kentucky.

    1. His name is_____
    2. Don't know_____

---

*
*21. Score on knowledge index (0-6) _____ (Do not answer)   *
*

22. What kinds of things do you think the President does?_____

_____

23. What kinds of things do you think the Governor of Kentucky does?

_____

24. What kinds of things do you think the state legislature of Kentucky does?

_____

25. What kinds of things do you think the County Judge of Knox County does?

_____

26. What kinds of things do you think the Congress in Washington, D. C. does?

_____

---

*   *
*   Do not write in this space: Code for questions 22-26.   *
*   *
*   P. 1. Correct   *
*   *
*   P. 2. Incorrect   *
*   *
*   P. 0. Blank   *
*

In the following 15 question, indicate whether you agree, disagree, don't know or are undecided. If you agree, circle A next to the question. If you disagree, circle D next to the question. If you don't know or are undecided, circle ? next to the question.

		2 AGREE	1 DISAGREE	0 ?
27.	My blood boils whenever a person stubbornly refuses to admit that he's wrong.	A	D	?
28.	There are two kinds of people in this world: those who are for the truth and those who are against the truth.	A	D	?
29.	Most people just don't know what's good for them.	A	D	?
30.	Of all the different philosophies which exist in this world there is probably only one which is correct.	A	D	?
31.	The highest form of government is a democracy and the highest form of democracy is a government run by those who are most intelligent.	A	D	?
32.	I'd like it if I could find someone who would tell me how to solve my personal problems.	A	D	?
33.	Most of the ideas which get printed nowadays aren't worth the paper they are printed on.	A	D	?
34.	It is only when a person devotes himself to an ideal or cause that life becomes meaningful.	A	D	?
35.	Most people just don't give a "hang" for others.	A	D	?
36.	To compromise with our political opponents is dangerous because it usually leads to the betrayal of our own side.	A	D	?
37.	The present is all too often full of unhappiness. It is only the future that counts.	A	D	?
38.	The United States and Russia have just about nothing in common.	A	D	?
39.	In a discussion I often find it necessary to repeat myself several times to make sure I am being understood.	A	D	?
40.	Even though freedom of speech for all groups is a worthwhile goal, it is unfortunately necessary to restrict the freedom of certain political groups.	A	D	?
41.	It is better to be a dead hero than to be a live coward.	A	D	?

42. Do your teachers ever talk about politics or government in your school?

    1____ Yes
    2____ No

43. Does your teacher ever say anything about which candidates your parents should vote for?

    1____ Yes
    2____ No

44. Do you think that quite a few of the people running the government are a little crooked, not very many are, or do you think hardly any of them are?

    1____ Quite a few are
    2____ Not very many are
    3____ Hardly any are

45. Do you think that people in the government waste a lot of the money paid ·in taxes, waste some of it, or don't waste very much of it?

    1____ Waste a lot
    2____ Waste some
    3____ Don't waste very much of it

46. How much of the time do you think you can trust the government in Washington to do what is right--just about always, most of the time, or only some of the time?

    1____ Just about always
    2____ Most of the time
    3____ Some of the time

47. Do you feel that almost all of the people running the government are smart people who usually know what they are doing, or do you think that quiet a few of them don't seem to know what they are doing?

    1____ Almost all know they are doing
    2____ Quite a few don't seem to know what they are doing

48. Would you say the government is pretty much run by a few big interests looking out for themselves or that it is run for the benefit of all the people?

    1____ Run by a few big interests looking out for themselves
    2____ Run for the benefit of all

49. In your school do you say the pledge of allegiance to the flag every morning?

    1____ Yes
    2____ No

Have you ever been asked to memorize or recite any of the following?

50. The Declaration of Independence 1____ Yes   2____ No

51. The Preamble to the United States Constitution 1____ Yes   2____ No

172

52. The Gettysburg Address 1____Yes   2____No

53. Do you think that it is the <u>duty</u> of every person to vote?

    1____Yes
    2____No

54. Should the people be able to remove public officials from office it they do not like what they are doing?

    1____Yes
    2____No

Do you agree or disagree with the following statements:

55. "All men are created equal." 1____Agree   2____Disagree

56. When playing games one should do everything , even break the rules, in order to win. 1____Agree   2____Disagree

Do you belong to any of the following organizations:

		YES	NO
57.	Boy Scouts or Cub Scouts	1____	2____
58.	Girl Scouts or Brownies	1____	2____
59.	Future Farmers of America	1____	2____
60.	4-H Club	1____	2____

61. Other organizations (please name them)_____

62. Do you believe that people have the right to change the government if they don't like what it is doing, or do you think the government should be kept like it is?

    1____People have the right to change the government
    2____The Government should be kept as it is

63. Are any of your friends interested in politics or government?

    1____Yes
    2____No

64. Do you ever discuss politics or government with your friends?

    1____Yes
    2____No

65. What is the political party choice of most of your friends?

    1____Republican
    2____Democrat
    3____Other (Specify)_____
    4____Don't know

66. If you could vote, who would be best to ask for voting advice? (Check one)

1___ A friend your own age
2___ Brother or sister
3___ Father
4___ Mother
5___ Teacher
6___ Someone else_____
          (write in whether this person is a neighbor, relative, etc.)

Would you be satisfied or dissatisfied with each of these jobs?

Job	Satisfied	Dissatisfied
67. Restaurant worker	_____	_____
68. Lawyer	_____	_____
69. School teacher	_____	_____
70. Governor of a state	_____	_____
71. Mail carrier	_____	_____
72. Clerk in a store	_____	_____
73. President of the U. S.	_____	_____
74. Bookkeeper	_____	_____
75. Religious leader	_____	_____
76. School Superintendent	_____	_____
77. Police chief or sheriff	_____	_____
78. County judge	_____	_____

79-80   Blank

Do not write in this space.

Case number ___ ___ ___ ___   Card number 4 ___ ___
              1   2   3   4   5   6

---

7. How do you view your father's   1.___ likes almost everybody
   liking for people as compared   2.___ likes as many as most
   with most men?   3.___ doesn't like as many
                                           4.___ don't know

8. How do you view your father's   1.___ knows more
   knowledge as compared with most   2.___ knows about same
   men?   3.___ knows less
                                           4.___ don't know

174

9. How do you view your father
   as a person?

1. ____best in the world
2. ____good person
3. ____not a good person
4. ____don't know

10. How hard do you think the
    President works as compared
    with most men?

1. ____harder
2. ____as hard
3. ____less hard
4. ____don't know

11. How do you view the honesty of the
    President as compared with most men?

1. ____more honest
2. ____as honest
3. ____less honest
4. ____don't know

12. How do you view the President's
    liking for people as compared
    with most men?

1. ____likes almost everybody
2. ____likes as many as most
3. ____doesn't like as many
4. ____don't know

13. How do you view the President's
    knowledge as compared with most
    men?

1. ____knows more
2. ____knows about same
3. ____knows less
4. ____don't know

14. How do you view the President
    as a person?

1. ____best in the world
2. ____good person
3. ____not a good person
4. ____don't know

15. How hard does your father work
    as compared with the President?

1. ____harder
2. ____as hard
3. ____less hard
4. ____don't know

16. How do you feel about your
    father's honesty as compared
    with the President's?

1. ____more honest
2. ____as honest
3. ____less honest
4. ____don't know

17. How do you view your father's
    liking for people as compared
    with the President's liking for
    people?

1. ____likes almost everybody
2. ____likes as many as President
3. ____doesn't like as many as
        the President

8. How do you view your father's
   knowledge as compared with the
   President's knowledge?

1. ____knows more than President
2. ____knows about same
3. ____knows less than
4. ____don't know

9. Voting is the only way that people
   like my mother and father can have
   runs things.

1. ____strongly agree
2. ____agree
3. ____disagree
4. ____strongly disagree
5. ____don't know or no opinion

20. Sometimes I can't understand what goes on in government.

1.____strongly agree
2.____agree
3.____disagree
4.____strongly
5.____don't know or no opinion

21. What happens in the government will happen no matter what people do. It is like the weather, there is nothing people can do about it.

1.____strongly agree
2.____agree
3.____disagree
4.____strongly disagree
5.____don't know or no opinion

22. There are some big powerful men in the government who are running the whole thing and they do not care about us ordinary people.

1.____strongly agree
2.____agree
3.____disagree
4.____strongly disagree
5.____don't know or no opinion

23. My family doesn't have any say about what the government does.

1.____strongly agree
2.____agree
3.____disagree
4.____strongly disagree
5.____don't know or no opinion

24. I don't think people in the government care much what people like my family think.

1.____strongly agree
2.____agree
3.____disagree
4.____strongly disagree
5.____don't know or no opinion

25. Citizens don't have a chance to say what they think about running the government.

1.____strongly agree
2.____agree
3.____disagree
4.____strongly disagree
5.____don't know or no opinion

26. How much does the average person help decide which laws are made for our country?

1.____very much
2.____some
3.____very little
4.____not at all
5.____don't know

27. Do you feel that a person with ability has a good chance of achieving success in our society, or do you feel that ability has little to do with it?

1____Person with ability has a good chance
2____Ability has little to do with it
3____Uncertain

28. How important to you personally is it to get ahead in life?

1____Very important
2____Not very important

29. Realistically speaking, how good to you think are your own chances of getting ahead?

1____Excellent   2____Fair   3____Not much chance

Rank in order of importance those things which you would like to get out of like. Rank them by placing a number (1-6) on the line next to each.

30. ____Owning your own home
31. ____Having lots of money
32. ____Having a good education
33. ____Having lots of friends
34. ____Having people "look-up" to you
35. ____Having a good, steady job

36. Name a famous person you want to be like._____

37. Why do you want to be like him (her)?_____

_____

38. Name a famous person you do <u>not want</u> to be like. _____

39. Why don't you want to be like him (her)?_____

Think of a person you know who you want to be like (give his or her

occupation and relationship to you)._____

_____

40. Why do you want to be like him (her)?_____

_____

Name a person you know who you do not want to be like (give his or her occupation and relationship to you).

_____

41. Why don't you want to be like him (her)?_____

_____

These questions cover briefly many other topics. Indicate whether you agree or disagree with each statement. Circle A if you tend to agree with the statement; circle D if you tend to disagree; circle ? if you don't know or cannot make up your mind.

		2 Agree	1 Disagree	0 ?
42.	Public officials should be chosen by majority votes.	A	D	?
43.	If a Negro were legally elected mayor of your city or sheriff of your county, the white people should not allow him to take office.	A	D	?
44.	If a Communist were legally elected mayor of your city or sheriff or your county, the people should not allow him to take office.	A	D	?
45.	If a person wanted to make a speech in your neighborhood against churches and religion, he should be allowed to speak.	A	D	?
46.	If an admitted Communist wanted to make a speech in your neighborhood favoring Communism, he should be allowed to speak.	A	D	?
47.	A Negro should not be allowed to run for mayor of your city or sheriff of your county.	A	D	?
48.	People of different races should not dance together.	A	D	?
49.	Swimming pools should admit people of all races and nationalities to swim in the same pool.	A	D	?
50.	There should be laws against marriage between persons of different races.	A	D	?
51.	Hotels are right to refuse to admit people of certain races or nationalities.	A	D	?
52.	Pupils of all races and nationalities should attend school together everywhere in this country.	A	D	?

53. If you had a son would you like to see him go into politics as his life work?

1____Yes
2____No
3____No opinion

4. If you had a daughter would you like to see her go into politics as her life work?

1___Yes
2___No
3___No opinion

5. The American political system is a model that foreigners would do well to copy.

1.___strongly agree
2.___agree
3.___disagree
4.___strongly disagree
5.___don't know

6. The founding fathers created a blessed and unique republic when they gave us the constitution.

1.___strongly agree
2.___agree
3.___disagree
4.___strongly disagree
5.___don't know

7. Americans are more democratic than any other people.

1.___strongly agree
2.___agree
3.___disagree
4.___strongly disagree
5.___don't know

8. American political institutions are the best in the world.

1.___strongly agree
2.___agree
3.___disagree
4.___strongly disagree
5.___don't know

Thank you. Now would you print your name below. After these forms have been received at the University of Kentucky each name will be given an identification number. Then this sheet on which you have printed you name will be thrown away.

Please print your full name: _____ _____ _____
                              (First)   (Middle)   (Last)

Bibliography

BOOKS

Aberle, D. F. "Culture and Socialization," in F. L. K. Hsu (ed.). *Psychological Anthropology*. Homewood, Ill.: Dorsey Press, 1961, pp. 381–399.

Adorno, T. W., Else Frankel-Brunswick, Daniel Levinson, and R. Nevitt Sanford. *The Authoritarian Personality*. New York: Harper, 1950.

Almond, Gabriel A., and Sidney Verba. "Political Socialization and Civic Competence," in *The Civic Culture*. Princeton: Princeton University Press, 1963, pp. 323–374.

Almond, Gabriel A., and G. Bingham Powell, Jr. *Comparative Politics: A Developmental Approach*. Boston: Little, Brown and Company, 1966.

Anderson, Scarvie B., *et al. Social Studies in Secondary Schools: A Survey of Courses and Practices*. Princeton, N. J.: Educational Testing Service, 1964.

Bachman, Jerald G., *et al. Youth in Transition, Volume 1: A Blueprint for a Longitudinal Study of Adolescent Boys*. Ann Arbor, Michigan: Institute for Social Research, 1967.

Bakke, E. Wight. *Citizens Without Work*. New Haven: Yale University Press, 1940, esp. Chap. 6.

———. *Social Learning and Personality Development*. New York: Holt, Rinehart and Winston, Inc., 1963.

Bandura, Albert. "Behavior Modifications Through Modeling Procedures," in L. Krasner and L. Ullman (eds.). *Research in Behavior Modification*. New York: Holt, Rinehart and Winston, 1965, pp. 310–340.

———. "Vicarious Processes: A Case of No-Trial Learning," in Leonard Berkowitz (ed.). *Advances in Experimental Social Psychology*, Vol. 2. New York: Academic Press, 1965, pp. 3–55.

———, and Richard H. Walters. *Adolescent Aggression*. New York: The Ronald Press Company, 1959.

Barber, James David. *The Lawmakers: Recruitment and Adaptation to Legislative Life.* New Haven: Yale University Press, 1965, esp. Chap. 6, "The Development of Political Personalities," pp. 212–258.

Barker, R. G., and H. F. Wright. *Midwest and Its Children.* Evanston, Ill.: Row Peterson & Co., 1954.

Barker, Roger. *Big School–Small School: Studies of the Effect of High School Size Upon the Behavior and Experiences of Students.* Stanford: Stanford University Press, 1962.

Bell, Robert R. "The Adolescent Sub-culture," in Robert R. Bell (ed.). *The Sociology of Education.* Homewood, Ill.: The Dorsey Press, 1962.

Berelson, Bernard, Paul F. Lazarsfeld, and William McPhee. *Voting.* Chicago: University of Chicago Press, 1954, esp. Chap. 6, "Social Process: Small Groups and Political Discussion," pp. 88–117.

Berkowitz, Leonard. *Aggression: A Social Psychological Analysis.* New York: McGraw-Hill, 1962.

———. *The Development of Motives and Values in the Child.* New York: Basic Books, Inc., 1964.

Blalock, Hubert M., Jr. *Social Statistics.* New York: McGraw-Hill, 1960.

———. *Causal Inferences in Nonexperimental Research.* Chapel Hill: University of North Carolina Press, 1961.

Bone, Hugh A. "Political Socialization," in *American Politics and the Party System,* 3rd ed. New York: McGraw-Hill, 1965, pp. 23–39.

Brim, Orville G., Jr. "Personality Development as Role-Learning," in Ira Iscoe and Harold W. Stevenson (eds.). *Personality Development in Children.* Austin, Texas: University of Texas Press, 1960, pp. 127–159.

Brim, Orville G., Jr., and Stanton Wheeler. *Socialization After Childhood.* New York: John Wiley & Sons, Inc., 1966.

Bronfenbrenner, Urie. "Some Familial Antecedents of Responsibility and Leadership in Adolescents," in L. Petrullo and B. M. Bass (eds.). *Leadership and Interpersonal Behavior.* New York: Holt, Rinehart and Winston, 1961, pp. 239–271.

Brown, Francis J. *The Sociology of Children.* New York: Prentice-Hall, 1939.

Brzezinski, Zbigniew, and Samuel P. Huntington. "Socialization and Politization," in *Political Power: U.S.A./U.S.S.R.* New York: Viking, 1963, pp. 76–90.

Burdick, Eugene, and Arthur J. Brodbeck (eds.). *American Voting Behavior.* New York: The Free Press, 1959, esp. Chaps. 2, 8, and 14.

Burton, William. *Children's Civic Information.* Los Angeles: University of Southern California Press, 1936.

Campbell, Angus, Gerald Gurin, and Warren E. Miller. *The Voter Decides.* Evanston, Ill.: Row, Peterson and Co., 1954, esp. pp. 97–107, 199–206.

Campbell, Angus, *et al. The American Voter.* New York: Wiley, 1960, esp. pp. 146 ff.

Catlin, George E. G. "Propaganda as a Function of Democratic Government," in Harwood L. Childs (ed.), *Propaganda and Dictatorship.* Princeton: Princeton University Press, 1936, pp. 125–148.

Centers, Richard. *The Psychology of Social Classes.* Princeton: Princeton University Press, 1949.

Child, Irvin L. "Socialization," in Gardner Lindzey (ed.). *Handbook of Social Psychology,* Vol. 11. Cambridge, Mass.: Addison-Wesley Publishing Company, Inc., 1954, pp. 655–693.

Clausen, John A. (ed.). *Socialization and Society.* Boston: Little, Brown and Company, 1968.

Coe, George A. *Education for Citizenship: The Sovereign State as Ruler and as Teacher.* New York: Charles Scribner's Sons, 1932.

Coleman, James. *The Adolescent Society.* New York: The Free Press, 1965.

Coleman, James (ed.). *Education and Political Culture.* Princeton: Princeton University Press, 1965.

Dahl, Robert. *Who Governs?* New Haven: Yale University Press, 1961.

Davies, James C. *Human Nature in Politics: The Dynamics of Political Behavior.* New York: Wiley, 1963.

Davis, A. *Social Class Influences Upon Learning.* Cambridge: Harvard University Press, 1952.

Dawson, Richard. "Political Socialization," in James H. Robinson (ed.). *Political Science Annual: An International Review, Vol. I.* Indianapolis: Bobbs-Merrill, 1966, pp. 1–84.

Dawson, Richard E., and Kenneth Prewitt. *Political Socialization.* Boston: Little, Brown and Company, 1969.

Dean, T. M., and O. M. Bear. *Socializing the Pupil Through Extracurricular Activities.* New York: Sanborn, 1929.

DeGrazia, Sebastian. *The Political Community: A Study of Anomie.* Chicago: University of Chicago Press, 1948.

Dennis, Jack. *Recent Research on Political Socialization: A Bibliography of Published, Forthcoming, and Unpublished Works, Theses, and Dissertations, and a Survey of Projects in Progress.* Medford, Mass.: Lincoln Filene Center for Citizenship and Public Affairs, 1967.

Deutsch, Morton, and Robert M. Krauss. *Theories in Social Psychology.* New York: Basic Books, Inc., 1965.

Dollard, John, Neal E. Miller, Leonard W. Doob, O. H. Mowrer, and Robert R. Sears. *Frustration and Aggression.* New Haven: Yale University Press, 1939.

Doob, Leonard W. *Propaganda: Its Psychology and Technique.* New York: Henry Holt, 1935.

Easton, David, and Jack Dennis. *Children in the Political System: Origins of Political Legitimacy.* New York: McGraw-Hill, 1969.

Easton, David, and Robert D. Hess. "Youth and the Political System," in Seymour Martin Lipset and Leo Lowenthal (eds.). *Culture and Social Character: The Works of David Riesman Reviewed.* New York: The Free Press, 1961, pp. 226–251.

Edwards, Allen L. *Techniques of Attitude Scale Construction.* New York: Appleton-Century-Crofts, Inc., 1957.

Eisenstadt, S. N. Ghmuel. *From Generation to Generation.* New York: The Free Press, 1956.

Elazar, Daniel J. *American Federalism: A View from the States.* New York: Thomas Y. Crowell Co., 1966.

Elkin, Frederick. *The Child and Society.* New York: Random House, 1960.

Erikson, Erik H. *Childhood and Society.* New York: Norton, 1950.

Estes, W. K. "The Statistical Approach to Learning Theory," in S. Koch (ed.). *Psychology: A Study of a Science, Vol. II: General Systematic Formulations, Learning and Special Processes.* New York: McGraw-Hill, 1959, pp. 380–491.

Estvan, Frank J., and Elizabeth. *The Child's World: His Social Perception.* New York: Putnam's Sons, 1959, Chap. 19, "The Capitol," pp. 191–205.

Eulau, Heinz, and John D. Sprague. *Lawyers in Politics.* Indianapolis: Bobbs Merrill, 1964, esp. "The Political Socialization of Lawyers," pp. 56–64.

Ezekiel, Mordecai and Karl A. Fox. *Methods of Correlation and Regression Analysis.* New York: Wiley, 1966. 3rd ed.

Ferman, Louis, Joyce L. Kornbluh, and Alan Haber (eds.). *Poverty in America*. Ann Arbor: The University of Michigan Press, 1965.

Flavell, John H. *The Developmental Psychology of Jean Piaget*. Princeton: Van Nostrand, 1963.

Ford, Thomas R. (ed.). *The Southern Appalachian Region: A Survey*. Lexington, Kentucky: University of Kentucky Press, 1962.

Freeman, Linton C. *Elementary Applied Statistics: For Students in Behavioral Science*. New York: John Wiley, 1965.

Fetterman, John. *Stinking Creek: The Portrait of a Small Mountain Community*. New York: E. P. Dutton, 1967.

Friedenberg, Edgar Z. *The Vanishing Adolescent*. Boston: Beacon Press, 1959.

Giddings, Franklin H. *The Theory of Socialization*. New York: Macmillan Company, 1897.

Goldsen, Rose, K., *et al*. *What College Students Think*. Princeton: Van Nostrand, 1960.

Greenstein, Fred I. *Children and Politics*. New Haven: Yale University Press, 1965.

Grossholtz, Jean. *Politics in the Philippines*. Boston: Little, Brown & Co., 1964, esp. Chap. VIII, "Political Socialization," pp. 183–201.

Harrington, Michael. *The Other America*. Baltimore: Penguin Books, 1964.

Havinghurst, Robert J., and Bernice L. Neugarten. *Society and Education*. Boston: Allyn and Bacon, 1962.

Hess, Robert O., and Judith V. Torney. *The Development of Basic Attitudes and Values Toward Government and Citizenship During the Elementary School Years: Part 1*. Chicago: The University of Chicago, 1965.

Hilgard, Ernest R. *Theories of Learning*. 2nd. ed. New York: Appleton, 1960.

Himmelweit, Hilde T., A. N. Oppenheim, and Pamela Vance. *Television and the Child: An Empirical Study of the Effect of Television on the Young*. New York: Oxford University Press, 1958.

Hyman, Herbert. *Political Socialization: A Study in the Psychology of Political Behavior*. New York: The Free Press, 1959.

————. "Mass Media and Political Socialization: The Role of Patterns of Communications," in Lucian Pye (ed.). *Communication and Political Development*. Princeton: Princeton University Press, 1963, pp. 128–148.

————, *et al*. *Applications of Methods of Evaluation: Four Studies of the Encampment for Citizenship*. Berkeley and Los Angeles: University of California Press, 1962.

Jaros, Dean. *Children's Orientations Toward Political Authority: A Detroit Study*. Unpublished Ph.D. Dissertation submitted to the Department of Political Science, Vanderbilt University, June, 1966.

Kish, Leslie. *Survey Sampling*. New York: John Wiley, 1965.

Klapper, Joseph. *The Effects of Mass Communication*. New York: The Free Press, 1960.

Lambert, William W., and Wallace E. Lambert. *Social Psychology*. Englewood Cliffs, N. J.: Prentice-Hall, Inc., 1964.

Lane, Robert E. *Political Ideology*. New York: The Free Press, 1962, Chap. 17.

————. *Political Life: Why People Get Involved in Politics*. New York: The Free Press, 1959.

————, and David Sears. *Public Opinion*. Englewood Cliffs, N. J.: Prentice-Hall, 1964.

Langdon, Frank. *Politics in Japan*. Boston: Little, Brown and Co., 1967, esp. Chap. 8, "Political Socialization Process," pp. 201–218.

Langton, Kenneth P. *The Political Socialization Process: The Case of Secondary School Students in Jamaica*. Unpublished Ph.D. Dissertation, University of Oregon, 1965.

Lantz, Herman R. *People of Coal Town*. New York: Columbia University Press, 1958.

Lasswell, Harold, "The Selective Effect of Personality on Political Participation," in Richard Christie and Marie Jahoda (eds.). *Studies in the Scope and Method of the Authoritarian Personality*. New York: Free Press, 1954, pp. 197–225.

———. *Power and Personality*. New York: The Viking Press, 1962.

———. *Psychopathology and Politics*. New York: The Viking Press, 1960.

———. *Politics: Who Gets What, When, How*. New York: McGraw-Hill, 1936.

Lazarsfeld, Paul. F., and P. Kendall. *Radio Listening in America*. New York: Prentice-Hall, 1948.

Lazarsfeld, Paul F., Bernard Berelson, and Hazel Gaudet. *The People's Choice*. New York: Columbia University Press, 1944.

Lerner, Daniel. *The Passing of Traditional Society: Modernizing the Middle East*. New York: The Free Press, 1958.

LeVine, Robert A. "Political Socialization and Culture Change," in Clifford Gertz (ed.). *Old Societies and New States*. New York: The Free Press, 1963; pp. 280–303.

Lewis, Claudia. *Children of the Cumberland*. New York: Columbia University Press, 1946.

Lewis, Hilda. *Deprived Children*. London: Oxford University Press, 1954.

Lewis, Oscar. *The Children of Sanchez*. New York: Random House, 1961.

———. *La Vida: A Puerto Rican Family in the Culture of Poverty—San Juan and New York*. New York: Random House, 1965.

Lipset, Seymour Martin. *Political Man: The Social Basis of Politics*. Garden City, N.Y.: Doubleday, 1959.

Massialas, Byron G., and C. B. Cox. *Inquiry in Social Studies*. New York: McGraw-Hill, 1966.

Mead, Margaret. "Administrative Contributions to Democratic Character Formation at the Adolescent Level." in Clyde Kluckhohn and Henry A. Murray (eds.). *Personality in Nature, Society and Culture*. New York: Alfred A. Knopf, 1959, pp. 523–530.

Meine, Frederick J. "Radio and Press Among Young People", in Paul F. Lazarsfeld and Frank N. Stanton (eds.). *Radio Research 1941*. New York: Duell, Sloan, and Pearce, 1941.

Merriam, Charles E. *Civic Education in the United States*. New York: Scribners, 1934.

———. *The Making of Citizens: A Comparative Study of Civic Training*. Chicago: University of Chicago Press, 1931.

Miller, N. E., and John Dollard. *Social Learning and Imitation*. New Haven: Yale University Press, 1941.

Mitchell, William C. *The American Polity*. New York: The Free Press, 1962, esp. Chap. 7, "The Socialization of Citizens, pp. 145–178.

Mosel, James N. "Communication Patterns and Political Socialization in Transitional Thailand," in Lucian Pye (ed.). *Communications and Political Development*. Princeton: Princeton University Press, 1963, pp. 184–228.

Mowrer, O. Hobart. *Learning Theory and Behavior*. New York: John Wiley, 1960.

Newcomb, T. M. *Personality and Social Change: Attitude Formation in a Student Community*. New York: Dryden, 1943.

———, *et al. Persistence and Change: Bennington College and Its Students After Twenty-Five Years*. New York: John Wiley, 1967.

Parsons, Talcott, and Edward A. Shils. *Toward a General Theory of Action*. New York: Harper & Row, 1962. (Paperback edition.)

Parsons, Talcott, and Robert F. Bales. *Family Socialization and Interaction Process*. New York: The Free Press, 1955.

Patterson, Franklin (ed.). *The Adolescent Citizen*. New York: The Free Press, 1960.

Patterson, Gerald R. "Responsiveness to Social Stimuli," in Leonard Krasner and Leonard P. Ullman (eds.). *Research in Behavior Modification*. New York: Holt, Rinehart and Winston, Inc., 1965, pp. 157–178.

Pierce, Bessie Louise. *Citizen's Organizations and the Civic Training of Youth*. New York: Scribners, 1933.

———. *Civic Attitudes in American School Textbooks*. Chicago: University of Chicago Press, 1930.

Rokeach, Milton. *The Open and Closed Mind*. New York: Basic Books, 1960.

Rosenberg, Morris. *Society and The Adolescent Self-Image*. Princeton: Princeton University Press, 1965.

Rosenthal, Robert. *Experimenter Effects in Behavioral Research*. New York: Appleton-Century-Crofts, 1966.

Sears, Robert R., Eleanor Maccoby, and Henry Levin. *Patterns of Child Rearing*. Evanston, Ill.: Row-Peterson, 1957.

Seasholes, Bradbury. "Political Socialization of Negroes: Image Development of Self and Polity," in *Negro Self-Concept, The Report of a Conference Sponsored by the Lincoln Filene Center For Citizenship and Public Affairs*. New York: McGraw-Hill, 1965, pp. 52–90.

Schramm, W., J. Lyle, and E. B. Parker. *Television in the Lives of Our Children*. Stanford: Stanford University Press, 1961.

Siegel, Sidney. *Nonparametric Statistics*. New York: McGraw-Hill, 1956.

Sigel, Roberta S. "An Exploration into Some Aspects of Political Socialization: School Children's Reactions to the Death of a President," in Martha Wolfenstein and Gilbert Kliman (eds.). *Children and the Death of a President: Multi-Disciplinary Studies*. New York: Doubleday, 1965, pp. 30–61.

Smith, Ernest. *American Youth Culture: Group Life in Teen Age Society*. New York: The Free Press, 1962.

Spaulding, F. T. *High School and Life*. New York: McGraw-Hill, 1938.

Steiner, Gary A. *The People Look at Television: A Study of Audience Attitudes*. New York: Alfred A. Knopf, 1963.

Stember, C. H. *Education and Attitude Change*. New York: Institute of Human Relations Press, 1961.

Teune, Henry, "The Learning of Integrative Habits," in Philip E. Jacob and James V. Toscano, *The Integration of Political Communities*. Philadelphia: J. B. Lippincott, 1964, pp. 247–282.

Thibaut, John W., and Harold H. Kelley. *The Social Psychology of Groups*. New York: John Wiley, 1959.

Verba, Sidney. *Small Groups and Political Behavior*. Princeton: Princeton University Press, 1961.

Wahlke, John, *et al. The Legislative System: Explorations in Legislative Behavior*. New York: John Wiley, 1962. esp. Chap. 4, "Recollections," pp. 77–95.

Walker, Kenneth N. "Political Socialization in Universities," in Seymour M. Lipset and Aldo Solari (eds.). *Elites in Latin America*. New York: Oxford University Press, 1967, pp. 408–430.

Whiting, Beatrice (ed.). *Six Cultures: Studies of Child Rearing*. New York: John Wiley, 1963.

Whiting, John W. M. "Resource Mediation and Learning by Identification," in Ira Iscoe and Harold W. Stevenson (eds.). *Personality Development in Children*. Austin, Texas: University of Texas Press, 1960, pp. 112–125.

Wilson, H. E. *Education for Citizenship.* New York: McGraw-Hill, 1938.

Wiseman, H. Victor. *Politics in Everyday Life.* Oxford: Basil Blackwell, 1966, esp. Part 1, Chap. 6, "Political Socialization and Recruitment."

Yarrow, Marion Radke, and Harold L. Raush (eds.). *Observational Methods in Research on Socialization Processes: A Report of a Conference Sponsored by the Committee on Socialization and Social Structure of the Social Science Research Council.* National Institute of Mental Health, July 26, 1966.

ARTICLES AND PERIODICALS

Abrams, Philip, and Alan Little. "The Young Voter in British Politics," *British Journal of Sociology,* Vol. 16 (1965), pp. 95–110.

Adelson, Joseph, and Robert P. O'Neil. "Growth of Political Ideas in Adolescence: The Sense of Community," *Journal of Personality and Social Psychology,* 4, 3 (1966), pp. 295–306.

Agger, Robert E., Marshall N. Goldstein, and Stanley A. Pearl. "Political Cynicism: Measurement and Meaning," *Journal of Politics,* XXIII, 3 (August, 1961), pp. 477–506.

Allen, Doris T. "Growth in Attitudes Favorable to Peace," *Merrill-Palmer Quarterly of Behavior and Development,* Vol. 9 (1963), pp. 27–38.

Argyle, Michael, and Peter Delin. "Non-Universal Laws of Socialization," *Human Relations,* 18, 1 (February, 1965), pp. 77–86.

Babchuck, Nicholas, and C. Wayne Gordon. "The Child as a Prototype of the Naive Informant in the Interview Situation," *American Sociological Review,* XXIII, 2 (April, 1958), pp. 196–198.

Bach, George R. "Father-fantasies and Father-typing in Father-separated Children," *Child Development,* XVII (March, 1946), pp. 63–80.

Bailyn, Lotte. "Mass Media and Children: A Study of Exposure Habits and Cognitive Effects," *Psychological Monographs,* 73 (1959), No. 471.

Baldwin, A. L. "Socialization and the Parent-Child Relationship," *Child Development,* XIX, 3 (September, 1948), pp. 127–136.

Ball, Donald W. "Covert Political Rebellion as Ressentiment," *Social Forces,* Vol. 43 (1964), pp. 93–101.

Bandura, Albert, Dorothea Ross, and Shiela A. Ross. "A Comparative Test of the Status Envy, Social Power and Secondary Reinforcement Theories of Identificatory Learning," *Journal of Abnormal and Social Psychology,* LXVII, 6 (December, 1963), pp. 527–534.

Barnes, Earl (ed.). "The Development of Children's Political Ideas," *Studies in Education,* Vol. 2 (1902), pp. 5–24.

———. "Political Ideals of American Children," *Studies in Education,* 11 (1902), 25–30.

Barry, H., Margaret K. Bacon, and I. L. Child. "A Cross-Cultural Survey of Some Sex Differences in Socialization," *Journal of Abnormal and Social Psychology,* LV, 3 (November, 1957), pp. 327–332.

Bauer, Raymond A., and Alice H. Bauer. "America, Mass Society and Mass Media," *Journal of Social Issues,* 16, No. 3 (1960), pp. 3–66.

Becker, Howard S. "Social-Class Variations in Teacher-Pupil Relationships," *Journal of Educational Sociology,* XXV (April, 1952), pp. 451–465.

———, and Anselm L. Strauss. "Careers, Personality, and Adult Socialization," *American Journal of Sociology,* LXII, 3 (November, 1956), pp. 253–263.

Bender, Gerald J. "Political Socialization and Political Change," *The Western Political Quarterly*, XX, 2 (June, 1967), pp. 390–407.

Benedict, Ruth, "Continuities and Discontinuities in Cultural Conditioning," in Kluckhohn, Clyde, and Murray, Henry A. (eds.). *Personality in Nature, Society, and Culture,* New York: Alfred A. Knopf (1948), pp. 414–423.

Bennett, Jr., William S., and Noel P. Gest. "Class and Family Influence on Student Aspiration," *Social Forces*, XLIII, 2 (December, 1964), pp. 167–174.

Bereday, George Z. F. "Education and Youth," *The Satellites in Eastern Europe*, Roberts, H. L. (ed.). *The Annals of the American Academy of Political and Social Science*, Vol. 317 (1958), pp. 67–70.

———, and Bonnie B. Stretch. "Political Education in the U.S.A. and U.S.S.R.," *Comparative Education Review,* Vol. 7 (1963), pp. 9–16.

Bloom, Leonard, A. R. C. De Crespigny, and J. E. Spence. "An Interdisciplinary Study of Social, Moral and Political Attitudes of White and Non-White South African University Students," *Journal of Social Psychology*, Vol. 54 (1961), pp. 3–12.

Bowerman, Charles E., and John W. Kinch. "Changes in Family and Peer Orientations of Children Between the Fourth and Tenth Grades." *Social Forces,* 37 (March, 1959), pp. 206–211.

Breslaw, B. J. "Development of a Socio-Economic Attitude," *Archives of Psychology*, 32 (1938), Doc. 226.

Brim, Orville G., Jr. "Family Structure and Sex Role Learning by Children: A Further Analysis of Helen Koch's Data," *Sociometry,* Vol. 21 (September, 1958), pp. 343–364.

———. "The Parent-Child Relation as a Social System: I. Parent and Child Roles," *Child Development*, Vol. 28 (September, 1957), pp. 343–364.

Bronfenbrenner, Urie. "Freudian Theories of Identification and Their Derivatives," *Child Development,* 31 (March, 1960), pp. 15–40.

———. "Soviet Methods of Character Education: Some Implications for Research," *American Psychologist* 17 (1962), pp. 550–64.

Browning, Rufus P., and Herbert Jacob. "Power Motivation and the Political Personality," *Public Opinion Quarterly*, XXVIII, 1 (Spring, 1964), pp. 75–90.

Bruner, Edward M. "Cultural Transmission and Cultural Change," *Southwestern Journal of Anthropology*, XII, 2 (Summer, 1956), pp. 191–199.

Burchinal, Lee G. "Social Status, Measured Intelligence, Achievement, and Personality Adjustment of Rural Iowa Girls," *Sociometry*, 22 (March, 1959), 78–80.

Burton, Roger V., and John W. Whiting. "The Absent Father and Cross-Sex Identity," *Merrill-Palmer Quarterly*, 7 (April, 1961), pp. 84–95.

Burwen, Leroy S., and Donald T. Campbell. "The Generality of Attitudes Toward Authority and Non-Authority Figures," *Journal of Abnormal and Social Psychology,* 54 (1957), pp. 24–31.

Byrne, Donn. "Parental Antecedents of Authoritarianism," *Journal of Personality and Social Psychology*, Vol. 1 (1965), pp. 369–373.

Cammarota, Gloria. "Children, Politics, and Elementary Social Studies," *Social Education*, XXVII, 4 (April, 1963), pp. 205–211.

Campbell, Angus. "The Passive Citizen," *Acta Sociologica,* VI (Fascia 1 and 2, 1962), pp. 9–21.

———, and Henry Valen. "Party Identification in Norway and the United States," *Public Opinion Quarterly*, XXV, 4 (Winter, 1961), pp. 505–525.

Carlson, Rae. "Stability and Change in the Adolescent's Self-Image," *Child Development,* XXXVI, 3 (September, 1965), pp. 659–666.

Centers, Richard. "Children of the New Deal: Social Stratification and Adolescent Attitudes," *International Journal of Opinion Attitude Research,* IV (1950), pp. 315–335.

Chaffee, Steven H., Jack M. McLeod, and Daniel B. Wackman. *Family Communication and Political Socialization.* Paper presented to Theory and Methodology Division, Association for Education in Journalism, Iowa City, Iowa, August, 1966.

Chapman, Ames W. "Attitudes Toward Legal Authorities by Juveniles," *Sociology and Social Research,* Vol. 40 (1956), pp. 170–175.

Child, I. L., E. H. Potter, and Estelle M. Levine. "Children's Text-books and Personality Development: Exploration in the Social Psychology of Education," *Psychological Monographs,* 44 (1949), pp. 303–314.

Chorost, Sherwood B. "Parental Child-Rearing Attitudes and Their Correlates in Adolescent Hostility," *Genetic Psychology Monographs,* LXVI, 1 (August, 1962), pp. 49–90.

Clausen, John A. "Research on Socialization and Personality Development in the United States and France: Remarks on the Paper by Professor Chombart de Lauwe." *American Sociological Review,* 31 (April, 1966), pp. 248–257.

Cohen, Yehudi A. "Structure and Function: Family Organization and Socialization in a Jamaican Community," *American Anthropologist,* LVIII, 4 (August, 1956), pp. 664–686.

Cole, David L. "The Perception of Lincoln: A Psychological Approach to the Public's Conception of Historical Figures," *Journal of Social Psychology,* Vol. 55 (1961), pp. 23–36.

Connor, Ruth, T. B. Johannis, Jr., and J. Walters. "Parent-Adolescent Relationships II; Intra-familial Conception of the Good Father, Good Mother, and Good Child," *Journal of Home Economics,* XLVI, 3 (March, 1954), pp. 187–191.

Converse, Philip E., and George Depuex. "Politicization of the Electorate in France and the United States," *Public Opinion Quarterly,* XXVI, 1 (Spring, 1962), pp. 1–23.

Cox, F. N. "An Assessment of Children's Attitudes Toward Parent Figures," *Child Development,* XXXIII, 4 (December, 1962), pp. 822–830.

Crandall, V. J., Anne Preston, and Alice Rabson. "Maternal Reactions and the Development of Independence and Achievement Behavior in Young Children," *Child Development,* XXXI, 2 (June, 1960), pp. 243–251.

Crandall, Virginia C., Suzanne Good, and V. J. Crandall. "The Reinforcement Effects of Adult Reactions and Non-Reactions on Children's Achievement Expectations: A Replication Study," *Child Development,* XXXV, 2 (June, 1964), pp. 485–497.

Crittenden, John. "Aging and Party Affiliation," *Public Opinion Quarterly,* Vol. 26 (1962), pp. 648–657.

Davies, A. F. "The Child's Discovery of Social Class," *Australia and New Zealand Journal of Sociology,* Vol. 1 (1965), pp. 21–27.

Davis, Allison, and Robert J. Havighurst. "Social Class and Color Differences in Child-Rearing," *American Sociological Review,* XI (1946), pp. 698–710.

Davies, James C. "The Family's Role in Political Socialization," *The Annals of the American Academy of Political and Social Science,* Vol. 261 (1965), pp. 10–19.

Davis, Kingsley. "The Child and the Social Structure," *Journal of Educational Sociology,* XIV, 4 (December, 1940), pp. 217–229.

———. "The Sociology of Parent-Youth Conflict," *American Sociological Review,* 4 (August, 1940), pp. 523–535.

———. "Adolescence and the Social Structure," *The Annals of the American Academy of Political and Social Science,* CCXXXVI (November, 1944), pp. 9–16.

De Charms, Richard, and Gerald Moeller. "Values Expressed in American Children's Readers: 1800–1950," *Journal of Abnormal and Social Psychology*, LXIV, 2 (February, 1962), pp. 136–142.

———, and M. E. Rosenbaum. "Status Variables and Matching Behavior," *Journal of Personality*, 28 (1960), pp. 492–502.

Dennis, Jack, *et al*. "Political Socialization to Democratic Orientations in Four Western Systems," *Comparative Political Studies* (April, 1968), pp. 71–101.

Dodge, Richard W., and Eugene S. Uyeki, "Political Affiliation and Imagery Across Two Related Generations," *Midwest Journal of Political Science*, Vol. 6 (1962), pp. 266–276.

Douvan, Elizabeth. "Sex Differences in Adolescent Character Processes," *Merrill-Palmer Quarterly*, VI (1960), pp. 203–211.

———, and Allan M. Walker. "The Sense of Effectiveness in Public Affairs," *Psychological Monographs*, LXX, 32 (1956).

Dubin, Robert, and Elizabeth Ruch Dubin. "Children's Social Perceptions: A Review of Research," *Child Development*, XXXVI, 3 (September, 1965), pp. 809–838.

Easton, David. "Function of Formal Education in a Political System," *School Review*, LXV (1957), pp. 204–216.

———, and Jack Dennis. "The Child's Acquisition of Regime Norms: Political Efficacy," *The American Political Science Review*, LXI, 1 (March, 1967), pp. 25–38.

———. "The Child's Image of Government," *The Annals of the American Academy of Political and Social Science,* Vol. 361 (1965), pp. 40–57.

Easton, David, and Robert D. Hess. "The Child's Political World," *Midwest Journal of Political Science*, VI, 3 (August, 1962), pp. 229–246.

Edelstein, Alex S. "Since Bennington: Evidence of Change in Student Political Behavior," *Public Opinion Quarterly*, 26 (1962), pp. 564–77.

Edwards, A. L., and Kilpatrick, F. P. "A Technique for the Construction of Attitude Scales," *Journal of Applied Psychology*, 32 (1948), pp. 374–384.

———. "Scale Analysis and the Measurement of Social Attitudes," *Psychometrika*, 13 (1948), pp. 99–114.

Eisenberg, P., and P. F. Lazarsfeld. "The Psychological Effects of Unemployment," *Psychological Bulletin*, 35 (June, 1938), pp. 358–390.

Elder, G. H., Jr. "Role Relations, Sociocultural Environments and Autocratic Family Ideology, *Sociometry*, Vol. 28 (1965), pp. 173–196.

Elkin, Frederick K., and W. A. Westley. "The Myth of Adolescent Culture," *American Sociological Review*, XX, 6 (December, 1955), pp. 680–684.

Engel, Mary. "The Stability of the Self-Concept in Adolescence," *Journal of Abnormal and Social Psychology*, LVIII, 2 (March, 1959), pp. 211–215.

Epperson, D. C. "A Reassessment of Indices of Parental Influences in the Adolescent Society," *American Sociological Review*, XXIX, 1 (February, 1964), pp. 93–96.

Estvan, Frank J. "Teaching Government in Elementary Schools," *Elementary School Journal*, Vol. 62 (1961–1962), pp. 291–297.

———. "The Relationship of Social Status, Intelligence and Sex of Ten- and Twelve-Year-Old Children to an Awareness Of Poverty," *Genetic Psychology Monographs,* XLVI, 1 (August, 1952), pp. 3–60.

Eulau, Heinz, William Buchanan, LeRoy C. Ferguson, and John C. Wahlke. "The Political Socialization of American State Legislators," in John C. Wahlke and Henry Eulau (eds.), *Legislative Behavior: A Reader in Theory and Research*. New York: The Free Press, 1959, pp. 305–313.

Fay, Paul J., and Warren Middleton. "Certain Factors Related to Liberal and Conservative Attitudes of College Students; II. Father's Political Preference . . . ," *Journal of Social Psychology*, Vol. II (1940), pp. 107–119.

Finney, Joseph C. "Some Maternal Influences on Children's Personality and Character," *Genetic Psychology Monographs*, LXIII, 2 (May, 1961), pp. 199–278.

Frey, Frederick W. "Socialization to National Identification Among Turkish Peasants," *Journal of Politics*, 4, 30 (November, 1968), pp. 934–965.

Froman, Lewis A., Jr. "Learning Political Attitudes," *Western Political Quarterly*, 15 (June, 1962), pp. 304–313.

————. "Personality and Political Socialization," *Journal of Politics*, 23, 2 (May, 1961), pp. 341–352.

————, and James K. Skipper, Jr. "An Approach to the Learning of Party Identification," *Public Opinion Quarterly*, XXVII, 3 (Fall, 1963), pp. 473–480.

Gage, Robert W. "Patriotism and Military Discipline as a Function of Degree of Military Training," *Journal of Social Psychology*, Vol. 64 (1964), pp. 101–111.

Garrison, Charles L. "Political Involvement and Political Science: A Note on the Basic Course as an Agent of Political Socialization," *Social Science Quarterly*, 49, 2 (September, 1968), pp. 305–314.

Geddie, Leanna, and Gertrude Hildreth. "Children's Ideas about the War," *Journal of Experimental Education*, Vol. 13 (1944), pp. 92–97.

Gilfand, Donna M. "The Influence of Self-Esteem on Rate of Verbal Conditioning and Social Matching Behavior," *Journal of Abnormal and Social Psychology* (1962), pp. 259–265.

Goldrich, Daniel, and Edward W. Scott. "Developing Political Orientations of Panamanian Students," *Journal of Politics*, XXIII (February, 1961), pp. 84–107.

Goodman, Mary Ellen. "Emergent Citizenship: A Study of Relevant Values in Four-Year Olds," *Childhood Education*, Vol. 35 (1958–1959), pp. 248–251.

Gough, Harrison G. "Theory and Measurement of Socialization," *Journal of Consulting Psychology*, XXIV, 1 (February, 1960), pp. 23–30.

————, Dale B. Harris, William E. Martin and Marcia Edwards. "Children's Ethnic Attitudes: I. Relationship to Certain Personality Factors," *Child Development*, 21, 2 (June, 1950), pp. 83–91.

Greenstein, Fred I. "The Benevolent Leader: Children's Images of Political Authority," *The American Political Science Review*. LIV (December, 1960), pp. 934–943.

————. "Sex-Related Political Differences in Childhood," *Journal of Politics*, 23, 2 (May, 1961), pp. 353–371.

————. "More on Children's Images of the President," *Public Opinion Quarterly*, XXV, 4 (Winter, 1961), pp. 648–654.

————. "New Light on Changing American Values: A Forgotten Body of Survey Data," *Social Forces*, Vol. 42 (1964), pp. 441–450.

————. "Popular Images of the President," *The American Journal of Psychiatry*, CXXII, 5 (November, 1965), pp. 523–529.

————. "Personality and Political Socialization: The Theories of Authoritarian and Democratic Character," *The Annals of the American Academy of Political and Social Science*, Vol. 361 (1965), pp. 81–95.

————. "Young Men and the Death of a Young President," in Martha Wolfenstein and Gilbert Kliman (eds.), *Children and The Death of a President: Multi-disciplinary Studies*, New York: Doubleday & Company Inc. (1965), pp. 172–192.

————. "College Students' Reactions to the Assassination," in Bradley S. Greenberg, and Edwin B. Parker (eds.), *The Kennedy Assassination and the American Public:*

Social Communication in Crisis, Stanford, California: Stanford University Press (1965), pp. 220–239.

Greenstein, Fred I. "The Psychological Function of the American President for Citizens," in Elmer E. Cornwell, Jr. (ed.), *The American Presidency: Vital Center,* Chicago: Scott-Foresman, (1966), pp. 30–36.

———. "Political Socialization," Article written for the *International Encyclopedia of the Social Sciences,* forthcoming.

———. "The Impact of Personality on Politics: An Attempt to Clear Away Underbrush," *The American Political Science Review,* LXI, 3 (September, 1967), pp. 629–641.

Harris, Dale B., Harrison G. Gough, and William E. Martin. "Children's Ethnic Attitudes: II. Relationship to Parental Beliefs Concerning Child Training," *Child Development,* 21, 3 (September, 1950), pp. 169–181.

Hartley, Ruth E. "Children's Concepts of Male and Female Roles," *Merrill-Palmer Quarterly,* 6 (January, 1960), pp. 83–91.

———. "Some Implications of Current Changes in Sex Role Patterns," *Merrill-Palmer Quarterly,* 6 (April, 1960), pp. 153–164.

———. "Sex Role Pressure and the Socialization of the Male Child," *Psychological Reports,* 5 (September, 1959), pp. 457–468.

Hamilton, Richard. "Skill Level and Politics," *Public Opinion Quarterly* (Fall, 1965), pp. 390–399.

Havighurst, Robert J., and Allison Davis. "A Comparison of the Chicago and Harvard Studies of Social Class Differences in Child Rearing," *American Sociological Review,* XX (1935), pp. 438–442.

Helfant, K. "Parental Attitudes vs. Adolescent Hostility in the Determination of Adolescent Sociopolitical Attitudes," *Psychological Monographs,* LXVI, 13 (1952).

Hennessy, Bernard. "Politicals and Apoliticals: Some Measurements of Personality Traits," *Midwest Journal of Political Science,* III, 4 (November, 1959), pp. 336–355.

Hennessey, Timothy M. "Democratic Attitudinal Configurations Among Italian Youth," *Midwest Journal of Political Science,* XIII (May, 1969), pp. 167–193.

Hess, Robert D., "The Adolescent: His Society," *Review of Educational Research,* 30 (February, 1960), pp. 5–12.

———. "The Socialization of Attitudes Toward Political Authority: Some Cross National Comparisons," *International Social Science Journal,* XV (1963), pp. 542–59.

———, and David Easton. "The Child's Changing Image of the President," *Public Opinion Quarterly,* Vol. 24, 4 (1960), pp. 632–644.

———. "The Role of the Elementary School in Political Socialization," *The School Review,* LXX, 3 (August, 1962), pp. 257–265.

———, and Irene Goldblatt. "The Status of Adolescents in American Society: A Problem in Social Identity," *Child Development,* XXVIII, 4 (December, 1957), pp. 459–468.

———, and Judith Torney. "Religion, Age and Sex in Children's Perceptions of Family Authority," *Child Development,* XXXIII, 4 (December, 1962), pp. 781–789.

Hill, David S. "Personification of Ideals by Urban Children," *Journal of Social Psychology,* 1, 3 (August, 1930), pp. 379–393.

———. "Comparative Study of Children's Ideals," *The Pedagogical Seminary,* XVIII, 2 (June, 1911), pp. 219–231.

Hoffman, Louis W. "The Father's Role in the Family and the Child's Peer-Group Adjustment," *Merrill-Palmer Quarterly*, 7 (April, 1961), pp. 97–105.

Hoffman, Martin L. "Power Assertion by the Parent and Its Impact on the Child," *Child Development*, 31 (1960), pp. 129–143.

Horowitz, Eugene L. "Some Aspects of the Development of Patriotism in Children," *Sociometry*, 111 (October, 1940), pp. 309–341.

———, and Ruth E. Horowitz. "Development of Social Attitudes in Children," *Sociometry*, 1 (1938), pp. 301–338.

Horton, J. E., and Wayne Thompson. "Powerlessness and Political Negativism," *American Journal of Sociology*, LXVII, 5 (March, 1962), pp. 485–493.

Horton, D., and R. R. Wohl. "Mass Communication and Para-Social Interaction: Observations on Intimacy at a Distance," *Psychiatry* (1956), pp. 215–229.

Iisager, H. "Factors Influencing the Formation and Change of Political and Religious Attitudes," *Journal of Social Psychology*, 29 (1949), pp. 253–265.

Inkeles, Alex. "Social Change and Social Character: The Role of Parental Mediation," *Journal of Social Issues*, II, 2 (1955), pp. 12–33.

Jahoda, Gustav. "Development of the Perception of Social Differences in Children from 6 to 10," *The British Journal of Educational Psychology*, Vol. 50 (1959), pp. 159–175.

———. "The Development of Children's Ideas About Country and Nationality, Part I," *British Journal of Social Psychology*, XXXIII (February, 1963), pp. 47–60.

———. "The Development of Children's Ideas About Country and Nationality, Part II: National Symbols and Themes," *The British Journal of Educational Psychology*, Vol. 33 (1963), pp. 143–153.

———. "Children's Concepts of Nationality: A Critical Study of Piaget's Stages," *Child Development*, Vol. 35 (1964), pp. 1081–1092.

Jahoda, Marie, and Neil Warren. "The Myths of Youth," *Sociology of Education*, XXXVIII, 2 (Winter, 1965), pp. 138–150.

Jaros, Dean. "Children's Orientations Toward the President: Some Additional Theoretical Considerations and Data," *The Journal of Politics*, 29, 2 (May, 1967), pp. 368–387.

———. "Measuring Children's Orientations Toward the President," Unpublished paper, Department of Political Science, University of Kentucky, Mimeo., 1967.

———. "Transmitting the Civic Culture: The Teacher and Political Socialization," *Social Science Quarterly*, 49, 2 (September, 1968), pp. 284–295.

Jennings, M. Kent. "Pre-Adult Orientations to Multiple Systems of Government," *Midwest Journal of Political Science*, XI (August, 1967), pp. 291–317.

Jennings, M. Kent, and Richard G. Niemi. "The Transmission of Political Values from Parent to Child," *The American Political Science Review*, LXII (March, 1968), pp. 169–184.

Johnson, Byron L. "Children's Reading Interests as Related to Sex and Year in School," *School Review*, 40 (1932), pp. 257–72.

Jones, Mary C. "A Study of Socialization Patterns at the High School Level," *Journal of Genetic Psychology*, 93 (1958), pp. 87–111.

Kagan, Jerome. "The Concept of Identification," *Psychological Review*, 65, 5 (1958), pp. 296–305.

———, and Judith Lemkin. "The Child's Differential Perception of Parental Attributes," *Journal of Abnormal and Social Psychology*, LXI, 3 (November, 1960), pp. 440–447.

———, and Harold A. Moss. "The Stability of Passive and Dependent Behavior from

Childhood to Adulthood," *Child Development*, XXXI, 3 (September, 1960), pp. 557–591.

Katz, Phyllis A. "Effect of Labels on Children's Perception and Discrimination Learning," *Journal of Experimental Psychology*, 66 (1963), pp. 423–428.

Kennedy, John L., and Harold D. Lasswell. "A Cross-Cultural Test of Self-Image," *Human Organization*, XVII, 1 (Spring, 1958), pp. 41–43.

Kish, L. "Some Statistical Problems in Research Design," *American Sociological Review*, 24 (1959), pp. 328–338.

Kohn, Melvin L. "Social Class and Parental Values," *American Journal of Sociology*, 64 (January, 1959), pp. 337–351.

———. "Social Class and the Exercise of Parental Authority," *American Sociological Review*, XXIV, 3 (June, 1959), pp. 352–366.

———. "Social Class and Parent-Child Relationships: An Interpretation," *American Journal of Sociology*, LXVIII, 4 (January, 1963), pp. 471–480.

Kornberg, Allan, and Norman Thomas. "The Political Socialization of National Legislative Elites in the United States and Canada," *Journal of Politics*, 27, 4 (November, 1965), pp. 761–775.

Kuroda, Yasumasa. "Agencies of Political Socialization and Political Change: Political Orientation of Japanese Law Students," *Human Organization*, Vol. 24 (1965), pp. 328–331.

Lambert, William, Leigh M. Triandis, and Margery Wold. "Some Correlates of Beliefs in the Malevolence and Benevolence of Super-Natural Beings: A Cross-Societal Study," *Journal of Abnormal and Social Psychology*, LVIII, 2 (March, 1959), pp. 162–169.

Lane, Robert E. "The Need to Be Liked and the Anxious College Liberal," in Sigel (ed.), *Annals*, pp. 71–80.

———. "Fathers and Sons: Foundations of Political Belief," *American Sociological Review*, 24 (August, 1959), pp. 502–511.

Langton, Kenneth P. "Peer Group and School and the Political Socialization Process," *The American Political Science Review*, LXI, 3 (September, 1967), pp. 751–758.

Langton, Kenneth, and M. Kent Jennings. "Political Socialization and the High School Civics Curriculum in the United States," *The American Political Science Review*, LXII (September, 1968), pp. 852–867.

Lapierre, Jean-William, and Georges Noizet. "Les jeunes Français devant l'objection de conscience," *Revue Française de Sociologie*, Vol. 4 (1963), pp. 259–274.

———. "L'information politique de jeunes Français in 1962," *Revue Française de Science Politique*, Vol. 14 (1964), pp. 480–504.

Lawson, Edwin D. "Development of Patriotism in Children: A Second Look," *Journal of Psychology*, LV, 2 (April, 1963), pp. 279–286.

Levinson, Daniel J. "The Relevance of Personality for Political Participation," *Public Opinion Quarterly*, 22 (1958), pp. 3–10.

Lazowick, Lionel M. "On the Nature of Identification," *The Journal of Abnormal and Social Psychology*, 51, 2 (September, 1955), pp. 175–184.

Leatherman, Daniel R. "The Political Socialization of Students in the Mennonite Secondary Schools," *The Mennonite Quarterly Review*, Vol. 36 (1962), pp. 89–90.

Levin, Martin. "Social Climates and Political Socialization," *Public Opinion Quarterly*, XXV, 4 (Winter, 1961), pp. 596–606.

LeVine, Robert A. "The Role of the Family in Authority Systems: A Cross-Cultural Application of Stimulus-Generalization Theory," *Behavioral Science*, V, 4 (October, 1960), pp. 291–296.

LeVine, Robert A. "The Internalization of Political Values in Stateless Societies," *Human Organization*, XIX, 2 (Summer, 1960), pp. 51–58.

Lewin, Herbert S. "Hitler Youth and the Boy Scouts of America: A Comparison of Aims," *Human Relations*, 1 (1947), pp. 206–227.

Lewis, S. L. "Political Heroes: 1936 and 1960," *Journalism Quarterly*, XLII, 1 (Winter, 1965), pp. 116–118.

Lippitt, Gordon L. (ed.). "Training for Political Participation," *Journal of Social Issues*, 16, 1 (1960), entire issue.

Litt, Edgar, "Civic Education, Community Norms, and Political Indoctrination," *American Sociological Review*, XXVIII, 1 (February, 1963), pp. 69–75.

———. "Education and Political Enlightenment in America," in Sigel, *Annals*, pp. 32–39.

———. "Political Cynicism and Political Futility," *Journal of Politics*, XXV, 2 (May, 1963), pp. 312–323.

Lynn, David B., and William L. Sawrey. "The Effects of Father-Absence on Norwegian Boys and Girls," *Journal of Abnormal and Social Psychology*, 59 (September, 1959), pp. 258–262.

Maccoby, Eleanor E. "Role-Taking in Childhood and Its Consequences For Social Learning," *Child Development*, 30 (1959), pp. 239–252.

———. "The Choice of Variables in the Study of Socialization," *Sociometry*, XXIV, 4 (December, 1961), pp. 357–371.

———. "The Taking of Adult Roles in Middle Childhood," *Journal of Abnormal and Social Psychology*, 63 (November, 1961), pp. 493–503.

———, Richard E. Matthews, and Alton S. Morton. "Youth and Political Change," *Public Opinion Quarterly*, XVIIII (Spring, 1954), pp. 23–39.

Marston, Benson H., and James C. Coleman. "Specificity of Attitudes Toward Paternal and Non-Paternal Authority Figures," *Journal of Individual Psychology* (1961), pp. 96–101.

Marvick, Dwaine. "The Political Socialization of the American Negro," in Sigel (ed.), *Annals*, pp. 112–127.

McClintock, C. G., and H. A. Turner. "The Impact of College Upon Political Knowledge, Participation, and Values," *Human Relations*, XV (1962), pp. 163–176.

McClosky, Herbert, and Harold E. Dahlgren. "Primary Group Influence on Party Loyalty," *American Political Science Review*, LIII, 3 (September, 1959), pp. 757–776.

McCord, William, and Joan McCord. "Effects of Parental Role Model on Criminality," *Journal of Social Issues*, 14 (1958), pp. 66–75.

McGinnis, Robert. "Randomization and Inference in Sociological Research," *American Sociological Review*, 23 (August, 1958), pp. 408–414.

McGranahan, Donald V. "A Comparison of Social Attitudes Among American and German Youth," *Journal of Abnormal and Social Psychology*, 41 (1946), pp. 245–257.

Merelman, Richard M. "Learning and Legitimacy," *The American Political Science Review*, LX, 3 (September, 1966), pp. 548–561.

Middleton, Russell, and Snell Putney. "Political Expression of Adolescent Rebellion," *American Journal of Sociology*, 68 (March, 1963), pp. 527–535.

———. "Student Rebellion Against Parental Political Beliefs," *Social Forces*, XLI, 4 (May, 1963), pp. 377–383.

———. "Influences on the Political Beliefs of American College Students," *Politico*, 29 (1964), pp. 484–492.

Mischel, Walter. "Father-absence and Delay of Gratification: Cross-cultural Comparisons," *Journal of Abnormal and Social Psychology*, LXIII, 1 (July, 1961), pp. 116–124.

Mischel, Walter. "Preference for Delayed Reinforcement and Social Responsibility," *Journal of Abnormal and Social Psychology*, LXII, 1 (January, 1961), pp. 1–7.

Moore, Joan W. "Social Deprivation and Advantage as Sources of Political Values," *Western Political Quarterly*, 15 (1962), pp. 217–226.

Moss, H. A., and Jerome Kagan. "Stability of Achievement and Recognition Seeking Behaviors from Early Childhood through Adulthood," *Journal of Abnormal and Social Psychology*, LXII, 3 (May, 1961), pp. 504–513.

Mussen, Paul H. "Some antecedents and Consequences of Masculine Sex Typing in Adolescent Boys," *Psychological Monographs,* 75 (1961), pp. 1–24.

———, and Luther Distler. "Masculinity, Identity, and Father-Son Relationships," *Journal of Abnormal and Social Psychology*, 59 (November, 1959), pp. 350–356.

———, and Anne Wyszynski. "Political Personality and Political Participation," *Human Relations,* V, 1 (February, 1952), pp. 65–82.

Neblett, T. F. "Youth Movements in the United States," *Annals,* 194 (1937), pp. 141–151.

Neugarten, Bernice L. "Social Class and Friendship Among School Children," *American Journal of Sociology*, LI, 4 (January, 1946), pp. 305–313.

Newcomb, Theodore M. "The Persistence and Regression of Changed Attitudes," *Journal of Social Issues*, 19 (October, 1963), pp. 3–14.

Newmann, Fred M. "Adolescents Constructs of Authority Figures: A Methodological Study," *Journal of General Psychology*, LXXIV, 2 (April, 1966), pp. 319–338.

Nogee, Philip, and M. B. Levin. "Some Determinants of Political Attitudes Among College Voters," *Public Opinion Quarterly*, XXII, 4 (Winter, 1958–1959), pp. 449–463.

Orren, Karen, and Paul Peterson. "Presidential Assassination: A Case Study in the Dynamics of Political Socialization," *The Journal of Politics*, 29, 2 (May, 1967), pp. 388–404.

Parsons, Talcott. "The School Class as a Social System: Some of Its Functions in American Society," *Harvard Educational Review*, 29 (1959), pp. 297–318.

Patterson, Franklin K. "Political Reality in Childhood," *National Elementary School Principal*, 42 (1963), pp. 18–23.

Payne, D. E., and Paul H. Mussen. "Parent-Child Relations and Father Identification Among Adolescent Boys," *Journal of Abnormal and Social Psychology*, LII (May, 1956), 358–362.

Piaget, Jean, and Anne-Marie Weil. "The Development in Children of the Idea of the Homeland and of a Relation with Other Countries," *International Social Science Bulletin*, 3 (Autumn, 1951), pp. 561–578.

Pinner, Frank A. "Parental Overprotection and Political Distrust," *The Annals of the American Academy of Political and Social Science*, 361 (1965), pp. 58–70.

Pope, Benjamin. "Socio-Economic Contrasts in Children's Peer Culture Prestige Values," *Genetic Psychology Monographs*, 48 (1953), pp. 157–220.

Prewitt, Kenneth. "Political Socialization and Leadership Selection," *The Annals of the American Academy of Political and Social Science*, 361 (1965), pp. 96–111.

Prothro, James, W. and Charles M. Grigg. "Fundamental Principles of Democracy: Basis of Agreement and Disagreement," *Journal of Politics*, XXII (1960), pp. 276–294.

Psathas, George. "Ethnicity, Social Class, and Adolescent Independence from Parental Control," *American Sociological Review*, XXII (August, 1957), pp. 415–423.

Putney, Snell, and Russell Middleton. "Rebellion, Conformity, and Parental Religious Ideologies," *Sociometry*, XXIV (June, 1961), pp. 125–135.

Pye, Lucian. "Political Modernization and Research on the Process of Political Socialization," *Items,* XIII (September, 1959), pp. 25–28.

Queener, L. "The Development of Internationalist Attitudes, I, Hypotheses and Verification," *Journal of Social Psychology,* 29 (1949), pp. 221–235; II, "Attitude Cues and Prestige," pp. 237–252; III, "The Literature and a Point of View," Vol. 30, pp. 105–126.

Reading, Reid. "Political Socialization in Columbia and the United States: An Exploratory Study," *Midwest Journal of Political Science* (August, 1968), pp. 352–381.

Remmers, H. H., and Naomi Weltman. "Attitude Interrelationships of Youth, Their Parents and Their Teachers," *Journal of Social Psychology,* 26 (1947), pp. 61–68.

Rokeach, Milton. "Political and Religious Dogmatism: An Alternative to the Authoritarian Personality," *Psychological Monographs,* LXX (1956).

Rose, A. M. "Reference Groups of Rural High School Youth," *Child Development,* XXVII (September, 1956), pp. 351–363.

Rosenberg, Morris. "Misanthropy and Political Ideology," *American Sociological Review,* XXI (December, 1956), pp. 690–695.

———, "Self-Esteem and Concern with Public Affairs," *Public Opinion Quarterly,* XXVI (Summer, 1962), pp. 201–211.

———. "Some Determinants of Political Apathy," *Public Opinion Quarterly,* XXVIII (Winter, 1954), pp. 349–366.

Rushing, William A. "Adolescent-Parent Relationships and Mobility Aspirations," *Social Forces,* XVIII (December, 1964), pp. 157–167.

Schein, Edgar H. "The Chinese Indoctrination Program for Prisoners of War," *Psychiatry,* 19 (May, 1956), pp. 149–172.

Schick, Marvin, and Albert Somit. "The Failure to Teach Political Activity," *The American Behavioral Scientist,* 6 (January, 1963), pp. 5–8.

Scoble, Harry M., and Joan E. Laurence. "Ideology and Consensus Among Children of the Metropolitan Socioeconomic Elite," *The Western Political Quarterly* (March, 1969), pp. 151–162.

Sears, Robert R. "Relation of Early Socialization Experiences to Aggression in Middle Childhood," *Journal of Abnormal and Social Psychology,* 63 (November, 1961), pp. 466–492.

Selvin, Hanan C. "A Critique of Tests of Significance in Survey Research," *American Sociological Review,* 22 (October, 1957), pp. 519–527.

———, and Warren O. Hagstrom. "The Determinants of Support for Civil Liberties," *British Journal of Sociology,* 11 (1960), pp. 51–73.

Sewell, William H. "Social Class and Childhood Personality," *Sociometry,* XXIV, (December, 1961), pp. 340–356.

———. "Some Recent Developments in Socialization Theory and Research," *The Annals of the American Academy of Political and Social Science* (September 1963), pp. 163–181.

Siegel, Alberta E. "The Influence of Violence in the Mass Media upon Children's Role Expectations," *Child Development,* 29 (1958), pp. 35–56.

Sigel, Roberta S. "Image of a President: Some Insights into the Political Views of School Children," *The American Political Science Review,* LXII (March, 1968), pp. 216–226.

———. "The Effect of Partisanship on the Perception of Political Candidates," *Public Opinion Quarterly,* XXVIII (1964), pp. 483–496.

———. "Assumptions About the Learning of Political Values," *The Annals of the American Academy of Political and Social Science,* 361 (1965), pp. 1–9.

Sigel, Roberta S. "Images of the American Presidency—Part II of an Exploration into Popular Views of Presidential Power," *Midwest Journal of Political Science,* X (February, 1966), pp. 123–137.

———. *Political Socialization: Some Reactions on Current Approaches and Conceptions.* Paper delivered at the 1966 Annual Meeting of the American Political Science Association, Statler-Hilton Hotel, New York City, September 6–10.

Simpson, Richard L. "The School, The Peer Group, and Adolescent Development," *Journal of Educational Psychology,* 32 (September, 1958), pp. 37–41.

Skipper, James K., Jr., Anthony L. Guenther, and Gilbert Nass. "The Sacredness of .05: A Note Concerning the Uses of Statistical Levels of Significance in Social Science," *The American Sociologist,* 2 (February, 1967), pp. 16–18.

Slater, Philip E. "Parental Role Differentiation," *American Journal of Sociology,* 67 (November, 1961), pp. 296–308.

Somit, A., *et al.* "The Effect of the Introductory Political Science Course of Student Attitudes Toward Personal Political Participation," *American Political Science Review,* XII (December, 1958), pp. 129–132.

Stagner, Ross. "Attitude Toward Authority: An Exploratory Study," *Journal of Social Psychology,* 40 (1954), pp. 197–210.

Steintrager, James. "Political Socialization and Political Theory," *Social Research,* 35 (Spring, 1968), pp. 111–129.

Stendler, Celia B. "Critical Periods in Socialization and Over Dependency," *Child Development,* XXIII (March, 1952), pp. 3–12.

Tannenbaum, Percy H., and Jack M. McLeod. "On the Measurement of Socialization," *The Public Opinion Quarterly,* XXXI, (Spring, 1967), pp. 27–37.

Tresselt, M. E., and J. Volkman. "The Production of Uniform Opinion by Non-Social Stimulation," *Journal of Abnormal and Social Psychology,* 37 (1942), pp. 234–243.

Triandis, Leigh M., and William W. Lambert. "Pancultural Factor Analysis of Reported Socialization Practices," *Journal of Abnormal and Social Psychology,* LXII (May, 1961), pp. 631-640.

Troldahl, Verling C., and Frederic A. Powell. "A Short-Form Dogmatism Scale for Use in Field Studies," *Social Forces,* 44 (December, 1965), pp. 211–214.

Tuma, Elias, and Norman Lawson. "Family Socio-economic Status and Adolescent Attitudes Toward Authority," *Child Development,* 31 (June, 1960), pp. 387–399.

Turk, Herman. "An Inquiry into the Undersocialized Conception of Man," *Social Forces,* 43 (May, 1965), pp. 518–521.

Ungs, Thomas. "Attitudes Toward Classroom Activism: A Note on Kansas Social Studies Teacher, *Social Science Quarterly,* 49, 2 (September, 1968), pp. 296–304.

Wasby, Stephan L. "The Impact of the Family on Politics: An Essay and Review of the Literature," *The Family Life Coordinator,* 15 (1966), pp. 3–24.

Weinstein, E. A. "Development of the Concept of Flag and the Sense of National Identity," *Child Development,* XXVII (June, 1957), pp. 166–174.

White, Elliott S. "Intelligence and Sense of Political Efficacy in Children," *Journal of Politics,* 30 (August, 1968), pp. 701–731.

Wiese, Mildred J., and Stewart G. Cole. "A Study of Children's Attitudes and the Influence of a Commercial Motion Picture," *Journal of Psychology,* 21 (1946), pp. 151–171.

Wilkinson, Rupert. "Political Leadership and the Late Victorian Public School," *British Journal of Sociology,* 13 (1962), pp. 320–330.

Witty, Paul A., *et al.* "A Summary of Yearly Studies of Televiewing—1949–1963," *Elementary English*, 40 (1963), pp. 580–597.

Wolins, Martin. "Political Orientation, Social Reality, and Child Welfare," *The Social Science Review*, 38 (1964), pp. 429–442.

Wright, Charles R. "Functional Analysis and Mass Communications," *Public Opinion Quarterly*, 24 (1960), pp. 605–612.

Wrong, Dennis H. "The Oversocialized Conception of Man in Modern Sociology," *American Sociological Review*, 26 (April, 1961), pp. 183–193.

Zeligs, Rose. "The Meaning of Democracy to Sixth-Grade Children," *Journal of Genetic Psychology*, 76 (1950), pp. 263–282.

Index

Index

Age:
  as factor in political socialization, 2-4,
    50-52
  conclusions on, 140
  mass media and, 120-121
  peer groups and, 71-77
  media exposure, attitudes and,
    150-151
  school as information agent and,
    95-99
Agents of political socialization (*see*
    Church; Ethnic origin and
    political socialization;
    Geographic region; Mass media;
    Parents; Peer group; School;
    Youth organizations)
Aggression:
  parental models and, 33-34
  peer models and, 77-78
Almond, Gabriel A., 104
Appalachian sub-culture, 24
  compared with Negro sub-sample,
    108
  contrasted with New Haven sample,
    44-45, 56, 77, 99-100
  extended family in, 52

father-absence in, 61-65, 112-113,
    139
influence of peers in, 76-77
matriarchal character of, 39-42,
    53-54, 57-58, 77, 90, 124-125,
    139-140
political cynicism in, 147-148
political efficacy in, 146-148
political sex roles in, 124-125, 135
role of teacher in, 99
summary of findings on, 65-66,
    76-77, 90-91, 114-115, 135,
    137-141
Argyle, Michael, 139-140
Attitudes, political:
  Appalachian and non-Appalachian,
    146-148
  father-absence and, 144-146
  media exposure and, 150-151
  school and, 149
  youth organizations and, 148
Australia, political socialization in, 9
Authoritarianism, 10, 15
Authority:
  attitudes toward, 10
  father-absence and, 7, 144

Authority figures, political, 9, 11, 18

Bandura, Albert, 22-23, 34, 46, 50, 77,
    118, 121, 145
  with Dorothea and Sheila Ross, 53
  with Richard H. Walters, 22, 33, 46,
    53, 71, 83, 100, 101, 104, 129,
    141-142
Belgium, political socialization in, 5
Berkowitz, Leonard, 61, 68, 126
Boy Scouts, 88-90, 148
Brim, Orville G., Jr., 23, 26, 68, 126
Brown, Francis J., 104-105, 122, 124

Chauvinism, political, 30, 109-110
  media exposure and, 150-151
  school as information agent and, 149
  youth organizations and, 148
Chile, political socialization in, 9
Church, as socialization agent, 6, 7, 23
Civics course, attendance in, 104-108
  orientation to media by, 107-108
  political efficacy and, 111
  school as information agent and,
    105-106
Civil rights score, 29
  father-absence and, 145
  media exposure and, 150-151
  youth organizations and, 148
Class and political socialization, 3, 6, 8,
    9, 23
Communication theory, 118, 129
Contiguity (see Modeling, contiguity
    factor in)
Converse, Philip E., 9
"Copying" (Miller and Dollard), 21
Cultural variable (see Appalachian
    sub-culture)
"Culture of poverty" (Lewis), 90
Cynicism, political:
  Appalachian and national, 147-148
  efficacy and, 146-147
  father-absence and, 145
  media exposure and, 150-151
  scale, 29
  youth organizations and, 148

Dawson, Richard E., 14
DeGrazia, Sebastian, 18
Delin, Peter, 139-140
Dennis, Jack (see Easton, David)

Depeux, George, 9
Deviancy, parental models and, 34
Discussion of politics with family, 47-50
Dollard, John, 21-22, 110
Doob, Leonard W., 57
"Drive" (Miller and Dollard), 21-22

Easton, David, 11
  with Jack Dennis, 5, 9-10, 14, 16,
    18-19, 29, 146
Educational status of parents, 58-61
Efficacy, political, 29, 110-111
  in Appalachia and elsewhere, 146-147
  cynicism and, 146-147
  father-absence and, 145
  media exposure and, 150-151
  school as information agent and, 149
  youth organizations and, 148
Elazar, Daniel J., 52
Elkin, Frederick, 129
Employment status of father, 57-59
Ethnic origin and political socialization,
    6, 8, 23, 108

Family, as socialization agent, 6-7, 9, 11,
    18, 23-24, 34-70, 112-113
  summary of findings on, 65-66,
    138-140
  (See also Father; Father-absence;
    Mother; Parents)
Father:
  child's relationship with: role of
    media and, 126-127
    role of peers and, 82-84
    role of school and, 111-112
  educational status of, 60-61, 69
  employment status of, 57-58
  as information agent: compared with
    media, 126
    compared with peers, 74-77
    compared with school, 111-112
  political office held by, 47-48
  as source of party identification,
    39-44, 53-58, 60
  as source of voting advice, 45-46,
    48-49, 52-57, 61
  (See also Father-absence; Parents)
Father-absence, 139, 151
  attitudes toward authority and, 7, 61
  political attitudes and, 144-146

political learning process and, 61-65
related to role of media, 127-128
related to role of peers, 83-87
related to role of school, 112-113
FFA, 88-90, 148
Fleck, S., 34
Fleron, Frederic (*see* Jaros, Dean)
4-H Clubs, 88-90, 148
France, political socialization in, 5, 9
Freudian influence on political
    socialization theory, 11, 18, 65
Friedenberg, Edgar Z., 92
Froman, Lewis A., Jr., 2
    on use of psychoanalytic thinking, 11

Geographic region, as socialization
    factor, 6, 23
Girl Scouts, 88-90, 148
Gough, Harrison G., 34
Government, four levels of:
    efficacy and, 147
    information transmission on, 34-37,
        120
        by media, 118-124, 126-128,
            130-132
        by parents, 47, 54, 58, 60, 62-63,
            113
        by peers, 72-75, 78-82, 84-86, 113
        by school, 95-99, 101-103,
            105-106, 113, 149
        summary of findings on, 139
        (*See also* Information transmission)
Greenstein, Fred I., 2-10, 92, 118, 122,
    124, 151
    on sources of voting advice in New
        Haven, 44-45, 53-56, 77,
        99-100, 128

Harris, Dale B., 34
Hess, Robert D., 9
    with Judith Torney, 6-8, 14, 19, 23,
        39, 68, 88, 92, 100, 144
Hirsch, Herbert (*see* Jaros, Dean)
Hyman, Herbert, 1, 20, 29, 129

Information level, political, 43-44
    attendance in civics course and,
        107-108
Information transmission:
    age and, 50-52, 72-75, 96-97

agents of, ranked by children, 34-39,
    72-74, 78-82, 96-97
conclusions on, 138-139
employment of father and, 57-58
father-absence and, 62-63, 84-87, 113
media as agent of, 118-136
    age and, 120-121
    family model contiguity and,
        127-128
    intrafamilial relationships and,
        125-127
    ranked by child, 119
parents as agent of, 34-39, 41-44,
    47-48, 50-54, 56-58, 60
    peer groups and, 71-77, 113
    school and, 97-98
peer group as agent of, 72-75, 78-81,
    83-87, 97-98
"personal" and "non-personal" agents
    of, 39
school as agent of, 93-106
    age related to, 95-99
    father-absence and, 112-113
    peers, parents and, 97-98, 113
    political chauvinism and, 149
    political efficacy and, 149
    relation to father and, 111-112
    sex related to, 100-101
    sex and, 53-54, 56-57, 100-101
Intrafamilial relationships:
    media as information agent and,
        125-127
    school as information agent and,
        111-112
    (*See also* Father; Father-absence;
        Family; Mother; Parents)

Japan, political socialization in, 9
Jaros, Dean, 8, 15
    with Herbert Hirsch and Frederic
        Fleron, 9, 15, 16, 144
Jennings, M. Kent, 34, 92-93, 105, 108,
    139
    with Richard G. Niemi, 29, 40-42,
        53, 68, 147

Klapper, Joseph, 150
Knowledge, political:
    attendance in civics course and, 108
    correlated with party preference,
        43-44

exposure to media and, 131-134
father-absence and, 145
Knox County, 27

Langton, Kenneth P., 71
with M. Kent Jennings, 92-93, 105,
108
Lasswell, Harold, 2
Learning:
citizen-role, 4-5
early political, 4-6, 9, 23
incidental, 129
"specifically political" (Greenstein),
4
subject-role, 5
Learning theory, 11, 19
(See also Social learning theory)
Lewis, Oscar, 90
Litt, Edgar, 30

Maccoby, Eleanor E., 50
Martin, William E., 34
Mass media, 8, 23, 118-136
civics course and orientation to,
107-108
as information agent: age related to,
120-121
father-absence and, 127-128
intrafamilial relationships and,
125-127
political learning and, 129-134
ranked by children, 34-39, 118-120
relationship with father and,
126-127
sex differences related to, 121-125
summary of findings on, 134-135,
138-139
latent operation of, 129-134
political attitudes and, 150-151
(See also Newspaper; Radio;
Television)
"Matched-dependent behavior" (Miller
and Dollard), 21
Media (see Mass media)
Merelman, Richard M., 19
Miller, N. E., 21-22
Mitchell, William C., 88
Modeling, 43, 46, 68, 141
age and, 50
Bandura on, 22-23, 34, 46, 50, 71,
77, 145

contiguity factor in, 61-65, 83, 90,
112-113
conclusions on, 139-141
ranking of media and, 127-128
sex differences and, 53-54, 77-78, 100
sub-cultural effects on, 39
symbolic (see Mass media; Symbolic
models)
(See also Father-absence; Parents;
Peer groups)
Mother:
educational status of, 60-61, 70
as information agent: compared with
media, 122-124
compared with peers, 74-77,
112-113
political office held by, 47-48
as source of party identification,
39-44, 53-57, 60
as source of voting advice, 45-46,
48-49, 52-57, 61, 112-113
(See also Appalachian sub-culture,
matriarchal character of; Father-
absence; Parents)
Mowrer, O. Hobart, 21

New Haven, study of, 44-45, 56, 77,
99-100
Newspaper:
attention to, civics course and, 107
as information agent: age of child
and, 120-121
exposure to, 131-134
father-absence and, 128
ranking of, 34-38, 119
relationship with father and,
126-127
sex of child and, 123-125
political attitudes and, 150-151
Niemi, Richard G. (see Jennings, M.
Kent)

Orientation to political stimuli:
conclusions on, 140
parental, 46-50
of peers, 79-83
by school, 104-111, 114-115
sex of child and, 124-125, 135
teachers', 101-104

Parents:
    educational status of, 59-61
    as information agent, 41-44, 47-48,
        53-54, 56-58, 60
    child's ranking of, 34-39
    compared with peer group, 71-77
    compared with school, 97-98,
        112-113
    intellectual status of, 58-61, 69-70
    orientation to political stimuli of,
        46-50
    party identification and, 39-44, 48,
        50, 51, 53-57, 69-70, 76-77
    as socialization agent, 7, 9, 34-70,
        138-140
    as source of voting advice, 44-46,
        48-49, 53-57
    (*See also* Father; Father-absence;
        Mother)
Party identification:
    age and, 50-52, 76-77
    conclusions on, 139
    employment of father and, 58-59
    father-absence and, 63-65, 86-87
    parents and, 39-44, 48, 50-52, 59-60
    peer groups and, 75-77, 79, 81
    school as information agent and, 98
    sex and, 53-57, 79
Patriotic rituals, exposure to, 109-111
Payne, Raymond, 15
Peer group:
    as information agent, 72-75, 78-82,
        85-86, 112-113
    child's ranking of, 34-39, 113
    orientation to political stimuli of,
        79-82
    party identification and, 75-77, 81,
        83, 87
    political attitudes and, 148
    as socialization agent, 7-8, 23, 71-91
    age of child and, 71-77
    sex differences and, 77-79
    summary of findings on, 90-91,
        138-139
    well-structured, 87-90
    (*See also* Youth organizations)
Personality variable, 8, 15, 151
Pinner, Frank A., 5
Political Socialization (Hyman), 1-2
Powell, G. Bingham, 104

Preference, party (*see* Party
        identification)
Prewitt, Kenneth, 14
Psychoanalysis, 11
Puerto Rico, political socialization in, 9

Questionnaire, development of, 28-29

Radio:
    attention to, civics course and, 107
    as information agent: age of child
        and, 120-121
    father-absence and, 127
    political attiudes and, 150-151
    ranking of, 34-38, 119
    rate of exposure to, 130-134
    relationship with father and,
        126-127
    sex of child and, 122, 124
Rebellion, adolescent, 51, 68
Revolutionary behavior, 10
Rosenberg, Morris, 8
Ross, Dorothea, 53
Ross, Sheila, 53

Sample, selection of, 27
School:
    as information agent, 93-106
    age of child related to, 95-99
    attendance in civics course and,
        105-108
    child's relation to father and,
        111-112
    child's ranking of, 35-36, 93-97
    father-absence and, 112-113
    other agents compared with, 97-98
    party preference and, 99
    political efficacy and, 149
    sex differences related to, 100-101
    teacher's discussion of candidates
        and, 106
    teacher's orientation to political
        stimuli and, 102
    orientation to political stimuli by,
        104-111
    political attitudes and, 149
    as socialization agent, 6, 7, 9, 23,
        92-117
    summary of findings on, 114-115,
        138-139
Schramm, W., 129

Self-esteem score, 150-151
Sewell, William, 3
Sex differences as factor in political
    socialization, 3, 52-57, 68
  aggression and, 77-78
  conclusions on, 140
  mass media and, 121-125
  peers and, 77-79
  school and, 100-101
Sigel, Roberta S., 10-12, 15, 18
Significance tests, 27, 31
Social Learning and Imitation (Miller
    and Dollard), 21-22
Social learning theory, 21-24, 137-138
  development of, 21-23
  on family, 33-34
  on parental orientation to political
    stimuli, 46-50
  political socialization and, 141-142
  on sex and political socialization,
    53-54
  on symbolic models, 118, 135
"Socializing contexts" (Hess and
    Torney), 6
"Specifically political learning"
    (Greenstein), 4
Status and political socialization, 3,
    57-59
Stimuli, orientation to (see Orientation
    to political stimuli)
Symbolic models, defined, 118
  (See also Mass media)
Systems theory, 18-19

Teacher:
  perceived orientation to stimuli of,
    101-104
  in poverty sub-culture, 99
  as source of voting advice, 98-100
Television:
  civics course and attention to news
    on, 107

as information agent: age of child
    and, 120-121
  father-absence and, 127
  ranking of, 34-38, 119
  rate of exposure to, 130-134
  relationship with father and,
    126-127
  sex of child and, 123-124
  political attitudes and, 150-151
Tests of significance, 27, 31
Teune, Henry, 19
Torney, Judith (see Hess, Robert D.)

Unemployment (see Employment status
    of father)

Voting advice, source of, 44-46, 53
  age of child and, 46, 52
  conclusions on, 139
  discussion of candidates in school
    and, 103-104
  discussion of politics in family and,
    48-50
  education of parents and, 60-61
  employment of father and, 58-59
  father-absence and, 64-65
  media and, 128
  peers and, 77, 81, 84, 86
  relationship with father and, 84, 111
  sex and, 53-57
  teacher as, 98-100, 102-103
  teacher's orientation to political
    stimuli and, 102-104

Walter, Richard H. (see Bandura,
    Albert)

Youth organizations:
  political attitudes and, 148
  as socialization agent, 23, 88-90

Ziblatt, David, 5